# *Praise for* THE ENDURING REVOLUTION

"Major Garrett has it right: the Contract with America, developed as a campaign platform, became an agenda for governing. Its provisions not only became law, largely with bipartisan support; they remain policy positions shared by the majority of American voters."
—HALEY BARBOUR, Governor of Mississippi, former Chairman of the Republican National Committee

"The Contract with America was the platform the Republicans used for the takeover of Congress in 1994. A decade later we're still dealing with its ramifications. Major Garrett has done a fine job analyzing this watershed event. Everyone who wants to understand the current Republican dominance of Capitol Hill should read this book."
—PAUL BEGALA, former Counselor to President Clinton, cohost of CNN's *Crossfire*

"As Major Garrett clearly and powerfully reveals in this book, big change is produced by big ideas. Garrett uncovers the inside story of the Contract with America and at the same time shows us how the Contract revolutionized the language and substance of American politics for a generation or more to come. A terrific, well-written, fascinating read." —PROFESSOR LARRY J. SABATO, Director of the Center for Politics, University of Virginia

"Major Garrett and I disagree on some political issues, but you can't help but admire his integrity and intelligence. Major always understood the importance of the Gingrich Revolution. Whether you cheered it on or were appalled that it happened, you need to read this excellent history to understand how 1994 changed our nation and our politics." —E. J. DIONNE JR., *Washington Post* columnist

"*The Enduring Revolution* helps us understand, with great clarity, how today's policy issues came of age and how the process works. Armed with this critical information, we can intelligently assess how best to move forward." —ALAN COLMES, cohost of the Fox News Channel's *Hannity & Colmes*

# THE
# ENDURING
# REVOLUTION

*How the Contract with America*

*Continues to Shape the Nation*

# MAJOR GARRETT

CROWN
FORUM
NEW YORK

To Julie

# CONTENTS

# THE
# ENDURING
# REVOLUTION

# PROLOGUE

It was a strange place to find the Contract with America.

Shortly before 9 A.M. on a rainy January day, I turned my rental car into the parking lot of the Davenport, Iowa, Holiday Inn. It was just days before the 2004 Iowa caucuses, the real kickoff of the race for the Democratic presidential nomination. A large crowd had squeezed into the hotel's ballroom to hear a man who was suddenly emerging as a major candidate, perhaps the Democrats' great hope to reclaim the White House: Senator John Kerry of Massachusetts.

Hundreds waited shoulder to shoulder for the candidate in the suffocating room—ten minutes, twenty minutes, thirty minutes. But no one seemed to mind that the senator was making them wait. The anticipation only grew. These Democrats were pumped up for John Kerry. They were ready to defeat George W. Bush. And finally, when the candidate arrived, he told them how he was going to do it.

By embracing the Republicans' Contract with America.

Kerry didn't put it this way, of course. No self-respecting Democrat seeking the presidency ever would. But the plan he laid out to voters in Davenport that day could be traced directly to a program that congressional Republicans had made the centerpiece of their agenda fully a decade earlier.

"Some in this campaign want to repeal all the Bush tax cuts," Kerry told the crowd, referring to opponents Howard Dean, the former governor of Vermont, and former House majority leader Dick Gephardt. "I'm not one of them. I believe the middle class has enough problems. I will protect those middle-class tax cuts." At this, the assembled Democratic stalwarts erupted in applause.

What Kerry called the "Bush tax cuts" were really the Contract with

America tax cuts. Four conservative women had jammed the most important of these tax cuts, the $500-per-child tax credit, down the throats of House GOP leaders in the spring of 1994. House Republicans, still in the minority at the time, recognized the overwhelmingly positive public reaction to the tax credit and realized that tax cuts would be a potent political weapon against President Bill Clinton, who had promised middle-class tax cuts in the 1992 campaign but had failed to deliver them. (In fact, Clinton had *raised* gasoline taxes and Social Security taxes, both of which hit middle-class families.)

Kerry was even more emphatic the next day at a town hall meeting in Newton, Iowa. (It was at this meeting, incidentally, that Kerry first suggested Senator John Edwards of North Carolina as a possible running mate. Edwards was the only other Democrat running in Iowa to embrace the Contract-era middle-class tax cuts, though he did not make protection of the tax cuts nearly so significant a part of his campaign.) Arriving by helicopter in a weathered bomber jacket, rumpled khakis, open-collar blue dress shirt, and walking boots, Candidate Kerry had the studied look of the rugged individualist. His scratchy voice betrayed the endless, hell-for-leather campaigning he had done in Iowa. The caucuses were fast approaching, and Kerry stuck to his formula of embracing the Contract tax cuts.

As Kerry took questions, a self-described "undecided" voter asked him what he would do about taxes and the budget deficit, then exceeding $400 billion. "I roll back the Bush tax cut for the wealthiest Americans," Kerry responded. "But I don't do what some other candidates [Dean and Gephardt] want to do, which is roll the whole thing back, because I don't want to raise taxes on the middle class. If you roll the whole thing back, you wind up losing the child tax credit increase, [and] you reinstate the marriage penalty. I don't want to tax the middle class to get out of this hole."

Kerry's specificity could not have been a more compelling salute to the Contract with America tax cuts. The two most important tax cuts in the Contract, the ones Bill Clinton eventually signed into law (representing the first broadly distributed federal income tax cuts since 1981), were the $500-per-child tax credit and the reduction in the marriage penalty, a tax-law change that protected millions of couples from paying more in federal income taxes as a married couple than they would if they remained single.

As a political reporter covering these campaign events, I couldn't help but reflect on how profoundly American politics had changed in just a decade. Back in 1994, President Clinton and Democratic surrogates, including Kerry, had campaigned hard *against* these tax cuts. Yet just five *days* after the GOP's historic victory in 1994—when the Republicans took control of both houses of Congress for the first time in forty years—Clinton embraced the child tax credit. He signed the tax credit and other Contract tax cuts into law in 1997, and they were wildly popular. In 2001, 2002, and 2003, President George W. Bush added still more Contract-era tax cuts and expanded the ones already on the books.

As the Davenport and Newton speeches indicated, John Kerry put his support of Contract with America tax cuts at the forefront of his economic platform during the Iowa campaign. It was certainly an unconventional and risky approach for a Democratic candidate. After all, since the New Deal the Democratic Party had been committed to using government programs to solve the problems of the lower and middle classes. Kerry gambled, literally betting millions of his own money (taking out a loan on his Boston home) on the outcome at a time when he had been written off as a candidate, and when it seemed that Howard Dean was running away with the Democratic nomination. Kerry's gamble paid off. He used his support for the Contract tax cuts to great effect, particularly against Dean.

And the Davenport and Newton performances were not aberrations. Kerry invested heavily in a thirty-second television commercial featuring Elizabeth Hendrix of Des Moines, a widow raising her four children on an office worker's salary of $28,000. In the ad, Hendrix, sitting in her living room and looking straight into the camera, told Iowans that she supported Kerry because he would protect the middle class. She said middle-class Iowa families had been through enough, were facing tough times, and didn't need higher taxes. "John Kerry understands what's going on in my life," she concluded. It was one of the most effective ads in the Iowa caucuses and helped propel Kerry to victory. The Hendrix ad was so important to Kerry, he mentioned her story prominently in his victory speech in the historic Fort Des Moines Hotel on caucus night: "For those of you not yet part of this fight, I ask you to go to johnkerry.com and join me in fighting for an America where the people are in charge. Join me in fighting for people like Elizabeth Hendrix from Des Moines, who's working full-time, raising four boys, and earns $28,000 a year. We shouldn't be raising taxes on the middle class; we shouldn't be telling them to pay the bill for George W. Bush's mistakes."

Kerry's triumph in Iowa essentially decided the race for the Democratic presidential nomination, because no one seriously challenged him thereafter. In other words, Kerry's path to victory was paved in no small way by the tax cuts first brought to national attention by the Contract with America. That an issue central to the political success of Republicans nearly ten years earlier could play so pivotal a role in a Democratic presidential candidate's campaign to win the support of liberal party activists (not middle-of-the-roaders, as you would find in a general election) is nothing short of astonishing.

Other factors contributed to Iowa's victory, of course, not least of which was Kerry's four-month tour in Vietnam as a Swift Boat commander. Howard Dean himself contends that Kerry's support among veterans proved more important than tax cuts. "We've talked about this, and I know John believes that he benefited by espousing the middle[-class] tax cut," Dean told me in an interview just before the Democratic convention in 2004. "But I don't. I don't want to make the political point, but I don't think John's victory had anything to do with middle[-class] tax cuts, not among Democratic activists."

But Kerry's own polling indicated that the middle-class tax issue was enormously important to the Massachusetts senator's victory in Iowa, as Kerry pollster Mark Mellman told me. "The issue polled very well, and that's why we put the ad out and made it one of the last two ads in the campaign before the caucuses," Mellman says. "We also ran a veteran ad at the same time, and that worked better in focus groups and polling, but only marginally better." Now, Mellman is quick to add that the Kerry campaign considered these tax cuts to be "Clinton tax cuts because he called for them in the '92 campaign" and that "we didn't consider ourselves to be copying or endorsing Republican tax cuts." But he concedes that President Clinton never enacted a set of broad-based middle-class tax cuts until Republicans won control of Congress and pushed the cuts.

Despite Howard Dean's contention, the tax-cut issue became the most important issue in the Iowa race, separating Kerry from the two competitors who were thought to pose the biggest organizational and political threat to his campaign, Dean and Gephardt.

And it wasn't just on tax cuts where John Kerry embraced the Contract with America. Throughout Iowa, Kerry set out a platform many of those who first signed the Contract with America, on September 27, 1994, would have endorsed: aggressive pursuit of a balanced budget; welfare reform; a strong defense, including a budget that would not cut any of the spending increases originally sought in the Contract; using IRAs and refundable tax credits to pay for a college education; allowing seniors to work longer without facing higher taxes; using block grants to boost state and local law enforcement; eliminating parole for repeat violent offenders and establishing truth-in-sentencing laws that would require prisoners to serve 85 percent of their sentences; eliminating unfunded federal mandates (federal laws that required states to comply but did not provide the revenue to achieve compliance); and applying all federal workplace and civil rights laws to members of Congress.

It made little difference that Kerry had originally opposed many of these policies. He, like many other Democrats, was now claiming political and policy terrain to which the Republicans had first laid claim a decade earlier.

To be sure, Candidate Kerry often promised to do much more than this. He promised far greater aid to college-age students. He promised even larger middle-class tax cuts. He promised more police on the beat by increasing direct federal aid that required the hiring of more police officers. But Kerry did not call for removal or reform of a single component of the Contract with America dealing with taxes, spending, welfare, crime, defense spending (with the exception of ballistic missile defense), federal mandates, or congressional reform. He and the other Democrats railed against aspects of the Republican agenda, of course, but these were quarrels with Republicans *outside of the Contract with America.*

In April 2004, after locking up the Democratic nomination, Kerry unveiled what he called "A Contract with America's Middle Class." This new "Contract," an attempt to refocus Kerry's domestic policy and create wider voter interest, promised even larger middle-class tax cuts, aid for home ownership and college tuition, and job retraining. Kerry also promised no new spending without matching cuts in other federal programs and what he called a "real cap on spending." "When I put forward a new idea," Kerry told the American Society of Newspaper Editors on April 23,

2004, "I'll tell you how I'm going to pay for it." As this book will demonstrate, it was just these budget-cutting tactics employed by Republicans that led to the budget showdown with Clinton in 1995, a confrontation that fundamentally changed Washington's approach to spending, deficit reduction, and debt repayment.

With the exception of job retraining, all of Kerry's pillars were part of the original Contract with America. In need of a victory from Democratic partisans in Iowa, Kerry ran stealthily on the Contract. In pursuit of a broader general-election audience, he did it more overtly. Covertly or overtly, the lesson is the same: The Contract lives.

The Kerry campaign vowed that its commitment to Contract-era tax cuts was sacrosanct. For example, on October 10, 2004—less than a month before the election—Democratic vice presidential nominee John Edwards went on NBC's *Meet the Press* to declare that if Kerry, as president, was forced to choose between protecting existing middle-class tax cuts and preserving proposed domestic spending increases, Kerry would choose the tax cuts. "If we have done all those things [to try to cut spending] and, at the end of the day, it becomes necessary to make sure we do not raise taxes on the middle class, then we will roll back some of our ideas," Edwards said. "John's already said, for example, national service, which is something he's committed to, early childhood, things that are near and dear to us, and we think very important to the country, but, if it becomes necessary to meet that commitment, we will roll things back." The Contract-era tax cuts that lay at the heart of Kerry's tax-cut agenda (Kerry promised to expand some cuts and add still more) had grown in importance from simple campaign proposal to absolute governing priority. It's a path the tax cuts had traveled once before, in 1994. The only difference was that this time they became part of the *Democrats'* governing agenda.

As I covered the 2004 presidential campaign for Fox News, I was amazed to see how few people recognized just how dramatically the Republicans who came to power in 1994 had reshaped American politics, and America as a whole. Certainly not many of the Democrats who cheered John Kerry on would have acknowledged the debt the candidate owed to the Contract with America. Democrats had consigned the Contract to the ash heap of history when Bill Clinton won reelection in 1996. By 2004, many conservatives, too, had come to have reservations about the importance of what came to be known as the Republican Revolution. They brooded that many of the so-called revolutionaries had lost their spine and accommodated to Washington go-along-to-get-along folkways, and they despaired that the first unified GOP government (control of the House, Senate, and White House) since the first two years of President Dwight D. Eisenhower's presidency—long before there was a conservative movement—had failed to control spending or shrink New Deal, Fair Deal, and Great Society bureaucracies.

Most of us remember snippets of the high-octane days that were the Republican Revolution. Newt Gingrich of Georgia—the leader of the revolution, a force that seems to bend the universe in his direction—takes over as Speaker of the House. Congressional Republicans march lockstep through the first hundred days. President Clinton struggles for relevance. Budgets collide. The government shuts down. Then shuts down again. Republicans cave. Clinton rises, Republicans retreat. Clinton wins reelection. Republicans obsess over Clinton's sex scandal with Monica Lewinsky and lose House seats in 1998. Gingrich resigns. Revolution ends.

For most Americans, that's the story: a bright flash of power; bravado and hubris; a clash with an eloquent president; a few midcourse compromises; a massive political overreach on the budget; an inglorious retreat; and a reelected president.

But that's not the end of the story. Far from it.

"We live in a Contract with America world," University of New Orleans historian and Kerry biographer Douglas Brinkley told me. "And if you look at Clinton and George W. Bush, they are successful in response to co-opting or working within a Contract with America framework of less government, lower taxes, and aggressive foreign policy. The Contract with America is the most important domestic political document of the last forty years."

Brinkley explains how it could be that a Democratic presidential candidate could seize control of the race by adopting the Republican Contract with America. "Everyone now positions off the Contract. They are either for it or against it. It's like the hub of a wheel, and everything touches it and moves off of it. And Democrats have not been able to circumvent it."

As Brinkley points out, the Contract with America is still very much with us. To many critics—Democrat and Republican; liberal, conservative, and moderate—the Contract with America was simply a gimmick of electoral politics, and the so-called Republican Revolution was anything but revolutionary. But the 1994 election did indeed mark a seismic shift in American politics. The Republicans who swept into office in 1994 on the strength of the Contract with America won a victory no one could see. For forty years Republicans had been written off when it came to congressional politics. But these Republicans refused to accept defeat, and they defied all rational political tactics and tendencies. Their gamble was as audacious as any contemporary American politics had ever seen. And so, in early January 1995, Newt Gingrich accepted the Speaker's gavel from Democrat Richard Gephardt. Republicans suddenly had a voice they had not had in four decades: the voice of congressional power. The voice of the purse strings. The voice of tax law. The voice of congressional investigations. The voice of the people.

The first year of the Republican Revolution, 1995, was the most tumultuous year in legislative politics of the twentieth century. As congressional reporter for the *Washington Times,* I had an inside view of the historic developments that year, just as I had covered virtually every step leading up to the revolution.

The Republican Revolution is the most important political story in decades. But it is also one of the most misunderstood episodes in our political history. In many ways, despite the common view that the Republican Revolution quickly petered out, some of the most consequential moments of Republican rule of Congress occurred *after* 1995.

Undeniably, Newt Gingrich and the other Republican leaders made critical mistakes and suffered setbacks, which this book will explore and explain. But their achievements were much more significant and long-lasting. At a minimum, the Republicans who took control of Congress in 1995 fundamentally changed the American debate on a host of issues— welfare, taxes, abortion, defense, health care, education, entitlements, terrorism, gun control, and crime, among others.

Even more important, the Republicans radically reshaped our notions of what government can and should be doing. Even after the presidency of Ronald Reagan, who preached, "Government is not the solution to the problem; government is the problem," a government that had been dominated by Democrats for four decades still reflected President Franklin D. Roosevelt's New Deal ethos. Although Gingrich praised Franklin Roosevelt in his January 1995 speech on accepting the Speaker's gavel ("If you truly love democracy and you truly believe in representative self-government, you can never study Franklin Delano Roosevelt too much. . . . He was clearly, I think, as a political leader the greatest figure of the twentieth century"), the Republican Revolution was dedicated to the systematic dismantling of Roosevelt's New Deal and its successor under Lyndon Johnson, the Great Society.

In fact, many of the setbacks the Republicans experienced when they took control of Congress occurred because they confronted the New Deal and Great Society head-on. This proved politically disastrous. That does not mean they gave up the fight, however. Now the moves are far more subtle and incremental. But the direction is the same.

Grover Norquist, one of the Republicans' most innovative thinkers and effective political strategists, sketched it out to me over coffee at Washington's Mayflower Hotel: "Give me a lever long enough and fulcrum strong enough and I can move the world. You can do anything ten or twenty years from now and you can do nothing next week. You can't do ten-year or twenty-year projects unless you're planning on having control [of Congress] for a lengthy period of time. A lot of this, you've got to have operating control for long periods of time, so you plan." The Republicans plan on having that operating control—and for more than a decade now, they've protected it. In fact, Republican control of the House and Senate has outlived the most visible figures of the triumph that was the 1994 election. Though Newt Gingrich, Bob Dole, Dick Armey, and Trent Lott have either left Congress or assumed far less-visible roles on Capitol Hill, the GOP's control continues. And the Republicans continue to make impressive gains; in the 2004 elections they gained seats in both the House and the Senate, while also helping George W. Bush win the presidential race decisively.

Republicans honestly believe that dismantling the New Deal and the Great Society will make America better. They believe in the power of personal savings, in personal responsibility, and in shifting choices about health care and retirement to individuals. They disdain the notion of a universal safety net and scoff at the idea that wealthy retirees require the same Social Security and Medicare protections as the poor. And they have moved to rewrite the tax code to shift wealthy and middle-class Americans away from both. It's a profound change, one that challenges Roosevelt's view of America. The Contract with America set it in motion.

The Contract not only lives, it governs—on both sides of the aisle. Just as John Kerry built much of his 2004 presidential campaign around the Contract with America, President George W. Bush has taken his cues on domestic policy from the congressionally driven agenda laid out in the Contract.

From the distance of ten years, this much is clear: Our lives are different because Republicans took control of Congress in 1995 and held that control for the next decade. Our lives are far, far different from what they would have been if Democrats had continued their reign. As this book will demonstrate, Republicans have changed this country and our lives in startling ways. It doesn't matter who you are. Rich, poor, or middle-class. Conservative or liberal. Pro-life or pro-choice. Pro-gun or anti-gun. Globalist or protectionist. Hawk or dove. All of our lives have changed, and they changed for one reason: Republicans won an election in 1994, igniting a clash of ideas and political forces America won't soon forget.

It is time to revisit the revolution. Only by understanding exactly what happened and how it happened can we understand how Republicans have changed America, and how these changes will shape the nation's future.

# 1

# REVOLUTION

The 104th Congress, of 1995–96, was the most important Congress of the twentieth century. Quite possibly it was the most important Congress in American history.

Most Americans don't think much about Congress. And it's not just the general public. Historians love to rank presidents, but they never rank Congresses. Why? Because Congress typically doesn't matter. That is, Congress typically doesn't matter as much as the president with whom it interacts—the leader who can set the nation's agenda even if he can't pass the laws. Whereas the president is an individual with a clear vision and often with the ability to rally Americans behind that vision, Congress is a hulking, plodding legislative body. Congress is not generally responsible for new, provocative ideas; rather, it is where such ideas go to be watered down by endless compromises and attached to other costly programs by politicians eager to impress their constituents.

That is how it normally works, anyway. Even when Congress has had big clashes with presidents, it has almost always been when Congress has resisted bold new ideas or resented efforts to uproot or challenge protected industries or orthodoxies. In 1832, Congress resisted Andrew Jackson's effort to kill the National Bank. In 1903, Congress resisted Theodore Roosevelt's attempts to tame the trusts. In 1919, Congress dealt a crushing blow to Woodrow Wilson's League of Nations by refusing to ratify the Treaty of Versailles. A series of Congresses used political intimidation to prevent Presidents Truman, Eisenhower, and Kennedy from proposing civil rights legislation.

But the Congress sworn in in January 1995 was anything but typical. In fact, this new Congress was hailed as bringing a "revolution" to American politics. Part of it, of course, was that for the first time in four decades the Republicans had taken control of Congress. And in truth, the Democrats' dominion over the House of Representatives extended back much further than to 1954, the election in which the Democrats regained the numerical advantage in the House they had lost in 1952. Democrats had really seized the levers of government in 1930, at the dawn of the Great Depression, and spent more than six decades consolidating that power—through the New Deal, Truman's Fair Deal, the civil rights era, the Great Society, and the large, liberal, and activist Watergate class of 1974 that redefined Democratic congressional power for the next twenty years. The Democratic Party controlled the House of Representatives for sixty of the sixty-four years between 1930 and 1994, and the Senate for fifty-four of those sixty-four years. The Republican Congress elected in 1952, on Dwight D. Eisenhower's coattails, was, in essence, an accidental majority—the Democrats regained power in the next election. The same could be said for the Republican majority that was elected in 1946: Republicans offered no coherent political alternative to President Truman's efforts to expand the New Deal, which allowed Truman to run for reelection in 1948 against the "Do Nothing" Republican Congress. Divorced from an agenda and a political plan to consolidate gains, the Republican majority disappeared as quickly as it had appeared. (So uncertain of their majority status were House Republicans in 1946 and 1952 that GOP leaders kept the offices they held while in the minority, ceding the larger and more ornately decorated real estate to their Democratic betters.)

Yet something more was happening in the 1994 election. This time the Republicans would not quickly cede the ground they had taken, as they had after 1946 and 1952. Here was a different breed of Republican. The Republicans of the 104th Congress were first and foremost about ideas. Ideas drove the politics. Ideas drove the reforms. Ideas drove the agenda. Ideas drove President Clinton away from the leftist congressional barons who had hijacked the centrist agenda he campaigned on in 1992 and turned it (at times with far too much Clintonian complicity) into an unrecognizable hash of tax increases, pork-barrel stimulus spending, nationalized health care, costly and timid welfare reform, drastic defense cuts, and no middle-class tax cut—for even while Clinton publicly demonized the new Republican majority for his short-term political benefit, he was adapting to the new center-right political terrain defined by the 1994 election, and defined by the Republicans' ideas. Ultimately, the Republicans' ideas profoundly reshaped our nation—and continue to shape it to this day.

These ideas were codified in the Contract with America, which Republicans publicly unveiled at a September 27, 1994, event on the West Front of the U.S. Capitol. Many Americans remember the ceremony on the Capitol steps, as 337 Republicans who either were in the House already or were campaigning to win seats gathered to sign the Contract. But the Contract was not designed just for that one-day press event. It offered a detailed, comprehensive agenda touching everything from internal congressional reform to national defense, welfare to economic growth, term limits to balancing the budget, crime control to tort reform.

The Contract started with a unified set of principles for which these 337 Republicans stood: individual liberty, economic opportunity, limited government, personal responsibility, and security at home and abroad. From these principles arose a two-part agenda: The first part laid out eight "major reforms" that were "aimed at restoring the faith and trust of the American people in their government." These reforms applied to the management of Congress; for instance, the Republicans called for changing the rules in Congress so lawmakers had to live under all major federal regulations, cutting the number of House committees and the size of committee staffs, and requiring a three-fifths majority vote to pass a tax increase. The second part, a ten-point legislative agenda, was even more important. As this book will reveal, it was the result of intense intraparty debate, and the culmination of years of work on the part of numerous Republicans both inside and outside of Congress. And to show their commitment to the agenda, the Republicans vowed that if they took the majority, they would vote on all ten planks of the Contract within the first hundred days of taking power. "If we break this contract, throw us out. We mean it."

In the ten planks, the Republicans called for:

1. A balanced-budget amendment and a legislative line-item veto to restore fiscal responsibility to Congress
2. A strong anti-crime bill that expanded the death penalty and required longer jail sentences for felons
3. A "personal responsibility act" that would reform welfare by forcing able-bodied recipients off public assistance after two years and reduce welfare spending

4. A "family reinforcement act" that would, among other things, provide tax incentives for adoption and establish an elderly dependent-care tax credit

5. A $500-per-child tax credit, a reduction of taxes on married couples, and the creation of tax-free savings accounts available to help families cover the cost of college tuition, first-time home purchases, or medical expenses

6. A strong national security defense bill that would protect defense spending from further cuts, eliminate any possible United Nations command of U.S. troops, and call for the swift development and deployment of a national ballistic missile defense system

7. Allowing seniors to earn more without losing Social Security benefits

8. Eliminating federal unfunded mandates (that is, federal laws that require states or communities to take particular actions but do not provide the funds necessary for the actions) and passing other reforms to create new jobs and increase wages, such as reducing the capital gains tax and providing incentives for small businesses

9. Reducing damages awarded in civil cases and making other "commonsense legal reforms"

10. Term limits on senators and congressmen

The legislative language behind each and every plank of the Contract with America was already written before the Contract was unveiled—pages and pages of legislation, in fact. This may sound like a minor matter, but actually it is the most significant part of the story. The Contract was much more than an easy-to-read political manifesto. To be sure, the ten planks were reduced for public consumption to catchy, focus-group-tested phrases, much as other campaign manifestos are constructed. But Contract task forces produced a complete bill for each plank, one that voters could scrutinize *before* the election. It was an arduous process persuading lawmakers who had never been in the majority to stop thinking about issues from the perspective of Republicans playing off Democratic proposals and start thinking of bills they wanted to become law. Operating as the minority party, Republicans created a political agenda they believed would give them real legislative power. By painstakingly turning "issues" into legislative documents, the Republican authors of the Contract made it impossible for their agenda to disappear after Election Day 1994, as so many election-year manifestos do. With tax cuts, welfare reform, defense spending, ballistic missile defense, prison and crime reforms, and the line-item veto, Republicans changed the country through the power of ideas and the unshakable desire to implement them. Unlike any other political document in American history, the Contract lived a more important life after the last ballot was counted than it did before the first vote was cast.

Two other Congresses of the twentieth century can claim the mantle "historic"—the first New Deal Congress, which set Franklin Roosevelt's liberal agenda in legislative stone, and Lyndon Johnson's first Congress, which enacted most of the Great Society programs. But both of those Congresses followed the political lead of powerful presidents who had won landslide elections. The GOP Congress of 1995, in contrast, worked in defiance of an opposition president in his first term in office and only two years removed from unseating a Republican incumbent. No Congress in American history working from such a small toehold of power gave rise to a wider array of ideas or changed the country, its economy, its defenses, its culture, or its political processes more profoundly than the 104th Congress. Not all at once. But gradually, at times almost imperceptibly, Congress changed America from top to bottom. And it did so through the strength, grit, and idealism of a kind of conservative Republican America had never known before and in many ways is still getting used to.

The America we live in now is a reflection in more ways of the 104th Congress than it is of the presidency of Bill Clinton or George W. Bush. Indeed, that Congress radically altered the political course of Clinton's presidency and laid the intellectual and political foundation for Bush's. The presidents might have signed the laws, but the 104th Congress either proposed those laws directly or set in motion the process by which they became law. Many policies now part of the fabric of American life drew their intellectual inspiration and political impetus from the leaders and members of that first GOP majority elected in 1994.

This book is not about tactics but about trajectories. It seeks to measure not only what Republicans accomplished and failed to accomplish, but also something much more difficult but just as important—to wit, what happened that otherwise would not have happened had Republicans not been in charge.

It is not an idle question. In fact, it lies at the heart of any serious evaluation of what Republican rule in Congress has meant to the nation.

### Radical Conservatives

Despite the deep and lasting changes it has brought to this country, the Republican Revolution remains misunderstood. Yes, the year 1995 was a watershed in our history. Yet so much of the political analysis immediately after the Year of the Contract dismissed the Contract itself and the legions of Republicans who supported it as failures.

Academic books written one or two years later remarked how pathologically antipolitical the first GOP majority was in seeking to pass the Contract and implement other components of its agenda. The academics said that the Republicans were to a fault antipolitical—in other words, that they were so ideological that they were virtually impervious to standard political calculations measuring how one political position or a series of them would affect constituent relations, fund-raising, and their role with leadership. Congressional scholars seemed absolutely floored and more than a bit repulsed by the apparent unwillingness of some members of the new GOP majority to play Congress's typical political games. For instance, most academics found baffling the frequency with which the newly elected Republican members ignored basic political calculations and plowed ahead with unrealistic plans to close the Departments of Education, Commerce, and Energy. They marveled at the ease with which the new Republican majority threw aside polling data about the government shutdown in 1995 and demanded that its leaders continue on the same course, even as their own prospects for reelection grew ever more remote.

But the commitment to the ideas above all else was entirely the point. The new Republican majority, especially the seventy-three fresh-faced freshmen, considered themselves a majority rooted in ideas they were sure would create a better America. Many of these ideas had been kicking around GOP think tanks and policy shops for years. Congressional Democrats had ignored both the Republicans and their ideas, as had the national media. But Republicans kindled their dreams of a House and Senate majority around the glow of a few big ideas—all of which were incorporated into the Contract with America.

Indeed, the Republicans of the 104th Congress and the Congresses that succeeded it were profoundly idealistic. The terms "conservative" and "idealism" are almost never found in the same sentence. But among the many things it is important to understand about the Republican Revolution, one of the most critical is the commitment of the vast majority of the members of the 104th Congress to their ideas, their belief that their ideas were better than anyone else's. To most of them, ideas were more important than politics. They looked askance at the sort of political calculations normal politicians make every day, because such calculations would subvert their ideas and undermine their very purpose as political actors. This idealism is one of the reasons the most radical conservatives who came to power in 1995 proved so hard to manage.

Of course, it would be naive to believe that congressional Republicans did not also hunger for power. While they clearly expected that control of the House would allow them to radically alter the direction of domestic and foreign policy, they also intended to punish Democrats and those who cooperated or sympathized with Democrats. Of the hundreds of internal House GOP documents I reviewed for this book, one of the most startling was a section from a massive confidential document that the Republican leadership developed in the summer of 1994 to plan for how to use the institutional power of the House upon gaining majority control. Titled "Hearings/Oversight," the document (which can be found in this book's appendix) read:

> The purpose of this section is to explore how a Republican majority in the House should use committee oversight authority. . . . To do the job right, House Republicans have to start with the right job description. They should consider oversight hearings both a tool for building constituencies and a weapon to expose and punish bad people and their bad policies. Yes, bad people, not just people with whom we disagree. House Republicans must be willing to let the world know that great evil has been done in the Congress over the past 40 years of Democrat rule. To exaggerate a bit, this will be our Nuremberg. Month after shocking month, the Democrat past must be put on trial.

With the benefit of hindsight, it's easy to see that this document failed to influence the House Republican approach to oversight. When it came to exposing the "great evil" of past Democratic Congresses or investigating government waste or malfeasance, the Republicans did almost nothing.

But they did use their congressional power against the Clinton White House. "I never understood why Republicans, after having their best election in fifty years on an issue-based strategy, promptly spent the next six on personal attacks," former Clinton political adviser Paul Begala told me. "It is impossible to express the torture that those right-wing congressmen exacted in their endless, politically motivated investigations. I truly hate the way those politicians abused the legitimate oversight function of Congress. There is no doubt it was a political strategy." Begala takes the oversight part of the GOP agenda personally, since many of his friends found themselves on the other end of Republican subpoenas.

But even Begala does not question that the Contract itself was rooted in new and important ideas. "As a strategist, I thought it was damn clever," Begala says. "It was very smart for the Republicans to accentuate accountability and commitment. It was also based on ideas, not personal attacks." He also concedes that Republicans shaped welfare reform, proved far more aggressive in reforming Congress than Democrats, and shifted national policy toward more direct confrontation with Saddam Hussein's Iraq and did so long before 9/11.

The early reviews of the first GOP House majority in forty years missed the critical point of the Republicans' idealism. Instead observers took out their legislative scorecards and noted that in the first hundred days only two bills were signed into law: one applied all federal labor, health, and workplace safety laws to the congressional workplace; and the other prohibited federal unfunded mandates. Only one bill was signed into law in the next hundred days. For the entire first year of the 104th Congress, only 88 bills became law—the fewest laws passed in a session of Congress since 1933, when the Twentieth Amendment was ratified, moving the month of Congress's convening from March to January. In the twenty years prior to 1995, the number of laws passed in a legislative session had dipped below 200 only twice and had never dropped below 100. Congressional analysts looked at the 104th's initial output and sniffed. "Republicans scored very few achievements," concluded *Congressional Quarterly,* considered by many the most authoritative and unbiased chronicle of congressional matters.

Why so few laws passed that first year? The new Republican majority sought massive changes in almost every area of government. It sought to radically alter the understood order of things in Washington. Where Democrats wanted to spend, Republicans wanted to cut. Where Democrats wanted to cut, Republicans wanted to spend. Programs Democrats vowed to preserve just as they were, Republicans vowed to reform as radically as possible. A Democratic president who had allowed himself to be defined by the congressional Democratic majority he inherited in 1992 felt obliged to stop the radical Republican restructuring of government wherever he could. But as we shall see, the new Republican majority's aggressive policy agenda changed the Clinton White House far more than the Clinton White House changed the hard-charging Republicans.

In short, to judge that first Republican Congress based on how many laws were immediately passed is utterly inadequate. It was said at the time that the GOP Congress failed because only one-third of the Contract became law during the 104th Congress. It was also said that the Republicans failed because they lost the public relations war over the 1995 government shutdown and provided a beleaguered President Clinton the kind of political showdown that led to his rehabilitation and reelection. These measurements fit precisely within Washington's obsession with tactical advantage and its slavish devotion to offering instant winner-loser analysis of any political confrontation.

Judging the first Republican Congress simply by the number of laws passed also ignores just how active that Congress was and how significant its proposals were. The first ninety-three days of the 104th—in which the Republicans moved ten separate pieces of legislation to the floor for votes, the ten planks of the Contract—were, in fact, the most productive of any Congress since 1933, when Congress wrote Franklin D. Roosevelt's "First Hundred Days" legislation. But the 104th was actually more productive than even Roosevelt's Congress, which simply redrafted bills passed previously that Roosevelt's predecessor, Herbert Hoover, had vetoed. In other words, Roosevelt's highly productive Congress was not staking out new ground, as the Republicans were in 1995. Moreover, in 1933, Congress was reacting to a national crisis, the Great Depression; no crisis existed in 1995, and thus Congress had no such mandate for radical change. Nor were the Democrats who controlled Congress in 1933 reacquainting themselves with the levers of power for the first time in decades. This is not a point to be taken lightly. The Republican majority of 1995 had no hands-on knowledge of how to run

Congress—how to organize committees, apportion committee staff, or bring legislation to the floor.* The Republicans started from nothing but a set of ideas and a notion that they wanted to govern differently and wield legislative power more effectively.

Another aspect of GOP success emerges when the 104th Congress is viewed through the longer lens of history. This Congress fundamentally changed Bill Clinton's approach to governing, driving him toward a balanced budget in seven years, persuading him to sign welfare reform legislation far more conservative than that which he originally proposed, leading him to dramatically boost spending on defense and intelligence programs, and forcing him to at least wrestle with Medicare bankruptcy by appointing a blue-ribbon panel whose chairman, Senator John Breaux, Louisiana Democrat, would years later play a pivotal role in writing a prescription drug benefit for Medicare on behalf of a Republican president. In addition, it set in motion intense congressional dialogue on ballistic missile defense that would create a wedge issue in the 2000 presidential campaign; it relaunched the career of one of the most powerful defense secretaries in American history (Donald Rumsfeld); it eventually generated a new global consensus on nuclear deterrence built around the concept of shared ballistic missile defense; it created the political impetus for the first middle-class tax cut in twenty-six years (those contained in Clinton's bipartisan budget deal with Congress in 1997); and it reversed a two-decades-long movement toward a center-left consensus on two of the most divisive social issues of our day—gun control and abortion. Finally, the 104th Congress or its immediate successors established the framework for nearly all of President George W. Bush's domestic agenda—most notably the three tax cuts passed during his first three years in office, but also Bush policy on education, welfare, health care, the environment, energy, Medicare, Social Secu-

---

* In fact, the only House Republican in 1995 who had actually witnessed GOP control of the House was the genial Congressman Bill Emerson of Missouri, who had been elected in 1980. Emerson saw it firsthand in 1954 as a House page for the 83rd Congress. He was sixteen. When GOP leaders convened a mock legislative session before taking formal control of the House on January 4, 1995, they had Emerson sit in the Speaker's chair because at least he could say he had seen a House GOP majority before and could speak with some credibility about what it looked and acted like. Emerson played the part of Speaker with aplomb, but when he walked down off the rostrum the footing was so unfamiliar, he lost his balance and fell, seriously injuring his ankle. No one considered it an omen, merely a reminder that the footing is trickier at the higher altitudes of power.

rity, defense, intelligence, crime, abortion, agriculture, regulations, and space exploration.

Many other ideas pursued vigorously in the 104th survive to this day. Many have changed the way you live your life. Many will change the way your children will live. Consider how many changes in American life are a direct result of actions taken by the 104th Congress or set in motion by it or later GOP congressional majorities:

- Everyone now pays lower federal income taxes.
- 25 million taxpayers pay on average at least $480 less in taxes because of the implementation of the child tax credit.
- 30 million married couples pay on average at least $369 less in taxes because of the implementation of the marriage penalty relief.
- Every soldier has better equipment and better pay because of annual increases in this type of defense spending first initiated by the 104th Congress and continued by every successive GOP-led Congress. The positive implications of these spending increases on the nation's ability to prosecute the War on Terror will be discussed in detail later in the book.
- The U.S. intelligence community acquired more spy satellites, hired more agents, and operated more aggressively in more nations because of annual increases in CIA and other espionage funding initiated in the 104th Congress and continued by every successive GOP-led Congress. The positive implications of these funding increases on specific tasks carried out to prosecute the War on Terror will be discussed in detail later in the book.
- America is now building a ballistic missile defense system to protect parts of the country from the launch of a ballistic missile carrying a nuclear, biological, or chemical warhead. The creation of this system led the United States to abandon the 1972 Anti-Ballistic Missile Treaty, a move that led to a dramatically different global debate on the future of nuclear deterrence. Eventually Russia, China, and Europe agreed that ballistic missile defense was neither destabilizing nor counterproductive. This reevaluation of strategic approaches to deterrence ushered in a new global consensus on the subject, the first such shift since the dawn of the Cold War.
- 2.3 million former welfare recipients now have jobs, 3.5 million fewer families live in poverty, and 2.9 million fewer children live in poverty as a result of welfare reform passed in 1996. States and the federal government have

saved hundreds of billions in lower welfare costs as a result of dramatically reduced welfare rolls since 1996.

- 17 million seniors over the age of sixty-five now have prescription drug coverage they never had before.
- Every American can now set aside tax-free money every year (up to $2,000) for unexpected health expenses, roll over unused portions, and transfer the entire accumulated sums to his or her heirs.
- Education spending increased 142 percent, from $23 billion to $56 billion, from 1996 to 2004. Funding for special education—a federal mandate since 1975—has increased 282 percent since Republicans took control of Congress, with spending in 2005 exceeding $10 billion.
- Every student in America will be tested for reading and math comprehension starting in the third grade and continuing through the eighth grade.
- For the first time since the Supreme Court's 1973 *Roe v. Wade* decision legalizing abortion, the federal government banned an abortion procedure. (The procedure is known as partial-birth abortion; President Clinton vetoed the ban twice, but President Bush signed the bill in 2003.)
- The federal criminal appeals process has been streamlined and the process of prosecuting death penalty cases and carrying out the death sentence if so ordered has been sped up.
- States are now required to increase sentences served by violent felons or lose federal funding for prison construction; as a result, tens of thousands of convicted felons have remained in custody for many more years, frequently fulfilling nearly all of their jury- or judge-imposed prison sentences.

Just as important are the policies and programs the 104th Congress and its successors stopped or reversed. After the Republican ascendancy in 1995, Congress

- Blocked creation of a patients' bill of rights to protect patients from decisions by health maintenance organizations (HMOs) that deny care or seek lower-cost care than the patient prefers or his or her doctor recommends. The blocked bills would have given patients broader access to sue HMOs for decisions that led to injury or death.
- Blocked moves to impose taxes of up to 50 cents per pack of cigarettes to fund federal health insurance and child care programs.

- Blocked all new attempts to expand gun control laws, such as requiring background checks at weekend gun shows.
- Blocked attempts to hold firearms manufacturers and gun sellers liable for injuries or deaths caused by a firearm the manufacturer produced or the gun seller sold.
- Allowed the ban on the domestic sale and importation of nineteen so-called assault weapons to expire in 2004.
- Rejected the Kyoto Protocol on global warming and conducted numerous hearings to question the validity of the underlying science identifying a sizable increase in global temperatures and the underlying causes thereof. This campaign of legislative and political rejection led George W. Bush to campaign against the Kyoto Protocol in 2000 and order the United States to abandon it almost immediately upon his taking office.
- Reversed six years of increases in funding for the Environmental Protection Agency (EPA), sought to reverse or reversed numerous specific regulations on clear air, clean water, and industrial waste, and when it could not reverse or kill the regulations, made several attempts to delete funding to enforce them.
- Canceled more than $1 billion in annual taxes assessed against corporations that were designed to pay for the cleanup of Superfund waste sites. The cancellation of taxes didn't mean the end of Superfund cleanups, but it relieved corporations of a tax burden and forced Superfund cleanups to compete with all other environmental programs, resulting in a cut of hundreds of millions of dollars each year to clean up Superfund sites where no responsible party could be found.
- Denied 935,000 legal immigrants access to welfare benefits. President Clinton originally sided with the 104th Congress on this point but prevailed two years later to partially restore the $3.7 billion in benefits on the grounds that legal immigrants were just as entitled to welfare as native-born Americans.
- Blocked efforts to lift the so-called gag rule that prevents doctors paid through Medicaid from discussing abortion with patients.
- Blocked increased funding for international family-planning programs that might counsel patients to have an abortion and, under President Bush, eliminated all direct U.S. aid to international family-planning programs that might counsel patients to have an abortion.

### Changing the Political Landscape

The 104th Congress changed more than policy. It changed the political landscape of America. The America we now understand as a Red and Blue nation first revealed itself in the 1994 midterm election that put the Republicans in power.

The tidal wave that swept Republicans into power was enormous, almost unimaginably large. Going into the 1994 election, Democrats held 258 of the 435 seats in the House and 57 of the 100 seats in the Senate; after the election, Democrats held only 204 seats in the House and 48 seats in the Senate (and they lost two more seats when Senators Richard Shelby of Alabama and Ben Nighthorse Campbell of Colorado switched parties). In the House, not a single Republican incumbent lost a bid for reelection. Thirty-four Democratic incumbents lost. This was the highest number and the highest percentage of losses suffered by the party in power in the House since 1948, when Republicans lost 75 seats and their recently won 1946 majority. It was also the most disastrous loss suffered by a president in his first term since Herbert Hoover in 1930, at the dawn of the Great Depression. And for only the second time in American history, a sitting Speaker of the House was defeated for reelection. Democrat Thomas S. Foley of Washington now shared this dubious honor with the Galusha A. Grow of Pennsylvania, who lost in 1862.

In races for governor, the GOP won 11 new seats, increasing their share of governorships from 19 to 30. This produced the first GOP majority in governorships since 1970. After the election, Republicans served as governor in 8 of the 9 most populous states (Florida being the only exception). These victories established another milestone, a majority of governorships in every region of the country, including the South, where Republicans had not controlled a majority of governorships since Reconstruction. As we will later see, the significance of the GOP congressional majority working with fellow Republican governors would figure prominently in the party's ability to transform domestic policy.

And those statistics only hint at the significance of the 1994 election. Some 70 million voters went to the polls in 1994, the largest midterm turnout in real numbers until that time. In the previous midterm election, in 1990, only 61 million voters went to the polls. In other words, the number of voters increased by 9 million, or nearly 15 percent, from one midterm election to the next, the second-biggest jump in American history. And Republicans reaped almost all of the benefits from this unexpected voting surge. Before the 1994 election, the GOP vote total in House races had never exceeded 28 million in any midterm election, which was the 1990 total. But in 1994, Republicans won 36.6 million votes, an increase of 8.6 million, or 31 percent, the largest midterm-to-midterm expansion of a party's House vote in American history. The GOP's share of the House vote, 52.4 percent, was the largest since 1946, when the party won control of the House during President Truman's first term. The Democrats, by contrast, received 1 million fewer votes than in 1990. From 1982 to 1994, the Democratic House vote declined from 35 million to less than 32 million. "The combination of shrinking vote totals for Democrats with an exploding GOP vote (nearly one-third larger than in 1990) was unparalleled since the Democrats' growth spurt in the 1930s during the Great Depression and the early days of the New Deal," *Congressional Quarterly* observed. And it was a vast turnaround from the previous election. In 1992, House Democrats collected more votes than the GOP in every region of the country. But in 1994, House Democrats lost every region except the East. It was the first time since Reconstruction that Republicans had won a majority of congressional districts in the Deep South.

These were stunning gains for the Republicans. Nothing like this had been seen even during Ronald Reagan's presidency. Republicans had gained control of the Senate in the 1980 election, as Reagan's landslide victory over President Jimmy Carter helped carry several Republican senators to narrow victories. But the GOP's gains in the Senate were linked almost entirely to Reagan's appeal and did not reflect a larger political realignment. Proof of this came when Democrats regained control of the Senate in 1986.

Just as Americans don't think much about Congress, we tend to underestimate the significance of congressional elections. We often treat House races as quaint exercises on the margins of federal governance, since a race for one seat out of a universe of 435 seems only slightly more important than a race for city council or county commission. (In some large cities, the congressman is in fact far less powerful than a city councilman or a county commissioner.) But House elections are, it is worth remembering, the world's oldest broadly popular elections. Americans began electing members to the House of Representatives in 1788 (fully 125 years before the Sixteenth Amendment would call for the popular election of senators). Historically, House elections are second only to presidential elections in highlighting political trends and conferring governing legitimacy upon those elected.

From a distance of ten years, we know that the shift in 1994 was real and profoundly important. For the next decade the Democrats tried and failed to eliminate the Republican majority. To be sure, the GOP's gains ebbed slightly in subsequent elections, but the Republican majority survived nonetheless. It survived Clinton's reelection in 1996, when the incumbent increased his vote total by 6 percentage points over 1992 and Democrats increased their congressional vote total by 4 percent. It even survived the 1998 elections. Speaker Newt Gingrich had predicted gains of at least 20 seats in the House in 1998, but defying historic trends, House Republicans *lost* 10 seats, while Senate Republicans won no seats. Gingrich, the leader of the Republican Revolution, announced his resignation shortly after the election.

Many observers view the 1998 election as the final blow to the Republican Revolution, the coup de grâce after they had already suffered setbacks during the 1995 budget showdown with Bill Clinton and Clinton's reelection in 1996. But in fact, that election only reinforces how central the core ideas were to the Republican ascendancy in 1994. In the immediate aftermath of the 1994 election, many Clinton loyalists and their multiple media apologists attributed the GOP landslide to blind anger at Clinton— the revenge, it was popularly observed at the time, of the "angry white man." Clinton defenders said the landslide had nothing to do with the Contract with America, nothing to do with decades of Democratic control of Congress, nothing to do with the voters' desire to see Washington under new management (something Americans *thought* they were voting for in 1992). If 1994 had simply been about anger at Clinton, then the Republicans should have run away with the 1998 elections. After all, as a party, Republicans ran in 1998 almost entirely on the Monica Lewinsky scandal. They ran on the outrage and disgust they were sure the report by Independent Counsel Kenneth Starr would provoke (which is why they rushed it to the public).

Of course, in seeking a repudiation of Clinton, the Republicans were themselves repudiated. They had sent a thunderous signal that GOP control of Congress was no longer about ideas, no longer about Washington under new management, no longer about advancing the center-right consensus enshrined in the Contract with America. The Republican majority had stopped identifying itself with the historic movement it had set in motion and fought so hard to advance only four years earlier. Instead, with single-minded zeal, the Republicans pursued Clinton's sexual foibles and did whatever possible to criminalize the subsequent denials. Moderates turned away, naturally and predictably. But in greater real numbers and in greater percentages, conservatives turned away as well. Conservatives recoiled from a party that appeared to have lost all sense of the responsibility of governing and all or certainly much of its interest in new ideas or new approaches to old problems.

Nevertheless, the majority survived. When I asked Gingrich his thoughts about the 1998 election, he replied, "Do I have regrets? Yes. Do I know what I could have done to solve it? No. My problem was with the Senate. I argued passionately in 1998 for an agenda of big ideas, and they said no. They said they didn't want any issues. Do I think we should have run on issues? Yes. Did I know how to get around the Senate? No. They wanted to pursue the exact same strategy that lost them the Senate in 1986, which was to run on nothing. We wanted to run on the merits of our ideas. They said no. And I battled against 125,000 [television and radio] ads run against me. And yet we kept control. So I often ask people about that election, 'Do you realize that what you're looking at when you're looking at Speaker [Dennis] Hastert is we have delivered the first decade of Republican control of Congress since 1920?' We propped that up. We had to choose: keep getting the crap beat out of us or keep control." In short, according to Gingrich, when Democrats focused all of their attacks on him, it tended to shield individual Republicans from political damage in their own districts. "So we took the beating and the heat and we kept control. In '98 I couldn't weigh in [with fellow Republicans] the way I had before. People were just tired. But I have no regrets about impeaching the president. If we had allowed a sitting president to lie under oath and gone with the political calculations, which were 'Don't do it, he's too popular, he'll never be removed from office,' then we would have been applying a sick principle by allowing him to beat back the rule of law. We would not do that, and we applied the rule of law and we had to pay a cost."

Not only the majority survived, but the ideas survived as well, even if the Republican leadership had temporarily deemphasized them. Republicans might have chosen to set those ideas aside in 1998, but it is important to note that American voters had not repudiated the ideas. Indeed, over the course of a decade the central ideas that animated the initial Republican Revolution became mainstream and, as noted, became the guiding principles of George W. Bush's presidency. A decade of Republican rule has not only influenced the daily nuts and bolts of legislating. It has enabled the Republican Party to dictate the terms of America's political debate and also to reinforce discipline within its ranks, recruit new party activists and leaders, generate long-term thinking, and generally create a sense of identity, direction, and purpose.

"You wonder if Republicans are headed to their forty years of control," says Larry Sabato, topflight political scientist at the University of Virginia. "The way they have been able to hold on is really a miracle. The campaign against them in 1996 could not have been more Democratic. They survived the disaster of impeachment. And they survived in 2000, when the last two weeks were all solidly Gore, and then in 2002 they defy history and come back and win seats. Something has to be going on. This Congress is often termed right-wing. In fact, it is closer to the views of America than the Democratic Congress it replaced."

Still, Democrats believed that Republican control of Congress was a phase that voters would soon grow tired of, that the ideas for which the Republicans stood were only incidental. The steady inroads the Democrats made in each election kept offering hope for a breakthrough. But in the 2002 elections, the Republicans gained seats in the House and Senate, even though midterm elections traditionally favor the party that does not control the White House. Democrats began to comprehend that they weren't as close to becoming the majority party again as they had thought. And they began looking for ways to redefine the party and give the party back the energy it had lost first in the 1994 election and again when George W. Bush beat Al Gore in 2000.

As the 2004 elections approached, it became clear that the Democrats, having been out of power for a decade, were fighting to reestablish their party's identity and purpose. For most of the twentieth century, the Democratic Party controlled Congress and thus set the parameters of debate on a wide range of issues. They used these powers to create a separate space for debate and legislative dialogue that often reinforced larger party political aims. They had the power of communication, the power of investigation, and the power to use the media to get out their message. With such dominion over the American political process, they did not have to pay much heed to Republican ideas. Republicans were not setting the terms of debate; they were on the defensive, merely reacting to Democratic proposals. The revolution came when they asserted their own ideas rather than simply critiquing the Democrats'.

Even Bill Clinton, as the titular head of the Democratic Party in the 1990s, did not clearly set out what the party stood for upon winning the presidency. As will be discussed at length, he fought with the party's more liberal congressional majorities in the House and Senate and found his own senior staff frequently divided on what would become the most important accomplishments of his presidency (cutting taxes, balancing the budget, and reforming welfare). Often the political pressure congressional Republicans brought to bear was what moved Clinton toward the positions he eventually staked out. This process carried a name: "triangulation." It wasn't a policy, a belief, or a philosophy. It was a political device, as even top Clinton advisers now concede. "I always believed in the Third Way and hated triangulation," Paul Begala, a top Clinton political adviser, told me. "One is a philosophy born of the notion that we can achieve liberal, activist ends through nonbureaucratic means. The other is simply posturing and positioning—you figure out where Jesse Helms is and where Jesse Jackson is and split the difference. Triangulation is bullshit. It is the antithesis of leadership and should never be confused with the Third Way." Even so, Clinton spent the last six years of his presidency "triangulating" Republicans on a variety of issues: tax cuts, welfare, defense spending, crime control, education, and entitlements. On some of these issues, Clinton moved much closer to the "radical" Republican majority than he ever wanted to (tax cuts, welfare, and defense), while on others, Republicans failed utterly to budge Clinton (education, the environment, and entitlements).

Finally, during Bush's presidency, Democrats recognized that they needed to get their own ideas out to Americans. Prominent Democrats who used to work in the Clinton White House created a new think tank in Washington in 2003, the Center for American Progress. It was designed, its leaders said, to fill a void in Democratic thought. But it had another purpose. It would not only create ideas but also sell them aggressively to the media. The Center for American Progress was, in essence, both think tank and war room. These Democrats looked around and found no centralized place where ideas and policy positions were formulated. "We can't do this through Congress like we used to," they said. "We need something new." It was among the many signs that Democrats were finally coming to grips with all that they had lost being in the minority. They needed to rebuild from the wreckage of the 1994 election.

At the 2004 Democratic National Convention in Boston, nominee John Kerry of course was the toast of the town. But the party faithful still had a warm spot in their hearts for former Vermont governor Howard Dean, who received an earsplitting ovation before he addressed the convention. Alone among Democrats running for the presidency in 2004, Dean identified two evil forces in American politics: President Bush and the congressional Republican majority. What's more, alone among Democrats, Dean devoted enormous energy to recruiting and supporting candidates to run in congressional races throughout the country, precisely the tactics that Newt Gingrich and other Republicans began employing years ago as they plotted to one day control Congress. In fact, Dean considers Gingrich and Ralph Reed, former chairman of the Georgia Republican Party and for years the chief political operative of the Christian Coalition, two of the most important political figures of the modern era.

"Ralph Reed and Newt Gingrich understood what they had to do and executed the plan," Dean told me. "They knew you've got to run outside the battleground states; you've got to go off the traditional map. If you don't send the message to voters everywhere, you can't compete and you can't pressure the other party to spend money and force it to compete. They were incredibly effective. You have got to admire the craft. They were the central figures in the change. They created a real opposition party. [Gingrich] and Reed created a real success for the right wing."

Dean told me that he considers the 1994 GOP victory the central political trauma for the Democratic Party in the post–World War II era. He considers it one of the three most important elections of the twentieth century, ranking it alongside the 1932 election that elected Roosevelt and ushered in the New Deal and John F. Kennedy's victory in 1960, which Dean argues set in motion Democratic liberalism and brought the country new civil rights laws, Medicare, Medicaid, and welfare. Dean concedes that the party fell into a deep intellectual and political funk after the GOP victory in 1994. He says that Clinton's triangulation allowed the party to ignore its own intellectual and political decay.

"Clinton in some ways papered over the problem," he says. "While Clinton was doing his jujitsu, the party just waited and the whole structure of the Democratic Party went flat and there wasn't much questioning about our direction. We were lulled into complacency. And when I ran, I tapped in to something. I think Democrats were angry because the Democrats in Congress had largely disappeared as an opposition party. They looked a lot more like Bob Michel [the GOP minority leader before Gingrich's ascension]. They were lulled into complacency and were not fighting back and not challenging the Republicans. But now, finally, we see the emergence of a real opposition party, one that is trying to become a majority party. But it's been very slow. [House Democratic leader] Nancy Pelosi is finally getting that. She's a much more polarizing figure. Luckily it took only ten years to recover instead of the forty years it took the Republicans."

Another sign that Democrats were trying to rebuild from 1994 was the creation of a liberal talk-radio network to combat the rise of supposedly right-wing media giants, such as my employer, the Fox News Channel. Despite millions of dollars in backing, a roster of left-wing celebrities as hosts, and a launch greeted with great fanfare by the mainstream media, the Air America radio network struggled mightily after its rollout. The troubles Air America encountered only underscored the Democrats' inability to fully grasp the role that the media play in the American political process. The media aren't suddenly right-wing or right-of-center, but rather the agenda of the nation has moved in that direction. Why? Because since 1994, congressional Republicans have set the political debate in America. First they changed Bill Clinton into a budget-balancing, tax-cutting, welfare-reforming centrist, and later, with George W. Bush in the White House, they had even more power to direct the nation's agenda.

The media didn't suddenly become captives of conservative group-think; they simply filtered the dominant political action of the day, which to a very significant degree was directed by a Republican president and a Republican Congress. In the modern media era, dominated by radio and TV, America has not seen Republican ideas and Republican means of governance exercised for so long a period of time as they have been in the past decade or given the expansive media coverage, analysis, and credibility they receive today. For the country, for Republicans, for Democrats, this has been a transformative experience.

Another searing example of this phenomenon was the 2004 Democratic National Convention, when prominent party leaders said almost nothing about bedrock liberal cultural issues such as abortion rights and gun control. In a post-9/11 environment, the Democratic Party was eager to prove itself on national security issues. But party leaders—including John Kerry and running mate John Edwards—extolled the virtues of the Contract's middle-class tax cuts, welfare reform, and a strong national defense and vowed to use market mechanisms, not federal mandates, to expand health insurance. Kerry and Edwards did not resurrect Al Gore's "people versus the powerful" campaign from 2000, and neither did they adopt the agenda that Bill Clinton pursued before the GOP breakthrough in 1994. Instead they embraced the agenda Clinton adopted when confronted with a unified Republican majority in Congress and a realigned, center-right political consensus.

The election of 1994 changed America in more ways than anyone could have known at the time. Many critics have suggested that the Republicans' claims about a "revolution" in 1994 were hyperbolic, but a closer examination from the distance of a decade suggests that the choices the nation made in 1994 dramatically altered America's course. Ten years after the 1994 election, we know that the Republican Revolution endures. But to understand its true significance, we must go back to the beginning.

# 2

# CICADAS

The candidates stepped out into sunshine and rounded the corner of the U.S. Capitol, turning into a blinding curtain of light. The September sun shone down and warmed the gleaming white marble of the Capitol's West Front. The politicians shifted their gaze downward to avoid the bright sun, but they were met with the reflected glare only white marble can produce. Below lay the Capitol steps, where taped markers beckoned. The candidates had to stand just so, arrayed on the steps below their ideological, political, and some might even say spiritual savior. From those steps the Republicans pledged to cut taxes, increase defense spending, cut back congressional spending, reduce the size of government, increase private investment. They offered their new vision of Washington, their road map to peace and prosperity. On the lush lawn that cascades from the West Front steps, reporters dutifully recorded the high-sounding rhetoric, jotted down the archly conservative agenda, folded their notebooks—and rolled their eyes. Within weeks, however, many of the candidates on these very steps would score upset victories. Some would take their seats as part of a new Republican majority that fundamentally altered the balance of power in Washington and left political reporters and pundits gasping in disbelief.

You're thinking 1994, the Contract with America, and Newt Gingrich, right?

Wrong.

The year was 1980. The date, September 15. The agenda didn't even have a name; only the event did. It was called the Capitol Steps Event. The candidate was former California governor Ronald Reagan, now the Republican presidential nominee. The event featured Reagan; his running mate, George Herbert Walker Bush; Republican leaders in the House and Senate;

and more than 150 House and Senate candidates. They outlined a five-point agenda they promised to pursue if voters gave them control of the White House and Congress, both of which were under Democratic control.

The agenda, which at the time was described as a "statement of pledges":

1. "Substantial cuts in the money that Congress spends on itself, to set an example for the rest of the Government."
2. "Selective cuts in Government spending to reduce waste, fraud, and abuse, and to fight inflation."
3. "An across-the-board cut in individual income taxes and increased incentives for savings, investment, and capital recovery."
4. "All-out efforts to encourage more private investment and more permanent jobs, especially in the central cities."
5. "Stepped-up military efforts to make the nation's foreign policy credible and to secure peace and stability in the world."

Press coverage was sparse; *serious* press coverage nonexistent. Only the *New York Times* and the *Washington Post* wrote stories the following day. The *Post*'s dispatch, in particular, dripped with sarcasm.

"Republican presidential nominee Ronald Reagan and GOP congressional leaders staged what amounted to a family portrait day on the Capitol steps yesterday—a picture of well-disciplined harmony to contrast with what Reagan called the 'legislative chaos' of the Democrats," wrote reporter Helen Dewar. "If it was a media event, the Republican made the most of it, even though the crowd was mostly congressional aides who did not exactly bubble over with spontaneous enthusiasm. Applause was frequent but thin."

Reagan spoke of the agenda as a road map for governing, a means by which the nation could judge his presidency and his party in Congress. While reporters sneered down below, Reagan stood with his party leaders in Congress (many if not all of whom were far more moderate than he) and spoke grandly of shared goals, shared responsibilities, and shared visions for the country. Looking out upon the verdant expanse of the National Mall, Reagan ignored conventional political calculations that advised against standing with "Beltway insiders" and asked for a mandate that he and his legislative partners could share.

"Each of us here pledges that if elected we will begin working the day after election as a solid, unified team, and we pledge that within a year from today we will achieve five major goals for America," Reagan said. "For the past nearly four years our nation has suffered under a presidency that has failed to lead and under a Democratic Congressional leadership that has failed to provide answers to the issues confronting our government."

The Democratic response? "Another cotton-candy media event," said Senate Majority Leader Robert C. Byrd of West Virginia.

Only David Broder, political reporter for the *Washington Post*, appeared to take the event at face value, study its contents, and offer a serious appraisal. In fact, Broder was the only observer to describe the set of pledges as a "contract" with the voters. It's a word even Republicans didn't use at the time. "The process of presidential campaigning has been so corrupted by 'media events'—posing the candidates in settings that convey a message on a TV tube without verbal content—that there is a tendency to view all visual spectacles as essentially phony. . . . The 'contract' Reagan and the Republicans are offering can be seen as a cheap promise to make—just another 'media event' on the candidate's schedule. But the ceremony has substantive significance, at least in the minds of the junior House Republicans who concocted the notion and sold it to a somewhat reluctant Reagan campaign."

There was one essential link in what many Republicans now regard as the mystic chain connecting two sunny September days fourteen years apart that gave rise to a new era of conservative Republicanism: Newt Gingrich.

## Newt

A freshman congressman from Georgia named Newt Gingrich organized the Capitol Steps Event. Gingrich chaired the long-range planning committee of the National Republican Congressional Committee, which upon its creation was to the D.C. power structure what Pluto is to our solar system—it existed, but you had to look really hard to find it. Even so, Gingrich made it the incubator of GOP plans to retake the House. He reported to Representative Guy Vander Jagt, a Michigan Republican who would lose his seat in 1992 in a Republican primary to Pete Hoekstra, one of the legions (yes, legions) of architects of the Contract with America. Gingrich's title as chairman of long-range planning gave him no staff, no office, and no clout. He was, by his own admission, a nonentity annoyingly yapping at the heels of the powerhouse Reagan campaign. Gingrich sold the campaign on the idea of a unity event where Reagan could appear with other GOP candidates in hopes of creating a linkage. Gingrich was confident Reagan would have coattails and he wanted to show home-state reporters that hundreds of Republican House and Senate candidates stood with Reagan and he with them. But there was a problem: That's all the Reagan campaign wanted Reagan to do, stand with Republicans.

"It was fascinating because the Reagan people were very unwilling to do anything but a dog-and-pony show," Gingrich told me. "So about two weeks out, I got Guy Vander Jagt's approval to tell the Reagan campaign we were canceling the event. And Bill Casey [Reagan's campaign manager] called me. I'd never really talked to him, and he said, 'Young man, I gather you wanted my attention.' I told him there had to be substance; for this thing to have any real impact, candidates had to lead with something common."

The year before, Gingrich had begun studying Margaret Thatcher's victory in 1979, when she became Britain's most conservative prime minister since World War II. He and then–GOP chairman Bill Brock brought to Washington the advertising firm that had worked on Thatcher's campaign.

"We understood how Thatcher had used ideas to win this decisive, stunning election in Britain," Gingrich recalls. "And that model was the framework for the Capitol Steps Event."

Reagan won, and Republicans won 33 seats in the House. More important, they won 12 seats in the Senate, gaining control of that body for the first time since 1952. Six Republican candidates who stood with Reagan on the steps defeated Democratic incumbents by a total of 241,277 votes out of 10.5 million cast.

"Say to yourself, What are the odds of these six guys, who all won their upsets, winning them without the kind of media attention that they got back home after having gone to the Capitol steps and standing next to Reagan and being part of the national sweep?" Gingrich says. "You can arguably make the case that that wouldn't have happened."

This is a point political scientists could spend hours debating. What's obvious is that the event identified Republican candidates with a concretely conservative agenda contrasted against a prevailing liberal Democratic agenda. This affirmative agenda pointed to a different future. It stood athwart the atmosphere of disillusionment and doubt of the Carter years.

Voters decisively chose the Reagan vision and the issues identified at the Capitol Steps Event. It wouldn't have worked without Reagan, the dominant change agent. It wouldn't have worked without the profound sense of distress among voters, fostered by presidential missteps and perpetual infighting with Congress. And it wouldn't have worked without a clear, visible, and unifying conservative Republican alternative.

If you were to subject the 1994 Contract with America to a political DNA analysis, the dominant genetic fingerprint would be the Capitol Steps Event. The Republicans of 1994 would ultimately fashion something larger and more ambitious, but the link to the Capitol Steps Event is undeniable. In fact, when the Contract with America was in its early planning stages in the late spring of 1994, "we kept calling it the Capitol Steps Event," remembers Kerry Knott, who was then chief of staff to Representative Dick Armey, who was at the time the chairman of the House Republican conference, the number-three position in the leadership. (The name "just didn't roll off the tongue," Knott says in explaining why the Republicans changed it.) Perhaps it is not surprising that the Republicans would resurrect the idea. After all, as Gingrich postulates, the Capitol Steps Event may well have created the Senate Republican majority in 1980, and by 1994, House Republicans had spent *forty years* mired in the minority.

The concept enshrined in the Capitol Steps Event did not reappear right away, of course. It went underground for a full fourteen years, emerging later in a slightly more evolved form. Gingrich used a fitting metaphor to describe the Republican leadership's process: "We planned in cicadas," referring to the insects that hibernate in seventeen-year cycles. In the case of the Contract, the cycle was fourteen years. Like the cicada, the concept of the Contract really did disappear. As it stayed underground, the political world above it went through tumultuous changes. The world it rejoined was barely recognizable compared with the world it had once known.

In 1980 Reagan's Republican Party was conservative because *he* was. Left to their own devices, Republican leaders would have continued their post–World War II ways of supine accommodation to New Deal and Great Society liberalism and the congressional Democrats who devoted their lives to remaking the laws and customs of government in the image of Roosevelt and Johnson. Reagan imbued the party with optimism about the future and an instinctive mistrust of government schemes to remake society or mankind. But his party's congressional leadership was chockablock with moderates who nodded agreeably at Reagan's rhetoric but disdained it as a political philosophy and never for a moment considered it the basis to rejuvenate the party or put it on a course toward majority status.

Things were decidedly different in 1994. No longer were congressional Republicans content to stand by as Democrats set the nation's agenda. They were committed to communicating their ideas to the American people so those ideas could govern the nation's future.

Because Newt Gingrich is the obvious link between the Capitol Steps Event and the Contract with America that propelled the Republicans to power in 1994, it is easy to claim that Gingrich himself was the reason for the Republican ascendancy. Numerous commentators have said that the Contract with America was Gingrich's idea; that he named it; that he wrote it; that he sold it to Republicans; that he developed the idea of a signed document, a contract; that it was his idea to put the Contract in *TV Guide;* that he paid to put it in *TV Guide;* that his own pollster, Frank Luntz, did all the polling to guarantee that all Contract items were supported by 70 percent of the public; and that he was the first Republican to see the majority coming in 1994.

None of it is true. These are among the many myths that have built up around the Contract with America, the Republican Revolution, and Newt Gingrich. And no one will be more relieved of the burden of these myths than Gingrich himself.

## The Gingrich Myths

There is an archaeology to the Contract with America; it was not created by one man. Yes, Gingrich was a central player in the Republican ascendancy, but at various turns he was neither pivotal nor decisive. Gingrich was one of hundreds who joined the effort to achieve a Republican majority in the House. Many gave as much of themselves as Gingrich did. Some gave more. At crucial times through the Reagan, Bush, and Clinton years, if just one of at least twenty players had turned Gingrich down, the majority probably never would have been achieved. Indeed, for much of the march to a Republican majority, Gingrich's *own colleagues* regarded him with derision. In significant respects, Gingrich did not draw followers to his cause but had his followers *driven* to him.

From 1982 forward, Gingrich believed the next election cycle was sure to produce a Republican majority. He was wrong six times in a row before he was right. That he never gave up hope did not mean a majority of his colleagues regarded him as insightful or courageous, or viewed his goal as achievable. In the beginning, you could literally count on one hand those who believed a Republican majority was possible. Many Republicans came to Gingrich simply because he was the only alternative. Even though he kept failing, he refused to give up pursuit of a majority. An increasing number of Republicans frustrated with the privations of being in the minority, and left with no other viable option, moved into Gingrich's circle. As that circle enlarged, it became stronger, more diverse, and better able to achieve concrete goals. Some of the most important innovations that led to the Contract and the House majority in 1994 came from others besides Gingrich.

Still, academics have settled on a theory of the Republican majority that portrays Gingrich as the modern legislative equivalent of George Washington, the indispensable man. In an essay in the 1999 book *New Majority or Old Minority?: The Impact of Republicans on Congress,* University of Oklahoma professor Ronald M. Peters said this about Gingrich's approach:

> Borrowing from contemporary management and military command theories, Gingrich sought to develop a doctrine for House Republicans that would unify them under his direction. In all of this Gingrich clearly believed that it was possible to shape member expectations. His premise was not that member expectations were a given (an independent variable); to the contrary, he believed that member expectations were bound to be shaped by someone or something and he was determined to make sure that the members took their cues from the leadership rather than anyone else.

This is only partially true. And it obscures the symbiosis between Gingrich and his closest allies among House Republicans and outside Republican actors. As we will see, the Contract and the majority created by the 1994 election were as dependent on *outside* actors (some Republican, others not) as they were on the Gingrich leadership team and its dozens of followers among House Republicans. Because Gingrich is a military brat, because he is fascinated with military planning, terminology, and history (and it's not a hobby—Gingrich is the longest-serving teacher in West Point history), political scientists have reached for convenient martial metaphors to describe Gingrich. At times he was a general. But many more times he was a scout, a grunt, a noncommissioned officer, a lonely soldier on impossible missions. He almost always operated on the very fringes of a larger battle plan. Yes, the plan was largely his, but he was no aloof, braided general moving troops on a map and surveying the action through field glasses. Gingrich and many others in the GOP leadership team waged the battle for the majority together, in the trenches. They shared few victories, many more defeats.

There is also a sneering, partisan analysis of Gingrich that inflates his role, minimizes the role of others, and portrays rank-and-file House Republicans as sycophants. It reached its zenith in Sidney Blumenthal's 2003 book, *The Clinton Wars:*

> He had brought House Republicans out of their wilderness—forty years in the minority—into their promised land. He was their mysta-gogue, a figure who, as Max Weber wrote, presents "magical actions that contain the boons of salvation." Gingrich was an avatar, not a deliberator; a man in search of a zeitgeist, not a compromise. He was intoxicated with the notion that he had a "mandate." By his lights, the congressional midterm election was a national referendum on him and his patchwork Contract with America—and he had won.

I don't suppose Blumenthal was trying to miss the point entirely, but he couldn't have missed by a wider margin if he was. Let us catalogue:

- Gingrich was not a mystagogue, a teacher of mystical doctrines. If any-thing, he studied and taught raw, down-to-earth politics: fund-raising, polling, issue development, team-building, candidate recruitment, can-didate training—the kinds of fundamentals that put the muscle behind ideas and allowed the party's emerging conservative consensus to aggressively compete in the public square. With the exception of Tom DeLay (often described affectionately by colleagues and menacingly by Democrats as the best Republican machine politician of the twentieth century), Gingrich may have been the most down-to-earth figure in the GOP ranks.
- Gingrich was not an avatar, a deity reincarnated in human form. Gin-grich thought himself brilliant and tireless, yes. But he did not see him-

self as a godsend, and neither did his closest allies or followers (a fact to which the withering quotes in this book will attest). The opposite may have been closer to the truth. Gingrich came to many more on bended knee, and he drew his eventual strength from his alliance with them rather than from their allegiance to him.

- Gingrich did not search for the zeitgeist, the fleeting moment of cultural consensus. Gingrich, his leadership allies, and those who followed them came to believe that out-of-step Democrats were clinging to a bygone, Great Society–era, center-left agenda in order to extend Washington's centralized powers. In other words, the emerging GOP believed the nation had moved center-right but was being governed center-left. Realigning center-right America with its federal legislature was the goal. In pursuit of that goal, Republicans would produce durable majorities and a new approach to government.

The truth is, Gingrich was neither the general nor the beguiling mystical leader of the Republican Revolution. He wasn't the only catalyst for the majority and he was not necessary for the majority to continue or flourish. In fact, the Republican majority has proven more durable without Gingrich than with him. Gingrich was not solely responsible for the 1994 election strategy, but he *was* responsible for the 1998 election strategy that led to historic GOP losses and cost Gingrich his Speakership. The GOP majority has grown larger and has accomplished more legislatively since Gingrich left Congress (with the exception, of course, of the first hundred days of the first GOP Congress in 1995). And even though Republicans lost seats in 2000, virtually all Republicans ran ahead of President George W. Bush. Bush "got it wrong" in 2000, top Republican lobbyist/activist Grover Norquist told me. "Bush thought he was more popular than the Republican House. Not on Election Day. They pulled him over. The Republican House electorally pulled him over the finish line. Once elected, he [Bush] adopted their entire agenda."

So let's dispense with the analysis that portrays Gingrich as the *sine qua non,* to use one of his favorite phrases. The story of the Contract with America and the Republican Revolution is the story of dozens of key players.

Did Gingrich lead? Yes. Did everyone follow blindly? No. Was Gingrich a figure of internal ridicule for years leading up to the 1994 election?

Yes. Did some of his closest advisers doubt him almost every step of the way? Yes.

### The Long Road to a Revolution: A Time Line

From 1980 to 1994, a number of significant events occurred that made the election of 1994 possible. Each was slightly more important than the one that immediately preceded it. All created a centripetal force that drove Republicans closer together. Some of the events were external, some internal. All added unity. Taken together, they go a long way toward explaining why Republicans were ready, willing, and able to organize themselves as they did to seize the unique moment that was the 1994 election.

### 1982

After the Republicans gain 33 seats in the House and 12 in the Senate in 1980, Gingrich goes into the 1982 election thinking a majority might be possible. But Republicans lose 26 seats in the House, and hopes of riding Reagan to a House majority disappear.

Senate Republicans cajole Reagan into raising income taxes. Gingrich dubs Bob Dole the "tax collector for the welfare state."

GOP pollster Fred Steeper and GOP consultants work with Gingrich to develop the model of "wedge" and "magnet" issues. Wedge issues divide the opposition party, while magnet issues attract those of the opposition who have been disaffected by the wedge issue. The model arises from a theory that effective politics is driven by binary choices—that is, if you believe in A and B, then you must chose C, not D. In the simplest formulation of the time, it translates roughly as, "If you believe lower taxes and more efficient government are best, then you must choose Republican, not Democrat." The binary-choice model will eventually be carried over into almost every issue and subissue.

Steeper's polls also search for broad, unifying themes around which to build rhetoric, policies, and agendas. The strongest theme by far to emerge is called "American exceptionalism." The phrase becomes an integral part of Gingrich's lexicon and an organizing philosophy from that point forward.

Several Republicans form the Conservative Opportunity Society. The founders are Jack Kemp of New York, Bob Kasten of Wisconsin, Trent Lott of Mississippi, Vin Weber of Minnesota, Bob Walker of Pennsylvania, and

Gingrich. At its core is a throbbing irritation with Reagan's drift away from cutting taxes toward reducing the deficit, always at the behest of moderate Senate Republicans. The name is drawn from a 1982 speech Reagan gave to the National Association for the Advancement of Colored People (NAACP) in Georgia in which the president stressed the importance of "hope and opportunity" for all, even in the midst of the deepest economic downturn since the Great Depression.

Representatives Nancy Johnson of Connecticut and John Kasich of Ohio are elected. Johnson will later become a moderate leader in developing the Contract. Kasich will eventually write the first balanced budget ever submitted by House Republicans and negotiate all Contract-related tax and spending cuts.

## 1983

Joe Gaylord becomes the executive director of the National Republican Congressional Committee (NRCC). Gaylord reports to work and is given one direct order by the committee chairman, Representative Guy Vander Jagt: "Guy Vander Jagt said to me, 'There is one obligation that you have in this job and that is you have to learn and understand what Newt Gingrich is all about and you've got to try to harness that activity for good. Because I believe he is the only person who understands how to get us the majority.' " Gaylord becomes one of Gingrich's closest advisers, and over the years he plays a pivotal role in linking this committee with the Republican National Committee (RNC) in pursuit of a majority.

## 1984

Reagan wins a 49-state landslide victory (59 percent and 525 electoral votes to Walter Mondale's 41 percent and 13 electoral votes) that translates to a paltry 14-seat House GOP pickup, leaving them only 8 seats ahead of where they were in 1978. Senate Republicans *lose* 2 seats, the worst same-party Senate performance in a reelection year since 1940 (Roosevelt's 55 percent and 449 electoral votes to Wendell Willkie's 45 percent and 82 electoral votes).

At the Republican National Convention in Dallas, two House candidates, both from Texas, make a big impression: Dick Armey from Dallas and Tom DeLay from Houston. "In '84, when we went to Dallas for the convention, a couple of the candidates who emerged and saw themselves in

our mold were Dick Armey and Tom DeLay," recalls Bob Walker, a founding member of the Conservative Opportunity Society. "But when they came
to Congress, to some extent they were talked into the you-don't-want-to-be-
with-those-guys wing of the party."

Armey doesn't have to be talked into steering clear of the Conservative Opportunity Society, and all other congressional groups for that matter. "I'm a loner, I've always been a loner," Armey told me. Armey
campaigns in a family pickup truck. "I was with him back when we used to
ride in his pickup truck from campaign stop to campaign stop," says Kerry
Knott, who would later, as Armey's chief of staff, give the Contract its name,
develop its legislative language, and create the transition plan for the GOP
takeover. "It was always, 'We got to get up there and get the majority.' It
wasn't just, 'I want to go serve my time.' "

When DeLay arrives in Congress, he seeks and soon wins a coveted
slot on the Appropriations Committee so he can steer as much federal
spending as possible to his Houston district. He also sizes up his clearest
path to a leadership slot and determines it is through an alliance with
Minority Leader Bob Michel of Illinois, whose leadership style puts the
emphasis on the party's *minority* status.

## 1985

Gingrich takes over the GOP Political Action Committee, commonly
known as GOPAC, and uses it to raise money, organize, and proselytize.

Senator Phil Gramm engineers the appointment of a fellow Texas
Republican, Representative Sam Hall, to the federal bench, creating an
open seat in a rural, gun-loving East Texas district that Reagan carried with
61 percent the year before. This one race will dramatically influence GOP
strategy for years to come. In the Lone Star State donnybrook, Republican
Ed Hargett, a former Texas A&M quarterback chosen by Gramm and RNC
chairman Lee Atwater, defeats the Democrat, Jim Chapman, a protégé of
then–House Speaker Jim Wright. But Hargett falls just short of winning
50 percent of the vote, making a runoff necessary. National Democrats and
Texas savings-and-loan tycoons pour millions into the campaign, and
Chapman wins the runoff. Though Hargett has mishandled two key issues,
trade and Social Security, Gingrich and other Republicans conclude that
the real problem was the GOP's weak approach to competitive House
races. They commit themselves to more fund-raising, better candidate

recruitment, and better candidate training. The NRCC and GOPAC develop the idea of using instructional tapes and manuals to prepare future Republican candidates for the intense media coverage close congressional races inevitably bring.

Meanwhile, a dispute over Indiana's Eighth District radicalizes Republicans as nothing ever has before. Democrat Frank McCloskey wins the first count, but the margin is so small that a recount is required by law. The recount declares Republican Richard McIntyre the victor, and state officials certify the result. Democrats step in and order another recount. A special panel with two Democrats (future Clinton chief of staff Leon Panetta is one) and one Republican is appointed. The two Democrats order the recount stopped when McCloskey is four votes ahead. On the day McCloskey takes his seat in Congress, Republicans storm out of the House en masse. "That process radicalized a third of the party, including Cheney," Gingrich told me, referring to then--House Minority Whip Dick Cheney of Wyoming. "It was the key to the majority." It also galvanizes moderates such as Steve Gunderson of Wisconsin and Marge Roukema of New Jersey to join Gingrich's activist wing of the party. The story of the "Bloody Eighth" will be retold every year at fund-raisers and recruiting functions. It will become an essential chapter in the GOP's oral history of repression at the hands of the despotic Democrats. And in a compelling twist of fate, it will play a key role in the defeat of McCloskey in the 1994 election.

The episode of the "Bloody Eighth" points to why it is myth that the Republican Party moved as robots to Gingrich's every command. Gingrich did challenge other Republicans to confront Democrats, but so did others—Bob Walker, Vin Weber, and Trent Lott chief among them. More important, those battle cries fell largely on deaf ears until episodes like the "Bloody Eighth" persuaded others that Gingrich might, in fact, be up to something.

## 1986

Gingrich again believes that the GOP can win control of the House. But the Republicans lose five House seats. They also lose control of the Senate after dropping 8 seats. Most of the Senate casualties are freshmen elected in 1980, in part by the Capitol Steps Event. In the campaign, the party has communicated no message except "Win one for the Gipper." After the election, Reagan's agenda is losing steam, and Republicans have 15 fewer

House seats and 8 fewer Senate seats than they had in 1980. Talk of a majority in either chamber is limited to what is widely regarded as the fever swamps of the Conservative Opportunity Society.

Dennis Hastert of Illinois, who for sixteen years taught history and government and coached the wrestling team at Yorkville High School in Yorkville, Illinois, is elected to the House. Hastert was chosen the GOP nominee only after the district's congressman, Republican John Grotberg, died unexpectedly of cancer.

## 1987

Vin Weber wins a low-level Republican leadership post. But other "activist" Republicans, such as Wisconsin's Steve Gunderson and Minnesota's Bill Frenzel, are thwarted in leadership races by Bob Michel's accommodationist wing of the party. Gunderson and Frenzel are themselves moderates, but they, like a small but increasing number of Republicans, are hungry to develop a conference-wide plan to win a House majority. They are not Gingrich acolytes. But frustration builds against Michel's perceived political lethargy and stasis. Another moderate, Representative Tom Tauke of Iowa, announces at a weekly meeting of moderates, "If we're serious about changing this party, we have to change the leadership."

On October 27, House Democrats, led by Speaker Wright, use the most diabolical tactics Republicans have yet seen to ram through a budget bill, further enraging moderates and sending them into Gingrich's activist camp. Wright has initially moved to bring the bill to a vote on final passage, but loses the procedural vote 217–203, a rare defeat that elates Republicans and infuriates Democratic leaders. Dozens of conservative Democrats have voted against the bill, because it contains tax increases and $9 billion in new welfare spending. Wright then kills the welfare spending and decides to bring the new bill back to the floor for a vote. But to do so *that day* would require a two-thirds vote of the entire House. To get around this rule, Wright orders the House adjourned and calls it back into session on a "new" legislative day a mere twenty minutes later. Even mild-mannered Republicans are incensed. Former Speaker Tom Foley, then the House majority leader, told me, "Dick Cheney came up to me and said, 'Tom, that's bullshit. That's fucking bullshit.' " Wright wins the vote, but only after sending an aide to find Representative Jim Chapman, the Texas congressman he saved in the 1985 special election, and dragging him back to the

House floor to change his vote and side with Wright. In their oral history of subjugation, Republicans add "Bloody Thursday" to the "Bloody Eighth."

## 1988

Going into the election, Gingrich again believes it's possible for House Republicans to win the majority. Although George Herbert Walker Bush wins the White House, the Republicans lose two seats in the House, while Senate Republicans gain no seats.

Representative Trent Lott leaves the House and his post as minority whip and wins a seat in the Senate.

Bill Paxon of Buffalo, New York, who will later chair the NRCC and develop the fund-raising concept that leads to literally dozens of GOP victories in 1994, wins a seat in the House.

## 1989

Bush appoints Senator John Tower of Texas as secretary of defense. Senate Democrats defeat the nomination over allegations of past drunkenness and infidelity. Wounded and in need of an easily confirmable replacement, Bush nominates Cheney, currently House minority whip. The vacancy sets off an immediate battle for the number-two slot and, as it turns out, the soul of the House Republican leadership.

Gingrich's phone rings at 3:45 P.M. that Friday. *USA Today* congressional correspondent Rich Wolfe tells him that Cheney has just been appointed defense secretary. "As soon as the receiver hits the cradle of my phone, I know I'm running," Gingrich later told me. Gingrich moves swiftly. His administrative assistant tells staffers they have one hour to call House members before they leave for the day. The calls continue all weekend. ("He contacted more than 120 members over the weekend, directly," Joe Gaylord told me.) On Newt's behalf, Representative Joe Barton of Texas calls thirty-five members. Early the next week, Michel, leader of the Illinois delegation and of the still numerically superior go-along-get-along wing of the party, informs Representative Henry Hyde that he cannot run for the number-two slot; instead, Michel's candidate is Illinoisan Ed Madigan. "If Henry had been allowed to run he'd have beaten me easily," Gingrich says now. Madigan chooses DeLay as his campaign manager and the battle is joined. Dick Armey sides with Gingrich, who wins, 87–85.

"When the Democrats killed John Tower, they set in motion the takeover of the House," Armey told me. "They killed Tower, Bush takes Cheney, and Bob Michel had been sitting there with a comfortable old-bull leadership, all the guys who well understood how comfortable it was to go along and get along. It wasn't the conservatives who beat Madigan. It was the activists. Newt was elected by moderate and conservative Republicans, but it was the activists that he won by." DeLay considers that election a turning point for Gingrich, the party, and, most important, himself: "You could consider that moment my downfall. But I think I helped myself right after. That same day Newt had to whip a vote. And on that very day I went into his office and I had to swallow my pride. I had to start from scratch. That's when I set my sights on a new path." A new path that would emphasize activism and conservatism over doling out dollars from the Appropriations Committee and protecting the old order.

In May, House Speaker Jim Wright resigns under Democratic pressure, a casualty, some say, of Gingrich's constant criticism, swirling ethics investigations, and a revolt among Democrats over his dictatorial treatment of *them*. House Democratic Caucus chairman Tony Coelho of California resigns a week later over financial improprieties. Taken together, the resignations appear to confirm the activists' argument of an ethically indifferent congressional leadership.

### 1990

Bush announces that he's willing to raise taxes to reduce the deficit. Negotiations with Congress drag on all summer. Armey, DeLay, Gingrich, and countless others rally Republicans to defeat the first compromise budget, ignoring Michel's pleas to stick with the president, in part because Bush and his top economic advisers never negotiate seriously with the rebellious Republicans. The White House considers it mutiny that the pugnacious congressman who has been the number-two House Republican for less than a year finds the nerve to tell the president and the leader of his party to go to hell. To Gingrich, the decision is easy. Bush broke his "no new taxes" pledge to the country and all elected Republicans. With that act of original betrayal, Gingrich and dozens of other Republicans believe, they have been released from any implied loyalty to Bush.

With Bob Michel lobbying hard for Bush and Gingrich rallying fellow Republicans to reject the compromise budget, the vote is, in essence, a shadow election for the next Republican leader—since everyone knows that Gingrich will challenge Michel eventually. The whole tax-increase ordeal also galvanizes Armey and DeLay, who are frustrated by being shut out of the negotiations. Both decide to aim higher, determined not to be locked out again. Armey sets his sights on the post of Republican conference chairman, which he wants to transform into an idea factory for his own brand of free-market Republicanism.

In the midterm elections, Republicans lose eight House seats and one Senate seat.

John Boehner of Ohio and Jim Nussle of Iowa win House seats. Boehner will become a key backer of the Contract with America in 1994. Nussle will later manage the GOP transition after the '94 election, a mistake-free transition that astonishes Democrats and gives the GOP even more confidence to aggressively push the Contract.

## 1992

In January, Armey challenges Representative Jerry Lewis of California for conference chairman. Lewis, part of Michel's wing, also backed Bush's tax increases. Armey defeats Lewis by two votes. At least two members of Lewis's own California delegation defect to Armey, an unfathomable breach of protocol. "When Newt Gingrich gets elected leader, this makes Michel very uncomfortable," Armey now says. "And then in '92 I decided to run for leadership and I took out Jerry Lewis, and that was another guy Michel was very comfortable with." Nevertheless, Armey now makes clear that he was not part of some Gingrich grand plan. "Newt and I were never in concert. People don't realize this. My run for leadership had nothing to do with Newt. I don't think we had more than a passing conversation between us. People somehow think we were in league, in concert, plotting, putting things together. I was flying solo in what I did. I don't mean to say there wasn't a symbiosis that came out—there was—but there wasn't a conspiracy going in."

At the August convention in Houston, the Bush team desperately tries to win back conservatives infuriated by his tax betrayal. They turn the program over to social conservatives, who pound Middle America with divisive rhetoric about culture wars, abortion, pornography, school prayer, and racism. The radioactive aftermath underscores the need for any future party platform to emphasize tax cuts, defense spending, deficit reduction, and reform.

In November, Bill Clinton wins the presidency, with independent candidate Ross Perot carrying 19 percent of the vote. Bush finishes second with 37 percent, down 16 points and nearly 9 million votes from 1988. Two weeks before the election, Arne Christenson, chief of staff to Representative Vin Weber, calls Dan Meyer, Gingrich's chief of staff, to tell Meyer that Gingrich has just made this upbeat prediction: "We face the very real prospect of President Bush and Speaker Bob Michel." Christenson shares this tale with other top GOP staffers, all of whom chalk it up to Gingrich's preternatural optimism, optimism that routinely unhinged itself from reality. "Newt had talked this up every two years," his former chief of staff, Dan Meyer, now recalls. "He predicted majorities every cycle all the way back to '82. Newt was the poster child of the guy who believed, because he always believed."

Jennifer Dunn of Washington State and Deborah Pryce of Ohio win House seats. Both will play vital roles as female conservatives pushing for the Contract. Dunn will become part of the leadership's kitchen cabinet. Pryce will eventually rise to Republican conference chairman in the post-Gingrich House.

### 1993

In January, the RNC is in shambles. Longtime members are in open revolt. Fund-raising letters are returned with scrawled obscenities.

"We had a deeply disillusioned party," recalls top GOP strategist Don Fierce, who at the time was the RNC's political director. Fierce offers this piquant condensed history of how the party of Reagan optimism had grown so angry:

"Reagan picked up Democrats in 1980. They got in his pickup truck and they rode with him for eight years. Then Bush comes along in his Volvo. They won't get in. But then he promises not to raise taxes and they get in the Volvo and ride with him until he raises taxes. Then they get out and they are pissed. We had lost our way, and I told [RNC chairman Haley Barbour] we have to say this. We need to go back to our people and tell them we lost our way. We did not have a leader. We didn't have a president. Republicans weren't going to listen to Dole, and precinct Republicans didn't know enough about Gingrich. Haley wasn't strong enough to describe the party's identity. I mean, our precinct Republicans were absolutely furious."

Fierce and Barbour set about rebuilding the RNC. Meanwhile, the NRCC next door is in worse shape. The organization through which Gingrich and others dream they will seize a House majority is negotiating its foreclosure. "When we took on the place in '93 we were broke," remembers Bill Paxon, who was then the newly minted NRCC chairman. "I had 93 employees. I cut staff to 26. We did massive layoffs. We got rid of consultants. But it wasn't enough." Banks are calling in overdue loans. The fundraising base has dried up. It's to become the first party committee in Washington history to close.

But that's not how it happens.

Within twelve months, Republicans will outline their plan to win a House majority.

Within fifteen months, the RNC will bankroll a national campaign with a goal of capturing the House, the Senate, and a majority of the governorships.

Within sixteen months, top GOP aides will begin assembling a transition plan to assume control of the House.

Within eighteen months, the Contract with America will be written, and within nineteen months, 337 Republicans will sign it.

Within twenty-one months, Republicans will score the most sweeping election victory in American history.

How could such a dramatic turnaround occur in a matter of months? The story begins on a February morning in Princeton, New Jersey, far removed from Washington's corridors of power.

# 3

# "WHO WOULD HAVE THE COURAGE TO DO IT?"

It was supposed to be a dull, discursive debate on the federal budget. Numbers, mind you. No strategy. But in many ways it was where the Contract with America was set in motion.

On February 26, 1993, the House Republicans had gathered at the Merrill Lynch corporate campus at Princeton, New Jersey. The Republicans were in the minority, as they had been for some four decades. But the situation in 1993 appeared even more dire than usual for the Republicans, since the Democrats controlled not only the House but also the Senate and the White House. The Republicans were on their heels, reacting to the agenda that Bill Clinton and the Democratic Congress were setting.

Three House Republicans with all of four years of Capitol Hill experience among them wanted to force the Republicans to completely change their long-standing way of doing business. Jim Nussle of Iowa and John Boehner of Ohio had been elected in 1990 and had already made a huge imprint on Congress as members of the so-called Gang of Seven, seven freshmen Republicans who challenged all variety of congressional customs. Nussle made national news when he spoke from the House floor with a paper grocery sack on his head, to protest the unwillingness of House leaders to release the names of lawmakers who misused the House bank; Boehner drew nearly as much attention when he condemned Democratic and Republican leaders for sneakily approving a pay raise. Martin Hoke, also of Ohio, had just been elected, and was eager to display similar nonconformity.

"A core group of members, Jim Nussle, John Boehner, and Martin Hoke, stood up and were saying, 'We have to be for something, we cannot just be against Bill Clinton. We have to provide an alternative vision of government,' " recalls Ed Gillespie, the chairman of the Republican National

Committee (RNC) through the 2004 elections, who was then Republican conference chairman Dick Armey's press secretary.

At that point in the debate, the energetic ranking Republican on the Budget Committee, John Kasich of Ohio, stood up and said, "We've got to propose our own budget."

This was a radical concept. Although the Constitution specifically delegates the power to tax and spend to Congress, historically Congress awaits the White House's recommendations and then sorts out the details in accordance with its own peculiar priorities. Members of Congress almost never propose an entire federal budget, because doing so tips Congress's hand as to where the votes lie, where the preferences are, where the weaknesses can be found. The idea of a majority party in Congress writing its own budget was laughable. The idea of the *minority party* doing it was insane.

Gillespie recalls the ensuing debate: "I remember [Kansas congressman] Pat Roberts standing up and saying, 'We don't have to do anything. It's their turn. They have to produce budgets.' "

Roberts's statement was a not-so-subtle reference to the hell Republicans had gone through trying to support President George H. W. Bush's budgets, especially during the tax-increase fiasco of 1990. It also spoke to a deeper division between old-guard and activist Republicans, a schism that would complicate future efforts to plan for a majority. Put briefly, old-guard Republicans considered talk of a majority worse than pointless: it was counterproductive. To pursue a majority meant picking fights with Democrats. Old-guard Republicans, by definition, had accumulated seniority and were in position to vie for some influence with powerful Democratic committee chairmen. Yet they overestimated the value of collegial relationships with the Democratic barons. If they received a favor or project, it was almost always an effort to placate. Democrats hardly ever shared the spoils of power out of kindness, any more than Republicans shared power when they took over. They did it to pacify, to tranquilize.

"We had a lot of problems," Dick Armey told me, recalling the early battles with old-guard Republicans. "I used to call it the dissertation syndrome. You live a crucial, critical part of your life where the most important person in the world for you to please is your dissertation adviser or supervisor. If he's not happy, you're dead. That's what the Democratic chairmen were to a lot of our more senior guys. That's who we were in the minority, with all of our ranking guys [the most senior Republican on any committee]. You watched our ranking guys and what they learned was, My best friend, the guy who can help me out with all of the reasons that I wanted to be on this committee in the first place, is the chairman. So they promised the chairmen a certain amount of complacency and mob control."

Former Iowa congressman Fred Grandy, who played Gopher on the 1970s television series *The Love Boat* and is now a radio talk-show host in Washington, described this problem succinctly: "The trouble with Republicans is they don't have anything and they won't share."

"That was so much of who we were," Armey recalls. "All the ranking [Republican] guys were getting taken care of and had great relationships. One of the reasons the young Turks were the people with the unrest is because they were the ones who weren't getting taken care of."

Young Turks. A better description of the Republicans who set the Princeton budget debate in motion—Nussle, Boehner, and Hoke—you could not find.

The Princeton budget placed the central question before the GOP conference: Would the Republicans be *for* something or simply *against* everything? Kasich took the question head-on. Gillespie recalls the Ohio congressman's summation: "Kasich says we have to have an alternative document that's legitimate and viable that we can point to and say this is what we are for, this is what the spending level and the tax level under our vision of government would be."

As Kasich now recalls, his determination to produce a budget alternative sparked "a very big fight about whether I should be able to put that forward or whether we as the opposition should just sit in the weeds and throw stones. It was vicious, the fighting over that was just vicious." But Kasich won that fight. He also won the burden of producing a viable Republican alternative to the Clinton budget.

The importance of this decision can scarcely be underestimated. In 1993, Republicans were demoralized and Clinton was ascendant. The easy course, the predictable course would have been to resist everything. (In fact, much later, Republicans would be portrayed as doing exactly that.) But the activists, the young Turks, won a crucial argument that required the conference to support a full-blown *alternative* budget. And the budget the Republicans produced was a credible alternative to the Clinton program. It was no coincidence that *every single House Republican* voted against the Clinton budget that year. Newt Gingrich and the rest of the House

Republican leadership never could have imposed the discipline necessary to rally a unanimous opposition without a viable alternative of their own. Republicans held the line against Clinton only because they held the same alternative budget line, one they had created after overcoming internal disputes and doubts.

Republican unity carried over to the Senate as well. Senate Republicans did not produce an alternative budget of their own, but they followed the lead of the young Turks in the House and unanimously opposed Clinton's budget. Afterward, Clinton's chief domestic policy adviser, Bruce Reed, dubbed the Republicans the "over-my-dead-body caucus." Other analysts have similarly focused on the unified GOP opposition to the Clinton budget and attributed it to a sort of mob political mentality by which Republicans were seized with a bloodlust to destroy Clinton's presidency. But if others missed the political lesson, the Republican leadership did not: The GOP achieved a substantial strategic victory not simply by opposing the Democrats and the White House but actually by setting forth a clear accounting of what it stood *for.*

Of course, Republicans would later turn their opposition to Clinton's budget into political success, not just tactical success. The 1993 Clinton budget passed the House and Senate by only one vote in each body. Fierce Republican unity and Clinton's inability to recruit any more than the bare minimum of support consigned every Democrat running for reelection in 1994 to the charge that he or she "cast the deciding vote" for a big tax increase. During the 1994 campaign, the GOP ran TV and radio ads across the country proclaiming that Clinton and the Democratic majority had "passed the largest tax increase in American history" (a fallacious charge— Ronald Reagan's 1982 tax increase, when adjusted for inflation, still ranks as the largest tax increase in American history). But the Republicans would never have reaped those political gains in 1994 if they had not taken the important step toward unity on the budget in that Princeton conference room in February 1993. It was the classic broccoli and ice cream sequence: You don't get the latter without the former.

## Setting Forth the GOP Vision of Government

The decision taken at the Princeton conference in February 1993 was critical for another reason: One could argue that the entire Contract with America flowed from it. The process of formulating a viable alternative budget allowed the Republicans to set forth their vision of a smaller government, and to set forth their three main goals—cutting taxes, reducing the deficit, and increasing defense spending. The policy choices were there for all to see.

The 1993 budget proposal was, for instance, where the Republicans first settled on all the spending cuts they would eventually propose in the budget wars with Clinton. It also showed that a balanced budget was an achievable goal, thus making Republican advocacy of a balanced-budget amendment—which would be a big seller in the Contract—appear far less cynical. It was, by political standards, a true root-canal budget document, full of spending cuts with virtually no tax cuts to ease the pain. It reflected almost entirely Kasich's vision of tackling the deficit by attacking government programs across the board, which meant sacred cows like Medicare, Medicaid, defense, farm subsidies, and veterans' programs. It utterly rejected the supply-side concept of cutting income taxes or investment-related taxes to reduce the deficit through economic growth and thus higher tax revenue. Kasich's energy and determination to focus fellow Republicans on ways to cut spending proved not only galvanizing but enduring as well. In the end, tax cuts were added to the '93 alternative, but they were far smaller in dollar amounts and political importance than the underlying spending cuts House Republicans were committing themselves to.

"The importance of the balanced budget in the long term was that we did have this discussion that if we want a balanced-budget amendment, we'd better be able to show we can do it, and it forced our people to accept Kasich's budgets that actually got you to balance," recalls former Pennsylvania representative Bob Walker, then the Republican chief deputy whip. "And in that sense it also sent out a signal to the Senate that this was really a serious matter. 'We're going to pass a balanced budget, and we're going to insist on balanced budgets whether there's a constitutional amendment or not.' "

### Plotting a New Course

While House Republicans were rallying around their budget, Haley Barbour, the new chairman of the RNC, devoted himself to cleaning up the mess left by the Bush White House. Believing that the party was in shambles, he set forth a four-part plan to return the party to national competitiveness in time for the 1996 presidential election. The plan called for:

1. *Creating self-sustaining state parties:* Barbour concluded that Republicans had grown too dependent on a party structure that took its cues for twelve years from Republican presidents.

2. *Recapturing small donors:* The party had raised a record amount of money in the '92 election but had done it from a much smaller donor base: From 1988 to 1992, the number of donors who gave small amounts of cash—less than $100—had fallen from 1 million to 500,000. Barbour recalls, "I used to tell people after Clinton won, 'We're not going to get any big contributions. We ought to build the party on belief money, not access money, because we ain't got anything to give people access to. We've got 176 members of the House, 42 members of the Senate; they've got the White House and our presidential candidate just got the lowest vote total for a Republican since 1912.' "

3. *Using technology:* Barbour wanted the party to comprehend the importance of television, and under his stewardship the party built its own state-of-the-art television studios and created its own programming for a channel called GOPTV. More than 500,000 Americans watched the 1996 Republican convention on the network. The RNC complemented the television programming with *Rising Tide* magazine and other publications. Barbour's group also instituted a cutting-edge blast fax program, which represented an important way to communicate ideas directly to the people in those days before e-mail was ubiquitous. The Republicans did not ignore the rapidly developing Internet, however. According to Barbour, the GOP became the first major political party to host its own website.

4. *Making the GOP a recognized "party of ideas":* The RNC chairman suspected that Clinton would run into troubles, since Republicans who had stuck with Bush were already against Clinton, and millions of Perot voters were up for grabs. Still, he believed that the Republican Party wasn't doing enough to actively appeal to voters. "We didn't have to tell our people that they did not like Clinton, but it was important to offer something to be *for*," he recalls.

Barbour began by commissioning a fifty-question survey to be sent to party members nationwide. The goal was to demonstrate that Republicans were united by a broad set of ideas. Barbour suspected that Republicans were not only dismayed by Bush's tax increase but were also uncomfortable with the perceived supremacy of social issues over economic and national security issues. Barbour felt that "Beltway Republicans," who had grown accustomed to power after twelve years of GOP control of the White House, had lost touch with rank-and-file party stalwarts.

Barbour had another reason for the survey: He was eager to revamp the image of the RNC as nothing more than a solicitor. "We had to stop and ask ourselves, 'When was the last time we sent out a mailer that didn't ask for money?' " recalls Barbour's chief deputy, Don Fierce. "No one knew." The survey explicitly said *not* to send donations.

Barbour sent out 400,000 surveys. There were fifty multiple-choice questions on policy and five open-ended direction/philosophy questions. The policy questions hit every topic. Barbour included abortion, asking members to rate its importance. Pat Robertson, head of the Christian Coalition, and Jerry Falwell, head of the Moral Majority, were furious and called to complain. They considered the party's antiabortion position set-tled and resented any "reopening" of the question. "Some prominent pro-life members of the party were afraid this was a secret way of changing the party platform on abortion," Barbour told me. "It never was, but they were very concerned. My ultimate answer to that was Henry Hyde [the Illinois congressman who was a pro-life stalwart]: I appointed him to chair the party's platform committee, and that ended all of that talk."

Barbour hoped to receive 5 percent of the surveys back. RNC head-quarters received nearly 20 percent back. Sacks of mail poured into Fierce's office. He moved the sacks into a spare office, which quickly filled up. Then another filled up. The mail appeared unstoppable.

"People [were] dying to participate," Barbour says. "They [were] just waiting for someone to give them a chance. I used to tell our state party people and our regional political coordinators, 'If you give people a chance to participate, they'll knock down your door.' "

The open-ended philosophy/direction questions sparked the most response. "I can't imagine how many barrels of ink got used on people writing on those surveys," Barbour says. "And every single note and letter was read and recorded. This was a massive focus group."

The survey showed deep reservoirs of support for fundamental GOP ideas: lower taxes, smaller government, balanced budgets, line-item vetoes, welfare reform, increased defense spending, congressional reform, fewer federal regulations. Social issues like gun control, abortion, and cultural decay were well represented too, but did not prove as unifying as those other issues. Barbour had just commissioned the largest Republican focus group in history to chart the party's new direction. Of course, it wasn't a new direction at all. It was a return to first principles. It was also a template for the Contract with America, though neither Barbour nor Fierce nor anyone else at the time realized it.

Barbour had watched Clinton campaign on many of these issues in 1992. He decided to plot a party strategy to capitalize if Clinton didn't follow through. He didn't expect this to result in immediate political gains in Congress or among governors. He merely saw it as a way to rebuild bridges with the rank-and-file and, not incidentally, fill depleted party coffers.

"We were flat on our back," Don Fierce recalls. "We had lost everything. We thought if we nationalized the election in '94, we could seize the moment. But we had no thought about winning the House or the Senate. We just did not. We just wanted to make some gains to prepare for the next election. We were just trying to get the party back in the game. We were trying to get the party out of its World War II mentality of the permanent minority. Newt Gingrich wasn't important to our plans. He was not central at this point at all."

With the survey data in his hands, Barbour began to crank up the fund-raising apparatus. He solicited funds the old-fashioned way: with Reagan. Barbour asked Reagan if he would lend his name to party fund-raising letters and play a more visible role in party-building activities. "Reaganism eliminated the wings of the Republican Party," Barbour says, explaining the former president's appeal to the party faithful. Reagan readily agreed, and Barbour made sure the RNC covered all expenses related to Reagan's political activity—thousands of dollars a month to defray the staff cost of processing and answering mail generated by Reagan's fund-raising appeals. In essence, the RNC chairman put Reagan on the party payroll. "He did political things for us," Barbour remembers. "So we paid Reagan's office to handle the costs of responding to all the letters his mailings generated. He might get five thousand letters a month. There was no reason for taxpayers to pay for the cost of reading and answering those letters." (Reagan would continue to help the Republican Party through 1994. In fact, he would share the dais with former British prime minister Margaret Thatcher at a huge party fund-raiser in Washington in February 1994. It would be

Reagan's last public appearance in the nation's capital; in November of that year he would announce to the country that he had been diagnosed with Alzheimer's disease.)

Barbour also began courting conservative constituencies shut out during the Bush years: small businesses, tax cutters, social conservatives, and gun owners, to name just a few. On their own, these same GOP interest groups initiated weekly strategy sessions at the offices of GOP activist/lobbyist Grover Norquist, president of Americans for Tax Reform, the group that created the no-new-taxes pledge Bush signed in New Hampshire in 1988 to defeat GOP rival Senator Bob Dole.

"At first it was stop health care," Norquist told me, referring to the Clinton administration's massive push for a nationalized health care system, but "then it became obvious you had to stop everything. So the gun people came in to stop the Brady Bill, the small-business groups came in on taxes and health care, and the social groups came in to stop abortion and gays in the military. You had every part of the coalition afraid that it was going to lose on the issue that most energized them and their slice of the coalition."

In the beginning, only a handful of conservative interest groups attended Norquist's meetings. Even so, he describes the movement as a raging bull. "When the bull comes into a bullfight, the picadors are the ones who throw little darts into him to irritate the hell of out him and make him mad and make him want to fight," Norquist says. "Then the other guys come in to cut the shoulder muscles and make him weak. The Clinton White House never got to the point where they passed anything that weakened us, just did the part, like the picadors, that pissed us off."

Barbour sent Fierce to Norquist's meetings, keeping the lines of communication open. Barbour also began a systematic campaign to win the support of H. Ross Perot. The Texas billionaire had captured 19 percent of the vote in 1992, and Barbour considered his support and that of his millions of followers up for grabs.

"We made repeated outreach to Ross Perot," Fierce recalls. "We looked at Perot as one of the pieces of getting our party back. He owned the Reagan Democrats. He had their faith, hope, and belief. And they were parking their vote with him."

The pursuit of Perot also marked the first coordinated political outreach Barbour did with Gingrich. One or the other would talk to Perot or his top political adviser, Russ Varney, at least once a week.

## Clinton's Missteps

While Republicans were beginning to reform their ranks, the Clinton White House and congressional Democrats prepared to rule Washington and the nation as a team for the first time since 1980. Key players on both sides are far more candid now than they were then on the early divisions that undermined Clinton's ability to govern as a centrist. Top Clinton White House officials now blame congressional leaders for undermining Clinton's desire for sweeping congressional reforms: staff cuts, congressional budget cuts, and campaign finance reform. They also blame congressional leaders for opposing early moves on Clinton's version of welfare reform.

"In the 103rd Congress, President Clinton took the advice of the congressional leaders that they knew how to get his agenda through," recalls Bruce Reed, Clinton's chief domestic policy adviser. "We couldn't convince the congressional leadership that our reform agenda was in their best interest—congressional reform and welfare reform. I mean, they simply didn't want to do it. They said they wanted to do health care first, but the truth is they didn't want to do welfare reform anytime soon. To be fair, some Democrats at both ends of Pennsylvania Avenue didn't fully understand that their agendas were different. Not that their issues or philosophies were necessarily so different, but the president's job is to get the country behind him so he can get things done. In the first two years of the Clinton presidency, we spent too much time trying to find the happy medium within the Democratic caucus instead of trying to put together a true working majority. They weren't used to having a president set the agenda, and they didn't realize how much better off the whole party would be if the president had some leeway to expand the party's appeal. That's not a subject that comes up in a Democratic caucus."

Congressional Democrats admit that they talked Clinton out of his reform agenda in part because they thought it unnecessarily demonized Democratic majorities. They advised Clinton not to pick fights with lawmakers he would need in the future. Clinton agreed, reluctantly.

Congressional leaders also admit that liberal Democrats had no interest in helping Clinton achieve his pledge to "end welfare as we know it."

"There was a tough kind of institutional resistance to overcome with a lot of liberal members of the Congress who were violently opposed" to welfare reform, recalls former House Speaker Tom Foley.

Before Clinton's inauguration, the House majority leader at the time, Richard Gephardt, advised Clinton over dinner in Little Rock, Arkansas, to focus his early energies entirely on the budget. Congressional reforms, welfare, and health care could wait, he counseled. Gephardt knew the budget would be tough enough.

"There is no doubt that the congressional wing debated with the president on what should be done," Gephardt told me. "We had this first meeting in Little Rock in '92 right after the election. It was a dinner we had in the governor's mansion with Bill and Hillary, [Senate Majority Leader George] Mitchell, Foley, and me. And when I had my chance to talk, I said, 'We've talked about campaign reform, health care, and all these other issues, but,' I said, 'the admission to the ballpark to play the economic game is to get the budget straightened out. And it's going to be hard.' "

At the time, Foley and Gephardt's advice made sense. There was no point in dividing the party from the outset. Stick with the liberal wing on the big issues, and fall back to centrism after the key fights on the budget and health care have been won. But Bruce Reed believes the decision weakened Clinton's presidency almost from the start because it forced him into the arms of the left wing of the party.

"Howard Paster [Clinton's chief congressional liaison] kept saying we should start left and let the congressional process move things to the center," Reed recalls. "And we'd never campaigned that way. In those two years we had a centrist agenda but we dressed it up as a more liberal one."

Moderate Democrats were devastated. Republican leaders eager to hold their party together were gleeful. They were terrified that Clinton would propose a budget that included his promised middle-class tax cut and follow that with centrist welfare and health care bills.

"We were achieving pretty fair unanimity in our conference on a lot of these issues simply because it was easy to be against nearly anything the administration wanted when it went hard left," recalls Bob Walker, then Gingrich's top floor leader. "Centrist Democrats became in play for us because some of what became the Democratic proposals were unsupportable in their districts." If Clinton had come at Republicans with centrist proposals, Walker and others are sure, the GOP would have splintered. "A centrist health care bill and a centrist welfare reform bill and we would have been in much deeper political trouble at that point," Walker says. "Probably we would have lost votes." They also feared a congressional reform push that would undermine their budding courtship of Perot.

Bruce Reed agrees with Walker and recounts the toll Clinton's deal with congressional leaders took on party centrists: "The moderates were miserable. After the '92 election there was 60 percent of America ready to sign up for something new—we ran against the brain-dead politics of Washington. The president had a chance to put together a much bigger coalition as a result. But the congressional leadership told him he'd never get his top priorities through unless he made some sacrifices. From the moment we caved on congressional reforms, we were giving up a big part of the independence that the voters had just given us. The decision to put off reforms turned us into a 43 percent presidency instead of a 60 percent presidency. Ross Perot was all about looking under the hood and changing Washington. We could have had the same result. It put us in the difficult position of looking like we opposed changing Washington. We could have broken down the Republican boycott early. But we were locked in to a strategy of getting to a majority only on our side of the aisle."

In Bruce Reed's view, "The Republican caricature of Clinton has it all wrong: Clinton wanted to do welfare reform, but the Democratic congressional leadership wouldn't have it."

All these years later, top congressional Democrats see it differently. They say it was impossible to move welfare because Clinton had saddled them with a ghastly health care bill.

"In retrospect," says Dick Gephardt, then the House majority leader, "doing a mandate was never going to happen and we were never able to get Republican votes. And then you had Newt, who, wisely, was trying to figure out how to keep us from doing it and so he was actively working against us. And we didn't have a plan that we could sell even to all the Democrats, much less Republicans."

Tom Foley concedes that he and other House Democratic leaders extracted concessions from Clinton but refuses to accept the blame for hijacking his presidency. Like Gephardt, he says that Clinton's early emphasis on the unwieldy health care bill stymied Congress for months, disabling it from helping the White House on other fronts. Though the bill was not formally introduced until September 1993, top Clinton aides had briefed senior lawmakers such as Foley that spring.

"If anything," Foley told me, "I thought the ambitiousness and the enthusiasm of the major health plan was something that we should have tried to curb and should have tried to channel into the post-1994 pragmatic Clinton administration—you know, the Clinton administration that was so-called triangulating. I remember [Clinton health care czar] Ira Magaziner coming up and saying that there were 740 decisions on the decision tree—this is industrial policy-speak—that had to be made before the bill could be drafted. This was April. And they wanted the bill passed by Christmas. It was totally unrealistic. The bill was a radical bill. It was an attempt to do a dramatic remake of the entire health care system of the United States, which was occupying 14 percent of the GDP, for God's sakes!"

Foley was not, of course, saying this at the time. Republicans were. And to this day many of those closest to the strategy behind the 1994 election give far more credit to Clinton's health care bill than to the Contract with America, or anything else for that matter.

"I always said Hillary's health care plan had more to do with us winning the majority in '94 than the Contract did," Armey told me. "Because I think the Democrats in '93 and '94 with health care scared the devil out of the American people. They did a grievous overreach. It's hard for people to remember how terribly, colorfully they put on the strut. And [Democratic] Representative George Miller I think said it best. We were having the committee hearing on Hillary's health plan. And George Miller got violently angry at us (and oftentimes did) and said, 'Now look, you guys, we've been waiting forty years to do this and we're going to do it.' Because they had all the marbles, see, that was their attitude."

The health care problem was not merely one of substance. It was also one of sequence. While the White House put the complex health care bill together, it decided to push for approval of the North American Free Trade Agreement (NAFTA). Clinton had campaigned on global free trade and was eager to make good on a pro-business campaign promise and to repair some of the damage he'd done by trimming back other centrist themes. The decision, like the ones to set aside congressional reforms, backfired, but for completely different reasons.

Rank-and-file Democrats, especially those in industrial and public service unions, were eager for a health care bill. They didn't need one as comprehensive as the universal health care package the White House was drafting, but the struggling middle class did want better health care coverage, or if that was too complicated, the freedom to move coverage from job to job. But while Democrats waited for progress on this front, Clinton came at them with NAFTA. Union Democrats hated NAFTA. The trade-off left them nonplussed.

"There was a big '93 debate within the White House and the Hill and with outside strategists about how to deal with NAFTA and health care," recalls Democratic media strategist Peter Fenn. "And the [health care] bill was too complicated. No one could work out all of the details. And some of us told the White House, 'If you're thinking about doing health care in '94, you're gonna get whacked. You won't get it done.' Health care was much more important to voters than NAFTA. Most people think NAFTA is an auto parts store. You felt it out there. People, they were pretty pissed. The fact is, politically, NAFTA could wait. Health care couldn't."

Congress approved NAFTA in November of 1993, about a month after the outlines of the health care bill were publicly released. Republicans provided majority support for NAFTA in the House and Senate, but withheld their support for months to extend Clinton's agony with his labor base. The NAFTA victory felt like a bipartisan breakthrough, but it wasn't. Republicans and much of the country regarded Clinton's agenda as more liberal than centrist. That was true of the budget, the health care bill, and the president's reluctance to lay out a bold new welfare bill. Republicans wanted NAFTA and weren't going to deny Clinton on that front. But by this stage, they were denying him everywhere else.

"It was a vastly more aggressive Republican conference that the Clinton administration was up against than anything anybody had seen prior to that," Bob Walker recalls. "Our technique, I mean my job as chief deputy whip, was to convince everybody that there was something in the bill they hated and that they couldn't explain back home. So even if they were willing to go along with one aspect of it, you'd simply go to another aspect and say, 'You don't want to go back home and defend this, do you?' "

Bruce Reed felt the political tug of GOP arguments against Clinton's natural House allies, moderate Democrats. "When you work just from your side of the aisle, every vote is a tough vote," he told me. "But with a big bipartisan coalition those votes are not tough at all. And you can only ask members in marginal districts to walk the plank so many times. There was easily a working coalition of 60 percent in both [the House and Senate] for the Clinton approach, but we didn't get there."

### "That's a Good Story, You Ought to Stick with It"

In October 1993, House Minority Leader Bob Michel announced that he would be retiring from Congress. Newt Gingrich had instructed his staff in August to begin preparing a campaign to run against Michel if he didn't leave Congress at the end of the year. "By God, in '94 we let [Michel] know we were running and to make his plans accordingly," recalls Tony Blankley, Gingrich's spokesman at the time. "Yes, he was given the old heave-ho."

Dick Armey, who at the time headed the GOP conference (the number-three leadership position), recalls his analysis of the political situation and what it might portend for the year ahead: "As soon as Bob Michel retires, I know a majority is possible, because the old bulls are going to get out of the way. Then there's a big question about who's going to run for whip [the number-two slot, which Gingrich had held since 1989]. And I decide fairly quickly that I'm not going to run for whip. Because one, I'd felt [with] the work we'd done in conference, we'd already eclipsed the whip in standing and stature. I was better suited for work in the conference. But when the other guys came around—Tom DeLay, Bob Walker, and Bill McCollum [of Florida]—I told them all, 'I'm not going to get into this race, but I want you to know that if we take over the majority, I'm going to run for majority leader, and I don't expect you to run against me if I stay out now.' They were willing to make that commitment, because they're saying to themselves, 'Armey just asked me to commit to a contingency that will never occur.' "

Armey's is the first known conversation where any Republican leader (a) predicted the coming majority in 1994 and (b) made a concrete personal political decision based on that assumption.

Days later, Armey joined other congressional leaders at the Clinton White House for a meeting on NAFTA. After the meeting broke up, Gephardt offered Armey a ride back to the Capitol in his congressionally provided Lincoln Town Car.

"He had, of course, security and a car; I did not," Armey recalls. "And Dick, being a nice guy, gives me a ride back. He turns to me and says, 'Dick, I'm real surprised you didn't get in that whip race.' And I said, 'Well, that's because I'm running for majority leader.' He laughed. He says, 'That's a good story, you ought to stick with it.' "

I asked Gephardt about this story in the spring of 2004.

"It's a true story. I've thought about it often."

I asked Gephardt what went through his mind on that drive back to the Capitol.

"I thought it was interesting. I didn't think they were going to win and I thought he was missing an opportunity. But it turned out he was right and I was wrong. He was very confident and I was impressed with his confidence."

Others, however, were not.

"At that time," Armey told me, "Newt came to me and said, 'Dick, you gotta quit talking about being in the majority, people are laughing at you.' I like to tell the story because you know, with Newt, things are always born with Newt. But he actually told me, 'People are ridiculing you.' And you know, my response was, 'If somebody doesn't dare say we can do it, we will never, ever try. So it might as well start with me.' What, are they going to call me stupid? I've got a Ph.D. in economics. Half of them couldn't even get through the course. Nobody can call me stupid. If I don't dare stand up and say it, nobody would. Who would have the courage to do it? You've got to be willing to be laughed at. I knew people were laughing at me."

Whether Gingrich was laughing is unclear. In interviews with all his top advisers, none said Gingrich predicted capturing a House majority in 1994, except for the grand I'm-dreaming-of-a-majority spasm that afflicted him every two years. Even so, Gingrich was now a player, and Haley Barbour dispatched Don Fierce to set up a working relationship.

"The first meeting we had with Newt was in the fall of '93, and Newt threw me out of his office," Fierce recalls. "We were thinking, 'Maybe we have an ally with Newt,' and Haley sends me over there to offer our services. You know, to build a new party. Not to win the House. But to create a solid foundation and solid footings for the party. He throws me out. He says I have no right to interfere with his plans and he wonders where I get off talking about rebuilding the party. He literally tosses me out of the meeting."

Gingrich would soon patch things up with Fierce and Barbour. And he would catch the fever of winning the majority in 1994—Armey's fever.

"I don't know what catharsis caught Newt," Armey says now. "Newt has an instinct, he's like a distance runner that just knows someone's closing on him and isn't going to let that guy get in front of him. So maybe Newt realized Armey's on to something here and I'm not letting him get ahead of me with this idea. So then we talked about, 'We ought to get together and plot this thing out.' And of course that's where the Contract all got started."

# 4

# MAKER'S MARK

Before the Contract with America had a name, the Republicans had a plan. And the plan took shape in the front seat of a black Nissan Sentra hurtling along U.S. Route 13 toward Salisbury, Maryland, on the morning of January 28, 1994.

Two top aides to Newt Gingrich, Dan Meyer and Len Swinehart, were on their way to Salisbury State University for the annual House Republican retreat. It had been a year since the Republicans had last gathered at Princeton, New Jersey, when the young Turks had pushed the leadership to put forward its own budget proposal. This retreat would be different. Meyer and Swinehart's boss, who was still number two in the Republican House leadership, had received permission from House Minority Leader Bob Michel to move away from the wonkery that typically characterized these retreats.

"The retreats until then had really been issue seminars, and Newt changed the old dynamic, the whole structure, the whole paradigm, and turned it into a planning retreat," Meyer told me.

So as Meyer drove and Swinehart hunched over a legal pad, the two staffers batted around ideas and concepts that would shape the Republicans' plan to seize the majority. "We were literally writing the agenda as we were going out to the retreat—in the car," Meyer remembers. "And one of the items was 'Designing an Agenda Worth Voting For.'"

At Salisbury, Gingrich and Armey wanted to introduce the idea of running on a specific legislative agenda that Armey had outlined in a December 1993 memo to Gingrich. (The memo can be found in this book's appendix.) As always, Armey deferred to Gingrich's ability to explain and "sell" the concept. That's why Gingrich had tasked Meyer and Swinehart with developing discussion points that could lead to a clear, unifying vision, then to a plan to achieve that vision, and ultimately to specific strategies and fine-grain tactics.

"That was kind of a productive drive," Swinehart recalls. "We were writing vision strategies. Newt had concluded that in a post-Michel conference, if he and Armey were together, they could get the conference to do anything. He concluded that they were the two power centers, and as long as they didn't fight, if they were a team, they could get anything done. Armey was a kind of loner congressman. It was a big change for him. In terms of the team, he was incredibly valuable."

Before the retreat, the Gingrich staff had outlined a ten-point legislative plan that melded Gingrich's thoughts about how to formulate a unifying policy/political vision for House Republicans with Armey's idea of introducing a specific conservative agenda Republicans should debate among themselves now that he and Gingrich were clearly in charge. The ten-point agenda didn't draw many enthusiasts.

"There was a lot of grumbling, a lot of bitching and moaning," remembers Jack Howard, a top Gingrich legislative aide who was at Salisbury. "The attitude was basically 'Don't bother us with this.' "

Meyer says most Republicans were still thinking like a minority party, the very malady Armey said in December the ten-point agenda had to confront.

"None of them believed we were going to win the majority, so they thought, What was the point?" Meyer says. "Even as a campaign tactic, they thought, 'What's the purpose? Because we aren't going to win the majority anyway.' "

"They thought it was another goofy Gingrich idea," Howard says.

But Gingrich and Armey knew they didn't have to persuade all House Republicans on this "goofy" idea.

"Newt's theory was, he said, 'If we can get 20 to 30 percent of the members to buy in to this, you might have 10 percent who will be hard-core against but the rest will just sort of go along.' He said, 'We just really need about 20 percent of the core.' There was an energetic but fairly small band of conservatives and then just a bunch of people who kind of went along. And Newt had done a really good job of bringing into the fold the ones who would be the most likely people to cause problems, the more liberal wing of the party [Republicans like Steve Gunderson of Wisconsin and Nancy Johnson and Chris Shays of Connecticut]. They were hungry for the majority. They were willing to look the other way on a few policy positions. And they bought in to the idea 'Hey, we have to win the majority.' All that had happened beforehand, so when we came out with this idea, it really did come out the way Newt said, where a lot of people were very excited about it, [but] most people thought it was a PR stunt. And I think one of the ways it was successful was that enough of the members who had real power, or were likely to get real power if we did take the majority, didn't take it that seriously."

Gingrich and Armey persuaded the targeted 30 percent of the GOP conference. Without much fanfare the entire conference agreed to develop a concept for the fall campaign tentatively and clumsily titled "10 Things House Republicans Will Do If We Take Over the Majority." Many suggestions for the items to be included in this list of ten were put forth in Salisbury, but no decisions were reached. At Gingrich's behest, however, Republicans agreed unequivocally to produce a comprehensive governing alternative for the fall campaign.

"I'll give Newt a lot of credit for this," recalls Kerry Knott, Armey's chief of staff. "He said we can run a purely negative campaign against Clinton in '94 and pick up a decent number of seats, but somewhere along the way it switched to where we thought, 'Hey, if we were to put a positive agenda together with the negative attacks on Clinton, that might be enough to actually make it all the way there.' Because nobody believed that if you ran a purely negative campaign you would pick up forty seats [which was necessary for a one-seat majority], and at some point the combination of the two started to give people hope that it could actually be done. That's where the idea came from to have . . . a ten-point plan. You know, ten is kind of a mythical number—you know, Ten Commandments. Newt said ten is a good number for this; we didn't have any idea what the ten planks would be at that point."

### "You'll Learn to Fly in Formation"

The tepid reaction from most Republicans at the Salisbury conference drove most of the early work on the manifesto underground.

"Everybody thought it was too hard and too complicated and could never be done," recalls Joe Gaylord, then Gingrich's top political adviser. "So we never talked about it again. And we just spoon-fed it after that."

In late January, shortly after Salisbury, Gingrich invited members of his core leadership team to dinner: Dick Armey, Tom DeLay, Bob Walker, and Bill Paxon. They met at the restaurant Head's (what is now Tortilla Coast), half a block south of the RNC headquarters and two blocks south of the Capitol. It was an odd group in many ways. Personally, only Gingrich and Walker were close friends. Armey worked with Gingrich but never considered him a friend. He was on speaking terms with Walker but always considered him Gingrich's alter ego and therefore a force to be dealt with delicately. Armey and DeLay knew each other but were not close. Paxon was known by all and found to be energetic and agreeable but nothing more. Aside from their hunger for majority power, the five would really have had nothing in common.

Armey, in particular, was reluctant to join the group. Priding himself on being a loner, he refused to commit to joining this new strategic planning team at that first dinner, he remembers. "I said, 'I have done very well in this body flying solo and I'm not ready to commit to flying in a formation until I know who I'm flying with.'" But Gingrich was ready with a response. "Newt said, 'You'll learn to fly in formation if you understand that your wingman will shoot you down if you break the formation.' Which I imagine is an old RAF saying that he got from Churchill."

As Walker relates it, "Newt put together this very small group of us who basically plotted the '94 election." Acknowledging the somewhat unusual makeup of the team, Walker says, "This was a group that Newt put together, and I think to some extent it was Newt reaching out to people who hadn't necessarily marched with us all the way along, in hopes of broadening the base. But there really was a coming together of that group."

Armey explains how the "coming together" began. At the second dinner, "we had one of these 'This is who I am and this is what my business is.' I always laughed and said, 'That was five people baring their soul and frankly, only two of the five lied, that wasn't too bad.' By my estimation, the truth tellers were me, Newt, and Bob Walker. We then got our smart guys around us. We got these guys around. We said we have to find some way to nationalize the election and so forth. We were saying, 'What kind of an instrument can we use?'"

The smart guys were the key staffers to Gingrich and Armey, all of whom would play herculean roles in developing the "instrument" that would later be called the Contract with America.

In late January, the Contract was little more than a concept. Although Gingrich had some definite notions about its potential content, he lacked a consensus. He knew the project needed much more substance. He also knew the party would need some real money to make any future "instrument" work in the '94 campaign. In late January, Gingrich had the ideas. What he didn't have was the cash. But that would soon come. Gingrich would find it in of all places a tavern in Annapolis, Maryland.

### The Seminal Moment

In early February, Senate Minority Leader Bob Dole organized a bicameral seminar in Annapolis to discuss GOP alternatives to the Clinton health care bill. At this point, Clinton's plan for universal health insurance was encountering quiet resistance within Democratic ranks, but Republicans like Dole remained open to a deal, in large part because they were unaware of the fissures developing across the aisle. Many conservatives mistrusted Dole and his chief of staff, Sheila Burke, a former nurse whom they considered a closet liberal always pushing Dole toward half-loaf deals with Democrats. Sure enough, Dole had crafted a bill that hard-line conservatives considered too close to Clinton's bill. Dole used the Annapolis seminar to rally House and Senate Republicans around his alternative, arguing that Republicans couldn't blindly oppose Clinton.

Newt Gingrich, Haley Barbour, and Don Fierce listened attentively, then whispered to themselves how they were watching the dying breaths of the old Republican Party. They couldn't wait to leave so they could start talking about the new Republican Party. Gingrich and political adviser Joe Gaylord, spokesman Tony Blankley, and pollster Bob Teeter agreed to meet Barbour and Fierce at a downtown Annapolis restaurant and bar for dinner and drinks.

Gingrich told me this meeting was "the seminal moment in the development of the Contract."

Barbour and Fierce were waiting when Gingrich and his entourage entered. Gaylord and Fierce headed to the bar to grab drinks for the group; their conversation quickly turned toward the '94 election.

"We want to nationalize this election," Gaylord said.

"No shit. We've been working on that all year," Fierce replied. "You get the hooch and we'll cut a fucking deal."

The two carried the drinks back to the table. There, Gingrich and

Barbour discussed how the Republican Party needed to run on a concrete set of ideas. When Gingrich summarized some of his ideas, Barbour seized on the concept of tort reform (using federal law to cap jury awards in civil suits) and flatly told Gingrich, "If you put tort reform in there, I'll bankroll the whole thing." On the question of political tactics versus Clinton, both men took Dole's point on health care, that the party must have alternatives. But they were pursuing a completely different vision—creating a stronger, more robust, truly national party, one that would eventually control Congress. As such, they drew an important distinction. Dole's plan was to create a Clintonian health care bill that Republicans could live with. The process kept Clinton in the driver's seat and forced Republicans to accept policy they would never propose themselves, thereby settling for derivative, watered-down Clintonism. The party had no future there, all agreed.

Gingrich let Barbour know about the plans he had laid out at Salisbury to develop a ten-point plan for House Republicans should they win a majority. Barbour was intrigued but didn't want anything to do with a House-only plan. The RNC chairman was trying to revive the party, and if he was going to be involved in *any* multiplank agenda, he wanted considerable say over its content. That meant a hand in the polling, fund-raising, media, and message. Gingrich agreed. He had no choice: Barbour had the money.

Since Salisbury, one idea had been bouncing around Gingrich's head. But it needed big money to work. And since the chat was going so well with Barbour, he blurted it out.

"Would you guys pay $50,000 for one page in *Reader's Digest*?"

Gingrich wanted to print the GOP's ten-point manifesto in Middle America's favorite magazine.

Barbour took a slow draw of Maker's Mark bourbon and suppressed a laugh.

"You want to nationalize the election through *Reader's Digest*?"

Gingrich nodded and explained that voters either subscribed to the magazine or picked it up at the grocery counter. Barbour, a native of Yazoo City, Mississippi, admired the populist thrust, though he and Fierce privately considered *Reader's Digest* a ludicrous venue to discuss a new Republican agenda for the country. They didn't have a ready alternative at the time, but they were sure that *Reader's Digest,* widely read though it was, lacked the market penetration and easy-to-read simplicity of the magazine the party would eventually settle on, *TV Guide.*

At meeting's end, Barbour and Gingrich agreed to coordinate all Contract-related efforts (even though the Contract had yet to be named). Barbour pledged heavy financial support, and promised to enlist outside pollsters and consultants to help Gingrich. Meanwhile, Armey and others would put together a full-blown strategy. This "fucking deal," as Fierce called it, would be among the biggest ever hatched in party history.

Shortly thereafter, on March 17, Kerry Knott, Armey's chief of staff, sent his boss a memo summarizing efforts to develop a post-Salisbury political and governing agenda and Gingrich's instructions for Armey to lead the effort:

Newt has asked Pete Hoekstra, John Boehner, and Jim Nussle (along with [staff]) to work in a small group to work out the plans to follow up [on] the ideas generated at Salisbury. This group is going to develop an overall plan for member and staff training, a "product development" plan (decide what new issues or bills need to be developed), a marketing plan, a communications plan, and a computerization plan. . . . One of the key products this group will develop is the "10 Things House Republicans Will Do If We Take Over in January." Newt asked you to take that project on in the [GOP Leadership] Roundtable today (culminating in a mass event on the steps of the Capitol in late September).

The memo mentioned two other crucial developments that would greatly influence the Contract. Knott noted continuing work on another House Republican alternative budget. This one would be even more specific than the '93 version, calling for a balanced budget in seven years. Though the '93 budget had familiarized Republicans with the broad policy choices they would have to make to fund the government, this budget, because of its specificity, would require much greater political courage to support. John Kasich and others would need to cajole Republicans, or when that didn't work, hold their hands. But in mid-March, the budget was still under construction. Knott offered this suggestion:

I suggest a companion bill . . . that would be the morality/family values/culture equivalent to [the budget]. I've not thought this through completely, but it should include such things as legal changes to strengthen the two parent family, support adoption not abortion, replace many of the welfare provisions with work ethic provisions, strong paternity language, an end to quotas, etc. Basically, it would be a bill to bias the laws toward personal responsibility, not irresponsibility. I think this could be done in a creative way that would not get into too many "federalist" problems.

Almost every one of Knott's suggestions in this memo would eventually become part of the Contract, and almost all would become law in some form.

## Epiphanies

While Dick Armey and others began to tease out the details of the ten items that would be in this all-inclusive agenda, no one was thinking particularly hard about what to call this manifesto. For weeks, Knott and other GOP staffers referred to it not as a thing but as an event. Knott wrote several memos updating Armey and other lawmakers about ongoing efforts to prepare for the "Capitol steps event." This harked back to Gingrich's event with candidate Ronald Reagan in 1980.

Sometime in late March or early April, at a meeting with Armey and senior staff, Gingrich confronted the obvious: This manifesto needed a name.

It was Kerry Knott who came up with the name "Contract with the American People." In this he is a historian's worst nightmare. Knott gave the manifesto its name, as all who were close to the project agree. But Knott can't remember the first day he said it, who heard him say it, or what the reaction was.

"I don't even know where it came from. I think we just talked about it enough. It can't just be a promise. It needs to be more than that, and the word 'contract' came from somewhere, and we just eventually put it together."

Before Knott came up with the name, Republicans were sure whatever title they chose for their manifesto would have to break through layer upon layer of political cynicism. Barbour was determined to find out how. He'd heard about Knott's "contract" idea and wanted to see what voters thought. He paid for two focus groups and sent top GOP pollster Brian Tringali to North Carolina with Dan Leonard, the spokesman and strategist at the National Republican Congressional Committee (NRCC).

"Voters were so cynical," Fierce says. "They had been screwed so many times. Three-card monte from politicians on so many issues. They were looking for some way to hold politicians accountable. They had decided you could not hold politicians accountable, even through the ballot box."

Tringali and Leonard conducted the sessions at L&H Focus Groups, Inc., in Raleigh, North Carolina. They walked in with what Tringali describes now as a "kernel of an idea."

Dan Leonard recalls the session, conducted with about a dozen voters seated around a table in a small conference room; Tringali observed on the other side of a two-way mirror as Leonard made the pitch.

"We asked, 'What if politicians promised to do something or some things?' There was no reaction. We said, 'What if they guarantee it?' There was no reaction. Then we said, 'What if they signed a piece of paper?' Then they started to say, 'Hmmm.' And right before we started, Joe Gaylord called down and told us to ask another question. 'What if they signed something and put it in *TV Guide*?' They really reacted to this."

Tringali said reaction to the word "contract" was a good start, and the even stronger positive reaction to placing the contract in *TV Guide* (where it would eventually end up) highlighted key strengths. But they weren't enough. Voters demanded more.

"We were selling fundamental change at the policy level," Tringali says. "Voters expected ten things. Three wasn't enough. Ten things sounded as if it was ambitious enough but not too much. No one was interested in more than ten things, because that sounded like too much and too hard to do. The focus groups showed that voters actually took it seriously."

The reaction in the second focus group mirrored that in the first. Tringali and Leonard knew they were on to something.

"We were pretty pumped," Leonard recalls.

"It was like an epiphany," Tringali says. "As we talked about a contract and signing it and ten items, they would go, 'Yeah, yeah.' Some would say, 'That will work, but they'll never do it. They won't have the guts.' From the focus group came the name 'contract.' And we started mocking up what the Contract would look like. We added a check box and a signature line."

Fierce says that until the focus groups were conducted, Haley Barbour was lukewarm to the idea of publishing the GOP manifesto anywhere. He thought it would be a waste of money. The focus groups made him a believer. Voters wanted something more tangible than sound bites, campaign mailers, and thirty-second radio and TV spots.

"They bought it because they could keep it," Fierce says. "In the group, the reaction to the contract idea, it's really good. But they don't trust it. But when we say vote us out if we don't do it, they love it. There are always equal parts cynicism and naiveté in politics."

But there was nothing naive about trying to keep the NRCC alive. The committee had avoided bankruptcy by slashing costs and suckling the RNC for months. "The committee was a mess; it was a creature of electability," says Bill Paxon, then the NRCC chairman. "It was just about keeping inertia. It was never about taking advantage."

But Paxon had seen the early plans for the ten-point manifesto, saw Gingrich and Armey's growing enthusiasm for the project, knew of the RNC's budding interest, and saw an opportunity to shine. He decided to see if he could translate all the theoretical talk of a House GOP majority into real campaign dollars. And Paxon would need a lot of money, because the NRCC had set out an audacious goal: recruiting a candidate for *every single one* of the 435 House races that year. This was a radical approach for the Republicans, who had never tried to compete *everywhere*. In the past, the party had picked a few dozen races that looked competitive a year ahead, recruited candidates, and fought the election out on very narrow grounds. Paxon wanted to force the Democrats to fight everywhere. He believed that if he could expand the field of battle, he could stretch Democrats to the breaking point, financially and tactically. If Paxon could find the candidates, it might work.

But there was one catch. In any election, candidates are reluctant to run unless they know they will receive at least some financial backing. In Republican political circles, the NRCC's financial woes were well known. Paxon knew that Bill Clinton's growing unpopularity gave the Republicans a fund-raising opportunity, but that alone would not solve the money problem.

So Paxon turned to Clarence Rappleyea. More precisely, he turned to Rappleyea's model.

Rappleyea was a member of the New York Assembly with Paxon in 1987. Republicans were meeting early that year to discuss how to try to win a June 16 special election for a state assembly seat in Republican-leaning Cattaraugus County. The state party didn't have any more money for a legislative race, so most Republicans were willing to write off the race. But as Paxon remembers, Rappleyea stood and up and said the party had a great candidate who had a chance to win the race and that everyone should pull together. He then said the people in the room would "chip in $1,000 apiece" to help the candidate, Patricia McGee (now a member of New York's Senate). After a bit of grumbling, the Republican members cut the checks, and McGee, given the cash to compete, won the race.

Paxon decided to bring the Rappleyea model to Washington. For the first time in party history, a reelection committee chairman ordered incumbents to raise money for Republican candidates.

"That was a huge change," Pennsylvania's Bob Walker told me. "A lot of this goes back to well before '92, because this whole learning process goes all the way back to '84, when we formed the Conservative Opportunity Society. One of the things we learned along the way was that unless you build a substantial financial base, you didn't have a chance of pursuing your policy ideas."

Paxon had no trouble selling the idea to Conservative Opportunity Society types, who were already solidly in Gingrich's camp. Many of the activist moderates were on board too, as were the young Turks. But almost none of these members—with the exception of Gingrich, Armey, and DeLay—had any fund-raising experience. And the most senior Republicans hated the idea. This was a big problem, because these Republicans held the highest committee posts and were therefore in the best position to raise large sums of special interest donations.

"Most members were *not* enthused," Paxon told me. "And the most powerful members were the least enthused."

That's putting it mildly.

"That was a huge cultural shift and not a pleasant process to go through," recalls Ed Gillespie, then Armey's press secretary and later chairman of the RNC. "But it was Newt and Armey and DeLay. When you had Newt and Armey and DeLay at the leadership table, that's when things really changed. That's when there were people at the table saying, 'I think Newt's right.' Until then he was all by himself. Old-line incumbents would say that's not how we do things [raise money for other candidates]. And the response would be, 'That's why we're in the minority!' We had to have a majority mentality."

"One member was very upset," Paxon remembers. "He said, 'My donors won't allow me to raise money and give it to some other candidate.' We said, 'Okay, but you can sponsor a fund-raiser for another candidate, right?' And he said he could. We weren't really hung up on how members contributed, as long as it was legal, and that they did it."

And that took some doing. Republicans in Texas and Florida were reluctant to break a détente with Democrats. Both parties in both states had agreed they would not raise money to help defeat anyone in the delegation. And since raising money for *other* candidates was virtually unheard of, the Republicans and Democrats essentially agreed to raise just enough for their races and to leave each other's races alone.

But the days of détente were ending. Gingrich was signing all NRCC fund-raising letters, and money had begun to trickle in. Armey was hitting up donors too. DeLay was creating a nationwide network of fund-raisers. Paxon recruited eager young members to raise money.

The old order remained on the sidelines, aloof and dismissive. That would last about two more months.

### The Contract Takes Shape

It was now mid-March and the battle over the budget was on. It wasn't Democrat against Republican but Republican against Republican. John Kasich's budget sought to balance the budget in seven years and included real spending cuts in almost every federal program, *including defense.* There were no sacred cows. Politically, the budget would be a big red bull's-eye on the back of every Republican who voted for it. But in keeping with the emerging philosophy of challenging Democrats with policy *and* politics, Kasich pressed on.

"The brilliance of all this was, we had an alternative," Kasich told me. "It was a moment in time when intellectual honesty counted for something. The idea was that if we would have taken power, we would be ready. I knew what the procedure was on these things. I'd been through it before. I'd been at it since 1989, when we first started discussing trying to cut spending. Those were nightmare times, trying to discuss. But in '94 it was about right. It wasn't about spending; it was about the idea that we didn't have the right to mortgage our children's future. But trust me, there's no constituency for cutting spending."

Before setting the final product before the Republican leadership, he met one last time with conservative activists—Michael Franc of the Heritage Foundation, Susan Hirschmann (who would later become Tom DeLay's chief of staff) of Phyllis Schlafly's Eagle Forum, Meghan Flaherty of the Family Research Council, Andrea Sheldon of the Traditional Values Coalition, Marshall Wittmann of the Christian Coalition, Scott Hodge of the Heritage Foundation, and Penny Young of Concerned Women for America. All were pressing for inclusion of more tax cuts, particularly the $500-per-child tax credit. Kasich had not pushed as hard for tax cuts as many conservatives wanted, because according to pay-as-you-go rules, for every dollar he cut in taxes he was compelled to take a dollar away in federal spending, and he was not eager for more fights over spending. Besides, Kasich was never a firm believer in supply-side economics. All he wanted to do was cut wasteful government spending. The tax code, Kasich thought, was mostly written by and for the wealthy. What real people needed, he believed, was a smaller government that didn't *need* to tax them so much.

The conservative activists came prepared to convince Kasich of the virtues of the child tax credit. They had already shared the data showing how many families would benefit on a district-by-district basis. Hodge then presented numbers related to one of the most reliable predictors of voting in any given district: the number of families with children above the poverty line (since parents of those children have a stake in the future and tend to vote to protect it). Hodge had run numbers showing that on average 123,300 families with children were above the poverty line in Republican districts and 113,300 were above the poverty line in Democratic districts. Hodge's numbers showed that the child tax credit could drive up party support among Republicans and possibly peel Democrats away from Clinton, who still had offered no middle-class tax cuts.

Still, Kasich was unpersuaded. The room got very tense. The four women then turned on Kasich.

"They just lit into him," Franc recalls. "They said, 'We demand this.' "

Kasich remained opposed to the tax credit. "There's a lot of truth to that," Kasich told me. "Early on, I wasn't for those tax cuts."

As Hodge recalls it, Kasich finally cracked under the pressure, lashing out at the Christian Coalition's Wittmann. After Wittmann made a pitch for the benefits families could enjoy from the $500-per-child tax credit, Kasich waved him off hotly, blurting out, "You greedy Christians." The room fell silent as other lobbyists bit their tongues, trying not to laugh. Wittmann was Jewish and Kasich had recently become a born-again Christian. "I almost fell on the floor laughing," Hodge recalls. "We all almost fell on the floor laughing."

Wittmann didn't take offense and continued pressing his point. The goal was to persuade Kasich that the socially conservative groups could generate sizable grassroots support for his balanced-budget plan if he had the courage to include tax cuts (primarily the child credit). Kasich was leery. A classic deficit hawk, Kasich saw it as his duty to produce a budget with nothing but spending cuts. But root-canal budgets produced no grassroots support at all. Instead they forced conservative lawmakers to defend spending cuts without offering anything in return. The socially conservative groups were trying to show Kasich he could create a countervailing constituency for a balanced budget, provided that he included tax cuts to motivate key parts of the GOP base.

Finally he relented, but that still didn't settle the matter. Hirschmann and company knew they had badgered Kasich, and no deal struck as a result of badgering had a chance of holding. They immediately activated their membership base to lobby Kasich and targeted Republicans and Democrats in advance of the floor vote on Kasich's budget. They wanted to prove to Kasich that support for the tax credit was real.

"What ensued," Franc says, "was a targeted phone-banking effort by these groups, and they inundated targeted members, some Democrats and some Republicans, saying, 'Support this tax credit.' Kasich's office received several hundred phone calls. And it created a buzz on the floor—you know, 'Everyone in our district is calling in about this.' "

The Kasich budget received 190 votes, the highest for any House Republican budget since 1981. (After 1981, Reagan's and Bush's budgets were declared dead on arrival by Democrats.)

"Kasich was ecstatic," Franc recalls, "and suddenly the $500-per-child credit from that point on was automatically in."

Not only was it in the budget, but eventually it would be the "crown jewel" of the Contract with America.

Ralph Reed, the former executive director of the Christian Coalition, told me that the victory achieved on family-friendly tax cuts marked the beginning of a new era. "All the pro-family groups made the tax cuts a priority and the top priority was the family tax credit. Getting that included in the Contract, to essentially make that a part of the Republican orthodoxy, was a huge moment for our groups. The social conservative movement had never before been allowed to infringe on the turf of the economic wing of the Republican Party. Before, social conservatives dealt with cultural issues, but now we were part of economic policy as well. That was a huge victory."

By April, the Contract was beginning to take shape. The ten items were always more or less in Gingrich's mind, but he let the process play out at the development level, always reserving his veto power. The key components had to be congressional reform, balanced budget, tax cuts, welfare reform, defense, crime control, and a line-item veto. Other items would come later, not the least of which was term limits. But these were the broad outlines. Gingrich, Armey, DeLay, Paxon, and Walker knew it from the start.

"Newt said, 'This is a wagon train going west,' " Joe Gaylord recalls, describing what would become the Contract. " 'And you can paint these wagons any color you want. But *this* is the wagon train and it's heading west.' "

From the beginning, Gingrich, Armey, DeLay, Walker, and Paxon sought battle-tested ideas with deep support among Republicans. But that wasn't enough. The ideas had to have a positive thrust.

"People sometimes confuse tactics and strategy," Gillespie says. "That strategy was to run for something, to be for something positive, to have a positive agenda as opposed to just being opposed to Clinton. We are the positive party. We are the party that gets things done. You know, the center-right party, there's a coherent philosophy to it, but in terms of the strategic change it effected, which is, 'We're gonna stop being "aginners" and we're gonna start being for something.' "

For this reason, GOP leaders intentionally avoided dragging the Contract down with divisive issues that would drive away independents and moderate Democrats. That meant no gun control, no abortion, no school prayer. This sounds so logical now. It didn't seem so at the time. Clinton had enraged most Republicans and many conservative Democrats on these very issues. They were hot. Conventional political analysis would have dictated including them in the document, particularly one that at this point had so little oomph. The temptation of base politics is almost impossible for most political leaders to ignore. In greater numbers, Republican were turning angrily away from Clinton. His numbers were soft among independents. Polling data showed real problems with conservative Democrats. Negativity was in the air. Clinton increasingly was becoming an object of public ridicule, and many Republicans wanted to pounce.

And Republicans did pounce. With increasing ferocity they criticized all of Clinton's perceived failures and made hay of issues that most divided Democrats—taxes, welfare, health care, gun control, and abortion. Many Republicans believed these typical tactics were more than enough to help the party pick up seats in '94. But by now the grander strategic goal had taken hold. The GOP leadership team was aiming higher, willing to risk everything, because, in reality, it had almost nothing to lose.

"Clinton certainly opened the door and gave the people the belief that we could pick up a serious number of seats," Kerry Knott recalls. "And for a lot of people that would have been enough, but I think the genius of the moment was 'Let's take a good hand we have been dealt and really try to turn this into something of historical significance. Let's take the majority, let's not just pick twenty or twenty-five seats.' And that was a gamble, because if it hadn't worked, we could have thrown away a pretty good hand. What if we had picked up just five or ten seats? It would have been a monumental mistake and we would all have been run out of town."

## A Manifesto

As the Democrats were privately haggling over the Clinton health care bill and a possible welfare reform bill (today, the Clinton team maintains that top House Democrats blocked the president's attempts at welfare reform, while House leaders like Dick Gephardt and Tom Foley claim that the White House's radical health care bill made it impossible for Congress to push welfare), Republican leaders were pursuing their own agenda. GOP leaders committed House members to the Contract *and* its specifics. The Republican hierarchy decided to err on the side of policy rather than politics. It was a bold step, since the natural inclination of every party is to reinforce its base, appeal to its strongest supporters first. A base-driven Contract would have looked far different from the one produced. Yes, the issues included in the Contract had strong popular support, as the polling and focus-group results indicated, but among Republicans, other issues would have had even *stronger* support. The key was to cause no internal division. Republicans knew they would be under constant attack in the fall campaign. They wanted no cracks in the line. They sought a document that unified all Republicans.

"The Contract with America said nothing about hate of the Clinton administration," Bob Walker recalls. "It was done for two reasons—to give us a positive agenda to run on and to give us a positive agenda to govern on. I mean, we were smart enough to know that if we did win this thing, we'd better have a coherent agenda. Otherwise everyone would believe they won it on their own issues and therefore it would be impossible to have a coherent program. We would have had a difficult time even organizing the Congress if we had that kind of fratricide inside our own ranks."

As the Contract developed, the GOP leadership team made another radical decision. The Contract would carry not just ten slogans but ten legislative bills that voters could evaluate *before* the election. Such a thing had never been done before.

"It was about policy, it wasn't about personalities," Armey says. "We said we could identify ten things that had a popular standing with the American people and that the Democrat Congress would not allow to even come to the floor for a vote."

This all seemed logical to the GOP leadership, as did the plan to require members to raise money for '94 challengers. But senior Republicans thought the manifesto idea was now getting out of control. They never imagined a majority was possible, at least not in the spring of '94. Most of these long-tenured leaders—the "old bulls," as the revolutionaries referred to them—assumed that it was a waste of time to write bills that would never see the light of day. So they did nothing but crack jokes behind the young Turks' backs.

"The old guys, the old bulls, they were laughing at us," Armey recalls. "But they didn't do it publicly. The fact of the matter is, we must have looked like a bunch of damn Don Quixotes to a lot of people. I'm sure there were a lot of people who thought that. And Newt had earned the epitaph 'gadfly,' and I think it would be real possible for a lot of guys who had been around saying, 'This is Newt off on one of his fantasy trips and he's got some of these goofy guys to go along with.' Well, it wasn't Newt's idea. I can't think of any time before or since when Republicans seemed to be speaking with one voice. I look back on it now as really quite remarkable. If there were dissenters, they zipped up. Why they did I don't know."

Had more senior Republicans taken the Contract seriously in its developmental stage, they might have been able to significantly alter its contents. By mostly ignoring the process of drafting Contract legislation, the old bulls left the field to younger Republicans who were generally more conservative and less risk-averse. The legislation behind the Contract reflected the revolutionaries' brand of take-no-prisoners conservatism that much later the old bulls would wish they had taken the time to soften.

"The Contract was really a compilation of ideas that had been out there for various amounts of time," says Michael Franc, now vice president of government relations at the Heritage Foundation. "You had sort of pent-up policy demands that were waiting to be unleashed under the right circumstances. A lot of these ideas have been developed, nurtured a bit, and fine-tuned, and [they had] no chance ever of passing, because the Democrats had such overwhelming majorities. There were these ideas sitting out there—welfare, crime, tax reductions. There were these ideas that were all dressed up but had no place to go. Then Armey and Gingrich had the luxury of all these proposals that were pretty well vetted and widely acceptable to the conservative base that were waiting to be enacted. The moderate part of the Republican caucus, they just thought, 'What are these crazy conservatives doing? I'm just running my reelection.' That was a really important nonact, because otherwise what would have come out of it would not have been at all compelling. That dynamic allowed the final product to be a lot more robust and clean than it otherwise would have been. It indelibly put the conservative stamp on the Republican majority."

But the manifesto had to do more. It had to suggest fundamental change in Washington. And it had to appeal to Perot voters. Republicans were feverishly trying to woo Perot voters to their cause. The Contract was devised at least as much to attract their attention as it was to rally the party faithful.

"I can say there was a conscious effort to attract the Perot vote in the '94 campaign, and one of the ways that manifested itself was there were no social issues in the Contract," Gaylord says. "Gingrich was very strong in saying, 'We don't want to turn anybody off with the Contract, so why would we put the most controversial things in there?' "

Pursuit of Perot voters led to an early decision, reached in the spring, to place the congressional reform agenda first. "The Contract led with the reform provisions, consciously—'We're going to reform Congress and the way it works,' " Gaylord says. "And I think that was hugely important to [Perot supporters]."

### A Glimpse of the Future

In May, top Republicans saw the first glimpse of a majority in 1994. They found it in central Kentucky, in a special election to replace Representative William Natcher, a legendary fixture in the House Democratic caucus, a powerful force on the Appropriations Committee, and the only lawmaker of his time to never miss a roll call vote—not one, from the day he arrived in 1953 until he died in May 1994. Democrats ran Joe Prather, who had served nineteen years in the Kentucky legislature, eleven as the Senate leader. Prather had extensive political connections throughout the state. Kentucky's senior senator, Wendell Ford, had cleared the field for Prather's bid to replace Natcher. Republicans ran Ron Lewis, a Baptist minister and Christian bookstore owner. Lewis had never won elective office.

The NRCC conducted a poll to see if Clinton was weak. It came back with 55 percent saying they were looking for someone new as president. That prompted a maximum effort from the NRCC and heavy support from the RNC. Paxon also dispatched his committee spokesman, Dan Leonard, to work on Lewis's race. "We were running to fill a seat vacated by a legend. The seat had been Democratic since before the Civil War," Leonard recalls. "The Democrat, Joe Prather, was running as the successor to Bill Natcher. And we said, 'Ron Lewis can't beat Joe Prather. But Clinton's negatives in the district were running between 60 percent and 70 percent.' We said, 'Ron Lewis can't beat Joe Prather, but Ron Lewis can beat Bill Clinton.' So we designed the morph ad to make Joe Prather turn into Bill Clinton."

The morph ad became legendary in the '94 campaign. The ad showed pictures of Prather that by degrees turned his face into Clinton's. The ad ran heavily, to devastating effect. "We had a positive ad for Ron Lewis cut too," Leonard says. "I think we ran the positive ad once just to say we ran a positive campaign too, but we ran that morph ad over and over." Lewis entered the race with name recognition of 13 percent. One month before election he trailed by 15 points. The morph ad began running eight days before the election. Lewis won by 10 points. "Anytime you have a public campaign on TV and radio that lasts eight days and you just blow out the opponent in a district you've never carried, you have to say this is something special," Gaylord recalls. "After the election was over, Gingrich turns to me and says, 'You better make sure this election is not a 35-seat-gain election, that this is a majority-winning election.' And I said, 'Yes sir, I'll work on it.' "

Peter Fenn, a Democratic consultant who worked on the Prather-Lewis race, saw seeds of potential destruction in the results, possibly far earlier than any other Democratic strategist.

"We kinda saw it coming," Fenn recalls. "Clinton's unpopularity made a lot more districts far more competitive."

## A Timetable and a Gamble

In June, Dick Armey sent a confidential memo that outlined the criteria for Contract items and a timetable for final approval.

Under "criteria," Armey listed the following:

- "Be sound public policy"
- "Excite our base and key allies"
- "Be dramatic enough to show real change"
- "Be easy to explain"
- "Not split our party"
- "Be do-able"
- "Fit within our overall message"

Armey's timetable for approval of Contract items was as follows: "First cut, immediately; second cut, July 15; final cut, August 12; full GOP conference approval, September 9."

Republicans followed this schedule precisely.

By mid-July, Gingrich and Barbour truly believed that if Republicans raised enough money to finance all their candidates, something historic might await them on November 8. Barbour continued to raise money and ordered Fierce to step up his long-running courtship of Perot. Meanwhile, in a memo sent to every Republican on July 18, Gingrich threw down the gauntlet on fund-raising: play or pay.

"Everyone Has a Part to Play," one of the memo's headlines read. The document informed members that Gingrich's fund-raising goal was an astonishing $8.5 million. The election was only fourteen weeks away; Gingrich was playing for keeps. Beneath the headline, the memo quoted Green Bay Packers coach Vince Lombardi, winner of two Super Bowls: "The team that doesn't break in the fourth quarter wins."

Early in the memo Gingrich summarized the state of play, pointing to numerous positive signs for Republicans.

President Clinton's *disapproval rating is 42%* with 30% strongly disapproving; right direction/wrong direction track is a devastating 32/65 in spite of the economic recovery for which neither the President nor the Democrats receive any credit. . . . At the National Press Club on June 22, 1994, [California Democrat Vic] *Fazio acknowledged that 175 seats are in play in 1994: he conceded that of the 30 Democratic open seats, only two are strongly Democratic and the other 28 are "extremely marginal" and could go either way. . . .* A record number of GOP incumbents are unopposed; GOP re-elects are running five points higher than Democrats (42% vs. 37%), according to a recent *Washington Post* poll [emphasis in original].

Gingrich said the fund-raising strategy "requires an unprecedented commitment from members. RNC and Chairman Haley Barbour have committed unprecedented candidate assistance to take advantage of this extraordinary opportunity. The minimum goal for candidate assistance is $8.5 million." Gingrich then laid out four fund-raising options for *each member:*

Option A: Commit $148,000 to challenger and open seats. . . .

Option B: . . . Raise $50,000 for the NRCC; contribute $5,000 to challenger/open-seat candidates.

Option C: Do both Option A & B.

Option D: Design a fund-raising program based on your personal strengths and interests that will yield $65,000.

The cover sheet advised members to "make decisions about what steps you can commit to achieving. Please plan to come to a meeting with your top political person and with your commitments thought through. My scheduler will call you to arrange a meeting as soon as possible."

Gaylord describes the unmistakable thrust of the pitch: "This is not a go-or-no proposition, this is a go proposition. How you want to be helpful and how you can make it better will be smiled upon. You can be an asshole and be opposed, but this is the gamble that we're staking this election on."

Gingrich, Gaylord, Paxon, and Barbour found many willing gamblers.

### Finalizing the Contract's Terms

By midsummer, the policy work on the Contract was nearly done. Only two issues remained to be resolved: school prayer and term limits—would they be in or out? Social conservatives were pressing hard for a constitutional amendment calling for prayer in school, seeing it as a necessary counter to the degradation of American culture. They also believed including school prayer would be a display of gratitude to the social conservatives for agreeing from the outset to keep abortion out of the Contract. But Gingrich's leadership team and Barbour were strongly opposed, wanting to keep the Contract focused on policy, not social issues.

"People generally agreed early on not to do abortion, but school prayer was in there for a while, it was on the table for discussion for a while, and people made a run to try to include it," recalls Kerry Knott, who was the policy gatekeeper for all Contract items.

"There was a big argument on the school prayer amendment," says Gingrich legislative adviser Jack Howard. "Paul Weyrich [a conservative activist with roots in the Reagan camp] and his crowd were just beside themselves over the fact that we didn't put the amendment in. I remember having to go over to one of their crazy lunches and they just tore me limb from limb over the school prayer constitutional amendment that wasn't in the Contract."

Ralph Reed, head of the Christian Coalition and a former Gingrich staffer, pressed the RNC to force Gingrich and his leadership team to swallow the school prayer amendment. Reed said the amendment was a long-standing priority for social conservatives, who would resent Republicans if it was kept out and a relatively new constitutional amendment, term limits, took its place. Without school prayer, Reed argued, the Contract would not speak to social conservatives but instead would suggest to them Republicans believed that they could win big only *without them.*

As a negotiating tactic, Reed never pulled abortion off the table. He kept pressing for abortion language and a school prayer amendment until the end, Barbour told me. "I told them, 'I'm begging you. If we put those things in there, we won't hold. We won't have unanimity. We'll just open wounds.' We had to find a compromise. You know what the compromise was? Henry Hyde."

Representative Henry Hyde, Republican of Illinois, was a champion of the pro-life movement, a tenacious opponent of abortion who was responsible for the first federal law to disallow federal subsidies for abortion services. Since 1976 the Hyde amendment had blocked the use of federal Medicaid funds to pay for abortions. Hyde was a hero among social conservatives. At Barbour's behest, Fierce proposed to Reed that Hyde would write the preamble to the Contract.

"We said, 'We'll give you Henry Hyde and the preamble and will you give us the rest?' " Fierce told me. "They said, 'You got a deal.' "

With that deal in place, only one issue remained: whether to advocate a constitutional amendment on limiting terms in the House to six years and twelve years in the Senate. Younger members pressed very hard for its inclusion, since the term-limits movement was sweeping the country and the young Turks saw it as reinforcing the Contract's message that Republicans favored bold changes. Senior Republicans like Gingrich, DeLay, Armey, Hyde, Bob Livingston of Louisiana, and Bill Archer of Texas vehemently opposed term limits, because they considered it an assault on the institution of Congress and an insult to voters. By supporting the Contract, they were committing only to participating in a vote on a term-limits constitutional amendment; they all made it clear that they would oppose the amendment when it came to the floor. But they recognized an unequivocal political advantage in highlighting the term-limits issue: In states where term limits had been placed on the ballot, voters had approved limiting the terms of their state legislatures by more than two to one. A *Wall Street Journal/NBC News* poll that spring showed that 80 percent of those surveyed supported term limits. In the end, term limits survived because the politics of the moment demanded it. Several Republicans now consider inclusion of term limits the only grossly cynical move in the entire Contract process.

"In the end, it polled the best but has meant the least," says Tony Rudy, a former top aide to DeLay and now a Washington lobbyist.

## The Courtship of H. Ross Perot

Once the Republicans had finalized those last disputes, the Contract's legislative language was written. And a good thing too. It would be essential in the on-again, off-again negotiations with Ross Perot. Barbour and Gingrich or their top aides kept in constant touch with Perot or his top political adviser, Russ Varney, calling at least once a week. Republicans knew what Perot's support could mean in the fall campaign. But they also feared his ego, paranoia, and desire to control everything.

"Perot is a very intimidating person," says Gingrich political adviser Joe Gaylord. "He makes you a little nervous."

Republicans lobbied Perot the best way they knew how—by appealing to his vanity. "There was a huge courtship of Perot," Fierce says. "Everyone was involved. We were telling him, 'You taught us something. You set a new

standard in American politics for communicating with the American people. Your information, your charts, your graphs—all of it taught us something.' " The GOP asked Perot to read the Contract and consider publicly
endorsing it. Perot was cautious. "Perot said, 'If it doesn't have substance,
I'm not buying it; I'm not in for the next political con game,' " Fierce
recalls. "We said, 'It will have substance but there's no veto. Take it or leave
it.' We're showing you this to win your approval. You're trying to take
advantage of us and we're trying to take advantage of you."

In late August, Perot sent Varney to Washington to inspect the Republicans' handiwork. As with everything with Perot, even the smallest matters
could be complicated. "We had all these discussions," Fierce says. "Could
they take it? Could they copy it? We agreed they could read all of it and
take parts Perot would need to think about. It was almost a legal transac-
tion. This was all about the elaborate courting of Perot. We told him we're
drafting all of this so we can pass it in the first hundred days."

Varney came to RNC headquarters and was escorted to Barbour's
conference room on the fourth floor, down a long hallway lined with por-
traits of every chairman in party history, the last being Rich Bond, who lost
his job in part because Perot ran against and helped defeat George
H. W. Bush in 1992.

Varney walked into the conference room and found a thick binder
with each Contract item, the legislative language behind it, the research
that underlay the policy, and all relevant polling data. It also included the
Republicans' transition plan for assuming control of the House. Within
GOP circles, a more sensitive document did not exist. And the GOP was
handing it over to the top adviser of one of the most slippery figures in
American politics. Such was the hunger, the desire, the palpable need for
Perot's blessing.

"It was like we were laying out the Torah, the Gospel, and the Dead
Sea Scrolls all at once," Fierce recalls. "Perot's guy was there for four hours
digging through all of the documents. We told them, 'You can't go public
with this. Not at all.' They were okay with that."

Varney reviewed everything, took copious notes, and never left the conference room until he was done. He promised to give Perot a full briefing.

Perot called less than a week later. "He says, 'I'm thrilled with what
you're doing,' " Fierce recalls. "He says, 'I'm stunned at the amount of
effort you've put in. The decency and honor of this process, it's unique in

American politics.' So Perot calls Haley and Newt and says, 'We've got to have a meeting.' "

Barbour and Gingrich agreed to meet Perot at the Crystal City Ritz Carlton in Virginia, just across the Potomac River from Washington and a stone's throw from the Pentagon. To give the meeting more heft, Gingrich and Barbour invited Bob Dole. The three most powerful men in the Republican Party would be going to Perot's suite on bended knee. Perot must have felt as if it he'd finally arrived in big-party politics. But it was not to be. The meeting did not occur as planned, in part because Barbour had second thoughts. Dole had been invited only as a courtesy, and in the end, only Gingrich, Gaylord, and Fierce made the meeting. It was Fierce's unpleasant duty to tell Perot that Barbour and Dole would not be there.

Fierce walked into the large suite to find Perot, Gingrich, and Gaylord seated around a small, brilliantly polished wooden table. "I walk in there and Newt, I can tell, is nervous," Fierce recalls. "Gaylord is scared shitless. Newt believes Perot controls his destiny. He's worried that this meeting gets pulled off all right. Then I come in and tell Perot I represent Haley and that Dole's not going to be there. And Perot has steam coming out of his ears. He is *pissed*. He says, 'I come all the way up here and I'm not going to see the chairman, I'm not going to see Bob Dole? I come all this way and they won't travel one mile to meet me? I'm doing all this to help the Republican Party. How could you treat me this way? And who are you? Can you cut a deal?' I say I can."

Fierce tried to get back in Perot's good graces. He did so by turning his attention to the two other men at the meeting, Home Depot co-founders Ken Langone and Bernie Marcus (Langone also took Perot's principal company, Electronic Data Systems, public). The two were there as the eyes and ears of the GOP's big-business backers. Fierce told Langone that the GOP was sick of big business taking the party for granted; he went on a long rant about the party's desire to cultivate stronger ties with the small-business community. Perot perked up at this, a billionaire who still cherished his small-business roots. Perot's hostility began to ebb.

"So I turn back to Perot and tell him, 'Mr. Perot, without you, we can't win,' " Fierce says. "I say, 'Mr. Perot, we need you to play a role. We're not interested in you funding this or that. We need your commitment.' I said, 'If you believe in Bill Clinton, send your supporters to him. They believe you. They'll follow what you say.' So Perot says, 'Well, how do I know you can win?' " He demanded to know why Republicans were so confident that they would take the House.

Gaylord, who confirms all of Fierce's recollections of this meeting, then took center stage. He explained the dynamics of every competitive House race from Maine to Washington, California to Florida.

"I was sort of the proof," Gaylord says. "I remember thinking, 'Let me get this out rapidly in a way that you can understand it, because you're not going to pay attention for more than two minutes.' We were looking for air-planes or dollars."

The presentation worked. Perot said he, too, was now a believer.

"Perot starts thinking, 'This could all be about me,' " Fierce says. "Perot was off to the races. It was game, set, and match. He looks at me and says, 'We'll take my jet, you and I, and we'll campaign. We'll fly all across the country, district by district, wherever this man over here, Joe Gaylord, tells us to go, that's where we go. I am committed to do this campaign.' "

In the end, by mutual consent, Perot did no such thing. The Republi-cans didn't know how much of his offer was bluster, but they were prepared only to spend Perot's money, not to make him a campaign front man. He was too volatile, too unpredictable for that.

"We had to be careful," Fierce recalls. "We couldn't turn the RNC and the House Republicans into a wholly owned subsidiary of Ross Perot. We needed and in the end we got his passive/aggressive support."

Gaylord says now that the encounter with Perot, as surreal and rich in drama as it was, ultimately proved a waste of time. "It was one of those things where these meetings did not a marriage make; you can't because he doesn't trust you and you don't trust him."

### *"The Sum Is Greater Than the Parts"*

Before they finalized the Contract with America, the Republican leaders had pollster Frank Luntz conduct focus groups on the concept and con-tents. First, he touched on the broad conclusions. "In politics, as in com-mercial advertising, it is rare for all elements of a market test to complement each other," Luntz wrote in a confidential memo to GOP leaders on September 2, 1994. "In this case, that is exactly what happened." Luntz then summarized the most important conclusions of surveys of 100 House Republicans, 100 House Republican candidates, and more than 1,000 registered voters:

Americans are skeptical of everything partisan and political, but "The Contract With America" is an exception. . . . I can say with confidence that *the "Contract" is our best hope of winning back Perot voters, disgruntled Republicans and conservative Democrats.* It is real, credible and deals with the issues most important to the electorate. Furthermore, the concept, wording and execution could not have been designed more effectively. . . . *While the notion that politicians would actually sign their name to a promise is valuable, what truly sets the Contract apart from past political documents is the "If we don't accomplish what we've pledged, throw us out—we mean it" clause. This graphically demonstrates our seriousness, and it will surely appeal to swing voters on Election Day* [emphasis in original].

Luntz offered these observations on voter moods and the Contract's ability to reach those who felt most disillusioned:

To say that the electorate is angry would be like saying that the ocean is wet. Voters in general and our swing voters in particular, have simply ceased to believe that anything good can come out of Washington. . . . The Contract is different. . . . *The idea that candidates—incumbents and challengers alike—would sign at the dotted line is highly appealing to the voters we wish to reach.* . . . Most of the phrases you see in the final Contract earned significant majorities, a strong indication that we really are using the best language possible [emphasis in original].

Luntz, at Barbour's instruction, had assembled a special Perot-centered focus group to road-test the Contract. These results proved more valuable than any other in committing top GOP leaders to the Contract.

A focus group of Perot voters and self-described "strong independents" was convened in Denver to determine the most effective "leverage points" available to Republicans in the Fall campaign, as well as to determine the correct layout for "The Contract." None had anything nice to say about Bill Clinton, Congress or either of the political parties. In fact, *they were literally the most negative, hostile voters I have ever assembled for a focus group* (and I have conducted 97 focus groups over the last three years). If the Contract can convince them, it can convince anyone. It did [emphasis in original].

For all the good news, there was one big catch.

One important caveat, however. *Not a single focus group participant liked the word Republican—not even the registered Republicans!* In fact, if the focus group had its way, the word Republican would have been removed from the text in its entirety. Again, *any appeal to partisan politics draws an equally strong negative* reaction from the very voters we need to win over. This is a difficult obstacle to overcome, and it should convince you that the party name should not (and does not) appear frequently. Readers should realize that this is a Republican document, but the party name should not be so prominent that it destroys the message. The document you now have strikes a perfect balance [emphasis in original].

The GOP had achieved this perfect balance by headlining the document "Contract with America" and mentioning the Republican Party only at the bottom, beneath all ten items and the promise that voters could throw them out if they violated the terms.

Luntz then offered this conclusion:

The Contract works not because of the individual components but because it is a complete package. In other words, the sum is greater than the parts. Remove a single component and you destroy the entire effort. To those voters who have had an opportunity to take part in the market testing, *the Contract represents the willingness of certain politicians to come together over a set of important issues and put their names and their careers on the line. This is an exercise in unity and integrity not seen in recent political memory.* That's why the "Contract with America" works [emphasis in original].

Armed with Luntz's polling data, Gingrich, Armey, DeLay, Barbour, and the rest of the party leadership felt confident that the Contract would work. The question was how well. The election was eight weeks away and only a few people really believed that a majority was possible. One of them was Tony Blankley, Gingrich's spokesman. He had a gnawing suspicion something big was afoot. And it affected the celebration of his tenth wedding anniversary with his wife, Linda.

"We were planning to go to France, and it was sometime in August that I told her I thought we were going to win and let's not make any plans and we'll celebrate some other time and some other place. I remember thinking that other than Newt, nobody thought that at the time. I remember thinking to myself, 'Am I a damn fool because I don't know anybody other than Newt who thinks this is going to happen and I'm telling my wife we're not going to celebrate our tenth wedding anniversary because I've got sucked into Newt's fantasy?' I felt like I was alone at the time, except for Newt. We engaged in it in the way spouses sometime indulge their other in whatever they take seriously and you love them too much not to take it seriously with them, but with a little bit of reserve. And when people started shifting from indulging Newt in his little fantasy into thinking this could actually be happening, I think it was very late in the process."

## A Campaign for Change

On September 9, 1994, just one week after Frank Luntz submitted his confidential report on the response to the Contract with America, the Republicans approved the Contract in final form. The Contract still wasn't a public document, but in keeping with Bill Paxon's vision of a fully engaged battle, Republicans had candidates running in 433 of the 435 House districts nationwide. Word of the Contract was spreading. Some candidates embraced it. Others were reluctant, in part because their consultants feared it would provoke too much controversy by forcing them to debate all sorts of complicated federal issues. Some consultants were much more comfortable riding the anti-Clinton wave. They weren't the least bit interested in specifics.

"Part of our challenge leading up to this was all of the consultants who didn't want to buy in to it," Kerry Knott recalls. "They were trying to tell their candidates, 'Look, we have a plan and let's stick to it.' "

Haley Barbour knew the Contract with America was a radical concept that Republicans would have a hard time selling, even with all the focus group data in their possession. Yes, they had plenty of candidates. Yes, most of them were hungry for an agenda. But the candidates wanted to know that the party was dedicated to the Contract and wouldn't cut and run in the face of inevitable Democratic attacks. To calm these fears, Barbour called GOP communications specialists Greg Mueller and Keith Appell, veterans of the Pat Buchanan campaign in 1992.

"They needed a proactive media campaign to sell the Contract," Mueller recalls. "They had to promote the human face of the Contract."

Mueller contacted Fred Sacher, a real estate developer in Sacramento, California, and asked him to bankroll a media campaign that became known as the Contract Information Center. It was designed to be a clearinghouse for all Contract-related publicity: all press releases, all speeches, all talking points, and all responses to media interview requests. Sacher agreed to pay $25,000 for the project, all of which built up to the September 27 event on the Capitol steps.

"It was the most significant marketing and selling of domestic policy since the New Deal," Mueller says of the entire GOP effort, in which he played a small part. "There are three great events in American legislative history: the New Deal, the Great Society, and the Contract with America."

The September 27 event went off without a hitch. "We all met in the Cannon Conference Room," Knott remembers. "The incumbents signed the Contract there, and we walked across the street and we get to around the East Front of the Capitol and start to walk around the back. And you kind of come around the top of the edge of the House side of the Capitol overlooking the West Side, and people saw this throng of people and like a hundred cameras and this stage set up and a band playing, and that's when they thought, 'Man, this is something different.' "

That same week, at the RNC, Barbour spent $1.6 million to place the Contract with America as a full-page ad in the October 22 issue of *TV Guide*. The campaign was joined.

Democratic reaction to the Contract was generally dismissive.

Gingrich adviser Jack Howard remembers watching the Contract ceremony winding down and being approached by two topflight Democratic Capitol Hill staffers. "They said, 'This is the biggest mistake you've ever made. You guys are crazy,' " Howard says.

"I thought, 'This isn't going to work,' " former House Speaker Tom Foley recalls. "I thought it was going to be effective but only as background music."

Most top Clinton advisers and virtually all congressional Democrats saw the Contract as a gift from heaven, a target they could aim at to take the attention and anger off Clinton. They attacked lustily on several fronts: the Contract was a fiscal fraud and warmed-over Reaganism (promising tax cuts, defense increases, *and* a balanced budget); the Contract was a stealth effort to undermine vital government programs; the Contract was another big GOP lie, just like Bush's no-new-taxes pledge; the Contract had turned every Republican candidate into one of Gingrich's robotic followers (Representative Charles Schumer of New York called them "Stepford candidates"); the Contract was grotesquely cynical because all it promised was a *vote* on the ten items, not that any of them would become law (the *ex post facto* Democratic reviews were much less forgiving, tabulating the precise number of Contract items that did not become law in the first hundred days). "They attacked it as warmed-over Reaganomics," Mueller remarks. "They just totally took the bait. They swallowed it whole. As soon as that happened, we said, 'They're taking the bait,' and our advice was just to push harder."

Democrats also tried to pin down first-time Republican candidates on the kinds of spending cuts that might be required *in their district.* Just as the backers of the child tax credit had predicted, most Republican candidates deflected questions about abstract cuts with the promise of pressing for a $500-per-child tax credit.

The Democratic attacks backfired in almost every case. In fact, as Joe Gaylord points out, the Contract provided "a message that was strong enough that candidates could actually talk about it as opposed to the usual horseshit that they talk about. The Contract in the climate we were in actually gave our candidates a lifeline. The big worry was you're going to saddle these candidates with these things and they're not going to be able to defend them because they don't know enough. What happened was they said, 'At least this is what I'm for. You won't even tell us what you're for.' "

By attacking the Contract with America, the Democrats also gave it something it had lacked before: credibility with the national media.

"I remember spending days and days lobbying all sorts of national reporters," Blankley recalls of the days leading up to the September 27 event on the Capitol steps. "I mean, I really broke my pick trying to drive this story onto the evening newscasts. One of the top producers for *NBC Nightly News* told me the day we had the Contract story it would be nothing more than a short anchor-read story accompanied by a flash of video showing all the Republicans on the Capitol steps. Then the White House attacked and we became a real story."

Media coverage focused heavily on Democratic criticism. For example, the Associated Press reported that California Democrat George Miller "said on the House floor that Gingrich was leading 'blindfolded candidates' to sign a pledge that will lead to mammoth new deficits." On CNN's *Inside Politics,* Judy Woodruff interviewed senior Democratic National Committee adviser Tony Coelho, who declared the Contract to be a "big error" on the Republicans' part. Some reporters even detected skepticism and unease within the GOP ranks—this reporter included. The day of the Contract's unveiling, I wrote this in the *Washington Times:*

> Republican House candidates hope the "Contract with America" they'll sign today will give them control of Congress for the first time in 42 years. Leading Democrats denounced it as an economic policy that's a proven loser, and even some in the GOP expressed reservations about the strategy. . . .
>
> "The Contract is complicated, and a week after this comes out no one will be talking about it or remember it," said a House GOP leadership aide who requested anonymity.
>
> A GOP campaign consultant who also requested anonymity agreed, saying, "Nationalizing elections hasn't worked for us in the last five tries, it gives Democrats a big target, it reveals our biggest weakness: We don't have philosophical unity to assure we would pass much of anything when we become a majority."

A couple of days later, an editorial in the *Cleveland Plain Dealer* sounded this cautionary note about the Contract with America:

> Republicans are quick to jump on Clinton for his many broken campaign promises. As they plot strategy for a campaign that marks their best bet at capturing Congress in decades, they might want to take some time to practice what they are so fond of preaching. Presidents are not the only politicians, after all, who can be haunted by broken promises. When congressional candidates campaign in unison, they should be prepared to be judged in unison.

But the GOP's willingness to "be judged in unison" was precisely what made the Contract so compelling as a political device and so significant as

a legislative document. Even so, it's easy to see why so many thought so little of the document. It defied all convention and forced the party to stand
together or suffer humiliation not once but twice—throughout the campaign and afterward, if their audacious dream of majority status failed to
materialize.

Many Democrats felt that forcing Republicans to defend the Contract
was better than having Democratic candidates defend Bill Clinton. Some
in the White House were uncomfortable, however. Unbeknownst to
Republicans, Clinton had toyed with a Contract-like document in the 1992
campaign. Some advisers thought now might be the time to bring it back.

"I thought from the very beginning of the Contract with America the
concept was an appealing one," says Bruce Reed, Clinton's chief domestic
political adviser. "When we were writing *Putting People First* [the 1992 Clinton-
Gore campaign tract], a couple of us produced a draft of 'Ten Big Ideas to
Revolutionize America.' But the campaign thought it was too bold and
rejected it. I thought we would respond with our own Contract, but instead
we decided to attack the Contract, and that completely backfired. Our strategy just said, again, we were against change. I mean, we argued against the
Contract specifically. We tried to get people to read it, and that's a useless
exercise in a campaign season. We should have produced our own alternative. I attended many meetings where we discussed producing our own alternative. I left the meetings believing we would produce our own alternative,
but we never did. The Democratic campaign was missing the point. People
elected Clinton because they wanted dramatic change. The 1994 election
came along and they wanted still more dramatic change."

Democratic consultants in the field had worries too. They could feel
that the Contract was gaining attention, acceptance, and traction.

"No one could remember what the details of all that were," recalls
Peter Fenn, who handled dozens of House Democratic races, "but the visual
of all those guys on the Capitol steps, the visual of the Republicans with a
plan, the anti-Washington, when you get the 'right direction'/'wrong track'
[polling] numbers way out of whack, when you get folks who are mad at
Washington, mad at politicians, mad at the insiders, then you play to that
outside card, which Gingrich did very, very effectively."

And the portrait of activism, of change, contrasted sharply with the
image of a Democratic Party riven by dissension, unsure of its direction,
and slowed by intellectual lethargy.

"There was a kind of sense, I think, out in the country that everything was falling apart," former Speaker Tom Foley recalls. " 'They can't do anything. What they concentrate on and achieve I don't like and what they concentrate on and don't achieve I do like.' It was a sense of failure. A sense of collapse. But it was the combination of the seeming collapse of unity and organization and leadership on the Democratic side and the plan on the Republican side. It was the fact that they had a national plan that they had a commitment to do certain things. These were things that people would say, 'Yeah, that's right.' It turned out to be brilliant. It was the first time that I can remember that there was a national appeal for congressional races in the House. It gave the contrast of a kind of collapse of vision or organization or expectations on the Democratic side and this kind of well-conceived popular program on their side."

All this was playing out in congressional districts across the country.

## Last-Minute Doubts

Despite the traction the GOP was gaining, some Republican candidates still resisted campaigning on the Contract as the elections approached.

In early October, Gingrich chief of staff Dan Meyer—who along with Len Swinehart had come up with "Designing an Agenda Worth Voting For" back in January—received a panicked phone call from Vin Weber, a former congressman from Minnesota and an early member of Gingrich's Conservative Opportunity Society.

"I got a call from Vin saying, 'This is really a stupid thing, because it's just going to give Democrats something to shoot at,' " Meyer remembers.

Out in Spokane, Washington, Republican challenger George Nethercutt was running a surprisingly close race against Speaker Foley. The Speaker had run afoul of some constituents for filing suit against a state initiative to approve term limits. The issue was resonating, and U.S. Term Limits, the nation's biggest and best-funded term-limits group, was pounding Foley, which was helping Nethercutt enormously. The last thing the Republican needed was a sticky debate about defense spending, crime, welfare, tax cuts, and the rest. "I hated the freaking Contract," Nethercutt spokesman Terry Holt recalls. "I told Nethercutt and told my friends in Washington, 'Keep it. We don't want it. We don't need it. It's dumb and it won't work.' "

After about two weeks of daily Democratic attacks, Barbour called in the party's top pollsters and strategists. Word was seeping out all over town that candidates should get off the Contract, run hard against Clinton, and forget that they'd ever signed anything. And this was not simpering yelps from wet-behind-the-ears consultants working their first campaign. This came from some of the most seasoned pros in the party.

Greg Mueller remembers an early-October meeting at RNC head-quarters where GOP pollsters Linda DiVall and Ed Goeas, whose firm did the early focus group work confirming the attractiveness of the Contract concept, both lamented that candidates they were working for were taking a terrific beating. They said it would be wiser for their candidates to dump the Contract or, at minimum, distance themselves from it as much as prac-ticable.

"Haley laid down the law," Mueller recalls. "He looked around the room. Hard. And he said, 'We're going to repeat it, and repeat it, and repeat it, and repeat it, and repeat it, and repeat it until we puke—and then we'll repeat it again. This is our package and we have to stick with it. We can-not run from this or it's over. We'd lose our base and our new voters.' "

Republicans did repeat it and repeat it and repeat it. In the end, it was the Democrats who puked.

### *Victory*

On Election Night, November 8, Newt Gingrich was in Georgia burning up the phone lines. It was already clear that the Republicans had won stun-ning gains, achieving the majority that Gingrich had long predicted and dreamed of. He was on the phone with Dick Armey, Tom DeLay, John Kasich, and Jim Nussle, setting the transition in motion. Gingrich would soon become the first Republican Speaker of the House of Representatives in forty years.

It was a remarkable night for Republicans. In Austin, Texas, George W. Bush rejoiced in defeating heavily favored Texas governor Ann Richards. In Spokane, Washington, Terry Holt basked in the glory of work-ing on only the second campaign in U.S. history to defeat a sitting Speaker of the House. In Buffalo, New York, a young Republican campaign worker, Tim Berry, gave up trying to watch election returns with friends in a Buf-falo bar and went outside to his freezing car to listen to returns on the radio, where he learned that his party had just made history.

In four years, Gingrich would step down as Speaker. In six years, Bush would become president of the United States. In nine years, Holt would become chief spokesman for Bush's reelection campaign. That same year, 2003, Berry would, as DeLay's chief of staff, shepherd through Congress a Medicare drug bill that conservatives would indict as the death of the Republican Revolution.

And in eight years, Barbour would be elected governor of Mississippi. But at 5 o'clock on the morning after Election Day 1994, in his suite at Washington's Renaissance Hotel, Barbour was dancing, whooping, and hollering, celebrating the victory with Fierce, his top political adviser. In his hand he cradled a freshly poured Maker's Mark bourbon, the very drink he had had when he and Gingrich agreed to "nationalize" the election less than nine months earlier.

Fierce looked up at him and said, "Haley, aren't you gonna get some sleep? You've got to go on the morning shows in less than two hours."

Barbour took a long draft of his Maker's Mark and said, "Hell no, what's the point of sleeping now? Who wants to sleep on a night like this?"

# 5

# THE HIDDEN VICTORY

Bob Dole walks into a room that his D.C. law firm, Alston & Baird, has set up for interviews and small, informal chats. He sees me sitting on the couch and plops down in the armchair to my right. As I click on my tape recorder, Dole synthesizes the messages he's been given by his staff about my book on what's become of the Republican Revolution:

"So you're doing a hatchet job on Newt, huh?" Dole asks, a wry smile crossing his face, a faint twinkle in his eye. "Wouldn't be hard."

This is where we've come, a decade since Haley Barbour and the rest of the Republicans celebrated their historic sweep of the November 1994 elections: Many observers, even some prominent Republicans, do not immediately think of major triumphs and transformations when they consider the revolution—they dwell on the setbacks.

To be sure, Bob Dole, like most Republicans, believes the revolution was important and accomplished far more than most people remember. But he has regrets as well. And dealing with Newt Gingrich was torture for him, the political equivalent of passing a kidney stone over and over and over.

"Newt was brilliant in many ways, but God, he was an anchor in many ways," Dole says now. "The feeling was, particularly when they got in the majority, was that we [the Senate Republican leadership] didn't know how to run the place, that we were all too soft and too old and too flexible and not hard-right enough."

Dole turns to the subject of the 1995 budget battle with the Clinton White House, which led to not one but two government shutdowns, the first in November and the other beginning in December and continuing into the new year. "I remember during all the budget battles I always thought [Dick] Armey was there to watch me, you know, that was his assignment, to keep an eye on Bob Dole so he wouldn't give up the store. God, it was Newt who was giving away the store in all these budget things."

Dole's sentiments about Gingrich's failures in the 1995 budget show-down are widely shared.

"The Clinton White House figured out how to play Newt," recalls Tony Rudy, a former chief of staff to current House Majority Leader Tom DeLay. "They would put the *Time* magazine cover with Newt as the Man of the Year on the coffee table in front of where they would have Newt sit. Newt would come back into leadership meetings from the White House and tell us how the White House understood his significance. And people would look around and say to themselves, 'Have you lost your mind?' "

Dole ruminates on the shutdown reluctantly, the mere mention of it causing him to wince. Dole was chairman of the RNC during Watergate, and he speaks of the shutdown in tones most Republicans reserve only for the series of political crimes that led to Richard Nixon's resignation.

"Tragedy," Dole says, shaking his head. "The first time is okay. Every-body does that. But then it sort of got to be a test of manhood. And I was not the man, of course; it was Armey and Newt who were holding the fort and were going to shut down the government for as long as it took. I kept saying, 'There's got to be some other way we can address this. You just don't cut people off at the knees.' I like to have fun up there and raise a lit-tle Cain. But in this case, the only winner was going to be Clinton. I don't know who made that decision that this was good politics. But it demon-strated to me that they didn't know anything about politics when it came to people. That hurt us a lot. You haven't noticed them shutting it down lately, have you? They learned their lesson."

Dole's assessment of the shutdown fits within the conventional wis-dom. His appraisal is also acutely personal. Dole suffered the shutdown's political consequences more than anyone. He had to run against Bill Clin-ton and the shutdown in the 1996 presidential election. Two opponents were more than Dole or probably any politician could defeat.

"Running for president almost made it worse," Dole remarks. "It was a factor in the '96 election. It was tailor-made for a guy like Clinton, who was sharp, and somebody saw it as a big thing and took it. Clinton just loved it. Hell, he didn't care how long he kept the government shut down. It helped him a lot."

For many, the 1995–96 shutdown fiasco marked the end of the short-lived Republican Revolution. President Bill Clinton, severely weakened after the catastrophic 1994 elections, came out of the 1995 budget showdown with a major political victory, according to the conventional wisdom. He emerged as a figure of strength, dexterity, and political acumen, while the Republicans, who had been so powerful in January 1994, suddenly seemed weak, fumbling, and politically tone-deaf. Newt Gingrich and his GOP allies had been vanquished, just months after they had promised to revolutionize American politics. After the shutdown, House Republicans would no longer be able to achieve the same unity of purpose. They were left chastened, their Speaker weakened, their sense of destiny hobbled.

This conventional view is accurate only to a point. Bill Clinton did indeed outmaneuver the Republicans during the budget showdown, which energized the Clinton White House and left House Republicans demoralized. Newt Gingrich never did recover the political power he had had before the budget fiasco. But Clinton's victories were *tactical* rather than substantive. To focus exclusively on tactical victories (as almost always happens in Washington, D.C.) is to offer an overly simplistic analysis. The only questions become *Who won? Who lost? And at what political cost?* Examining only tactical achievements ignores shifts in trajectories.

In fact, the Republicans dramatically changed the trajectory of the federal government during the 1995 budget showdown. As we will see, they made it possible for the United States to achieve balanced budgets and pay down hundreds of billions in public debt during the late 1990s. Those were incredible achievements, seemingly unrealistic just a few years earlier, but the Republicans made them happen. Nor was it simply a function of fortunate timing. The changes they forced on President Clinton—changes that a Democratic Congress certainly would not have sought—put the country in a far better position to digest the unprecedented prosperity of the late 1990s. Had the Republican Revolution not occurred, Clinton and the Democrats would have allocated those unexpected riches much differently. The Republicans of 1995 can even justifiably claim credit for rendering the government smaller, if not nearly as small as they had promised to make it; they forced more cuts than Clinton wanted and more than any Democratic Congress would have demanded.

In some ways, the tactical analysis of the 1995 budget showdown has the situation exactly backwards. While Clinton is generally regarded as the figure of strength in the budget battle, he was mostly weak, continually

giving ground to the GOP on key budget concepts. The secret of his tactical success was that he was more pliable than the House Republicans.
Unlike Clinton, the Republicans were firm in their convictions, strong
beyond comprehension. They were committed to the policy above the politics, which is ultimately why they stumbled in executing their plan. The
Republicans had a goal but no political strategy. The Clinton White House
had a political strategy but no goal—no specific budget for which it was
fighting or to which it was committed, only a few talking points culled from
incessant polling.

How many times has it been uttered—how many times have you said
yourself—that politicians should just do what they think is right and stop
playing politics, that political calculations should stop trumping true convictions? If ever there was a time in modern American history when such
calculations were abandoned, it was the 1995 budget showdown. But the
fact that Republicans ignored standard political calculations is precisely
why they are seen as the losers in the showdown with Bill Clinton. Their victories may not be as obvious, but they are far more consequential.

## What Was It All About?

In the popular wisdom, it all feels so futile now. The budget showdown of
1995 seems a huge clash about not much at all. Twice in just a matter of
weeks, the federal government was shut down as the two major political parties faced off against each other. It was a spectacle the likes of which Washington had never seen before. In a city that prefers hushed tones and the plastic
language of deference *("Will the distinguished gentleman yield?"),* the conflict
was raw, vengeful, angry, petulant, and loud. (In denouncing the Republicans and their budget, Democrats threw out terms like "whore," "fascist,"
"racist," "Hitler," and perpetrators of "genocide.") It was a circus, an opera,
WWF Smack Down, the Super Bowl. It was America's first reality series,
played out on the nightly news.

But what was it all about? To many, the fight over the budget seems
inconsequential, a needless, heedless exercise in Republican excess. They
might remember the Republicans as Visigoths, hordes of strange,
unkempt barbarians hell-bent on sacking and pillaging every government
program from the National Endowment for the Arts to the Appalachian
Regional Commission to the Legal Services Corporation. Many Republicans see it differently, but they would agree that the stakes seemed

unimaginably high, as the new GOP majority set its sights on ending forty years of fiscal recklessness, on toppling the spendthrifts who had mortgaged the nation's future, frittered away billions on feckless programs, undermined defense, confiscated trillions in taxes, and created this corpulent and sclerotic federal government. The Republicans who had risen to power wanted to reform virtually all federal programs, pursuits, and perquisites. The Republicans were taking on the New Deal and the Great Society at the same time, while also trying to cut taxes and increase defense spending in a return to Reaganism. Nothing was off-limits. The Republicans' budget even included calls to eliminate the Departments of Education, Commerce, and Energy.

"I signed on to all of this stuff," Dole recalls. "We were going to get rid of the Department of Education, the Department of Commerce, the Department of Energy." He looks away wistfully. "Then it just sort of—it's too hard, it's too hard. I think it demonstrated things are not as easy as they seem."

The Republicans' grand budget plans seemingly disappeared into the ether, which is why so many consider the Republican Revolution dead. Besides, the thinking goes, whatever the Republicans might have achieved back then has been obliterated under the apparent Republican profligacy of today. Conservative budget watchdogs have been among the most vocal critics of the Republican Revolution's failure to curtail government spending. In March 2004, for example, the Cato Institute issued a report entitled "The Republican Spending Explosion," which stated, "After only three years in office, President Bush is headed to the record books as one of the biggest spending presidents." In the first three fiscal years under the Bush administration, federal spending increased more than 8 percent annually, the report said. "By comparison, the average increase in the past 40 years is 1.7 percent." The criticism began even before Bush. A June 2000 Cato study entitled "The Return of the Living Dead: Federal Programs That Survived the Republican Revolution" revealed, "Many of the more than 200 programs that the Republicans pledged to eliminate in 1995 in their 'Contract with America' fiscal blueprint now have fatter budgets than they had before the changing of the guard. Overall, federal expenditures for 95 of the largest 'living-dead' programs have risen a total of 13 percent since 1994. Many of President Clinton's favorite programs have received substantial increases, often in excess of what the president has proposed."

Facts, as the saying goes, are stubborn things. But do they tell us the whole story? More pointedly, do they tell us the story that matters most? In the normal telling, the 1995 budget showdown is reduced to this: Republicans won a big election, overplayed their hand, ran into a master politician, and impaled themselves on the insane politics of government shutdowns in pursuit of a balanced budget.

But does the conventional wisdom tell us about the 1995 shutdown's lasting impact on politics and policy or about the underlying importance of the revolution and the causes for which it was fought? No, it doesn't.

First, consider the long-forgotten reality that Republicans actually did cut spending in significant ways, reversing four decades of Beltway tendencies.

"We immediately launched a mission to cut the previously committed budget for fiscal year '95; we cut $50 billion out of what had been previously voted on in the previous Congress," says former Appropriations Committee chairman Bob Livingston. "We had tremendous success at the outset, because we had knocked the Democrats off balance and the Clinton administration decided to co-opt us rather than work against us. As time went on, Clinton's people got much better at obstructing our cuts than they were at the outset. And our ability to cut back their deliberate attempt to spend more money was diminished. Our stick became smaller as we went forward in those years. But if you look at the amount that the government spent, both domestic and defense, it had been going up steadily for thirty or forty years and all of a sudden took a dip. The intent to scale back spending was achieved and we ended up in the early years eliminating over 300 programs, about 310 programs. Rather than a failing, you judge an era by results. And the results were that we shifted the mindset of government away from constantly promising and spending more to promising and spending less."

The actual number of shuttered federal programs was less than 200, according to Cato's June 2000 study. Nevertheless, the cuts were real. The report notes, "We find that in their first year in control of Congress the Republicans made impressive progress in downsizing the federal government by reducing or eliminating domestic agencies. Almost 200 programs were eliminated between fiscal years 1995 and 1997. Domestic discretionary spending actually declined in real terms from $259 billion to $250 billion after the first year of the Republican Congress."

Consider, too, that the Republican revolutionaries redirected the entire ship of state. Until the Republican Revolution, no major political party in post-Depression America had tried to use balancing the budget as an organizing political philosophy, as a true agenda. Pursuit of a balanced budget had never moved beyond rhetoric before 1995, and had only gained serious attention as a political goal in the 1992 presidential election.

"The deficit never worked as an issue," recalls Tony Blankley, Newt Gingrich's former press secretary. "Republicans had been beating our heads on it forever and nobody cared. And it was only Perot's launching of it that Newt borrowed that ended up defining the Clinton-and-Newt struggle. It was an odd issue for us to champion. It didn't deliver votes. There was just this brief moment, the Perot campaign in '92 and the Contract, that launched the deficit as an issue, that we somehow made the public care about briefly and was given credibility by Perot. Perot being the outsider made it a nonpartisan issue and we borrowed it and said this nonpartisan issue we're going to champion."

One of the central planks of the Contract with America was a balanced-budget amendment. And within the first hundred days of taking power, House Republicans had in fact passed a balanced-budget amendment, only to see it die in the Senate when one Republican voted against it and six Democrats who had previously voted for it switched their vote. By all normal political calculations, this should have been the end of the House Republicans' pursuit of a balanced budget. After all, they had fulfilled their Contract promise to bring the amendment to a vote. But they refused to let the game end there. Their raw, seemingly antipolitical pursuit of a balanced budget drove them deeper into the fray, far beyond what they had promised in the '94 election and far beyond what the political calculations of the time would have recommended. A majority that had been in the hands of others for forty years was now in the hands of House Republicans, and they were willing to *throw it away* in pursuit of one definable, all-encompassing goal: balancing the budget. They didn't throw it all away, but they did weaken their position. In the process, though, they fundamentally altered the terms of debate in this country, establishing a new set of center-right parameters on some of the most important issues.

This is what that dramatic clash in 1995 was all about. A long-suppressed political philosophy was slamming into a wall of resistance that had been built and reinforced over the previous four decades. Amazingly, the Republicans knocked down that wall, and this country is a much different place because of it.

## The Drive Toward a Balanced Budget

In February 1995, just days after he delivered the State of the Union address in which he declared that "the era of big government is over," President Bill Clinton submitted his budget, which projected deficits of $275 billion in the year 2000. As June O'Neill, director of the Congressional Budget Office (CBO), told the Joint Economic Committee on June 22, 1995, "The budget that the administration submitted in February for fiscal years 1996 through 2000 would not have substantially changed the projected budget deficits." Indeed, Clinton was most concerned with protecting core liberal spending. Meanwhile, however, House and Senate Republicans were cracking the whip and producing comprehensive, specific budget documents that, according to the same analysis that the CBO applied to Clinton's February budget, would achieve a balanced budget by 2002, in the space of just seven years.

The lines had been drawn. While Bill Clinton and the Democrats would later claim credit for balancing the budget, the budget they initially set forth in 1995 would have kept up the deficit spending that Democrats had been practicing for years. The Republicans had set out a clear, ambitious goal: a balanced budget to be achieved in seven years.

In the face of the Republicans' aggressive policy-making, Clinton had to retool and retrench. Politics dictated as much. Polls showed that the Republican majority was winning over voters once unsure about the Contract with America. An April 1995 CNN/ *USA Today*/Gallup poll showed Congress's approval rating at 58 percent compared with Clinton's 35 percent rating. And 49 percent said that Congress was doing the "right amount" of budget cutting and "not going too far," as Clinton political guru Dick Morris noted in a memo to the president. In his book *Against All Odds*, Morris recounts how Clinton shifted strategy on April 5:

> Frustrated by stagnant or dropping poll ratings and by his inability to project a centrist message, at the April 5 strategy meeting Clinton decisively turned away from the confrontational tactics urged upon him by his staff. . . . The April 5 agenda also marks the intro-

duction of the idea that the president might advocate a balanced budget but reject the GOP demand that balance be achieved in seven years.

Already, then, Clinton was coming toward the Republican side on the budget issue. But the adjustment would take time. White House chief of staff Leon Panetta, Clinton adviser George Stephanopoulos, and the entire economic team opposed supporting a balanced budget even in concept. Morris recognized that the resistance to a balanced budget was creating political problems for the president. In a memo dated May 16, Morris wrote:

> Error of past week—too orthodox Democrat; Created clear impression: Clinton opposes balanced budget; (a). Submitted a budget in deficit (b). He opposed balanced budget amendment (c). Now he's attacking Republican balanced budget plans (d). Conclusion: if it talks like a duck, walks like a duck, and looks like a duck—Clinton is a fiscal liberal

Morris, at war with senior White House staff, wanted to move Clinton toward a pro–balanced-budget position. Later he would push for achieving that goal by a certain date. For now, it was enough work to move Clinton from his outward hostility, reinforced by all senior staffers, and his apparent desire to delay balancing the budget forever. Morris's May 16 memo proposed a strategy, part of which was to attack the GOP's goal of balancing the budget in seven years:

> Outlines of plan in speech; 1 (a) Clear unambiguous statement of the need for zero deficit plan to be passed this year. (b) Praise for Republicans for finally leaving speechmaking behind and now joining serious work of budget balancing.

> 3 g. Attack 2002 deadline (1) "a date off a bumper sticker." (2) Attack prolonged delay, but suggest 2003 or 2004 might be more reasonable. (3) Demand that we show year-by-year progress deficit reduction

President Clinton adopted Morris's strategy. On June 13, he announced to the country that he was going to submit a new budget that would achieve balance by 2005. Just before Clinton's speech, Leon Panetta told reporters assembled in the White House briefing room, "The president has laid down a proposal now to achieve a balanced budget in ten years. I think that's a significant step for the president. We're saying, 'Look, we're willing to move towards a fixed date in terms of achieving a balanced budget.' "

But the step was not as significant as the Clinton White House portrayed it, according to the Republicans. The Republican-controlled CBO disputed Clinton's numbers, which had been fashioned by the White House Office of Management and Budget (OMB). The CBO said that Clinton's "updated" June budget wouldn't achieve balance in ten years, but that it aimed only to keep deficits under $200 billion from 1995 through 2005. In other words, even in June, Clinton had no plan whatsoever to achieve a balanced budget.

The discrepancy between the OMB's and the CBO's numbers was so great that the Republicans would insist that the CBO become the final arbiter of balanced budgets. It would become another key issue in the budget showdown.

While Clinton's revamped ten-year budget did not achieve balance, it did imagine reductions in the growth of key social welfare programs—the very programs Clinton had set out to protect. For example, the June budget provided $295 billion less for Medicare, $105 billion less for Medicaid, and $63 billion less for welfare. As it always does, the CBO compared the budget numbers with what is known as the baseline, which imagines existing programs continuing with no changes and increasing spending each year at the rate of inflation. Clinton's February budget tracked almost identically with the CBO's baseline through the year 2000 (less than $30 billion separated their 2000 deficit projections). By contrast, the projected 2000 deficit under the GOP budgets was nearly $200 billion smaller than the CBO baseline deficit. But what about Clinton's revised June budget? To counter the GOP's muscular fiscal austerity, the president's new-look budget undershot the CBO baseline *every year from 1996 to 2005*. It envisioned *$105 billion* less in spending from 1996 to 2000 than the president had proposed four months earlier and roughly *$840 billion* less in spending from 1996 to 2005.

I call this the first of many "Contract Dividends." To adequately measure what the GOP majority and its single-minded push for a balanced budget meant to federal spending, you have to first ask yourself what things would have been like had the GOP majority not existed in the first place. Clinton's own budgets and the CBO's analysis of them tell us quite clearly what the situation would have been like. The Clinton baseline would have resulted in deficits of more than $250 billion in 2000 (this even with the vaunted Clinton deficit-reduction act of 1993). And Clinton's budget "do-over" in June—with its "cuts" of Medicare, Medicaid, and welfare—still would have left the country with deficits of $200 billion until 2005 or, to use a well-worn phrase of the day, "for as far as the eye could see."

There is no shortage of evidence that the Republican majority drove Clinton to embrace the idea of a balanced budget. It is simply inconceivable that Clinton would have arrived at this policy objective any other way. Facing an aggressive GOP majority seemingly obsessed with the budget, Clinton in June still couldn't bring himself to endorse policies that brought the nation anywhere close to a balanced budget even by 2005. The closest he could come was a deficit of $175 billion! And yet within months he would embrace a seven-year balanced-budget model.

### *"We'll Shut the Government Down"*

The Republicans, with their goal clearly laid out, had already forced President Clinton to maneuver toward their position. But the political battle had barely begun.

As the months wore on, the Republicans showed how serious they were about balancing the budget by publicly threatening to shut down the government in the fall if the Clinton White House did not accede to their demands. And as it became clear that the U.S. government would reach its federal debt limit sometime in the fall, they decided to incorporate the debt limit into their plan to achieve a balanced budget. They began saying that they knew President Clinton would be legally obligated to seek congressional approval to increase the debt limit so the government could continue to service the debt on all present and future obligations. If Congress refused to extend the debt limit, the nation would be in danger of default. It was a high-handed way of telling Clinton that the only way he could prevent the government from lapsing into default would be to surrender to them on the balanced budget.

And surrender he might have, had it not been for the "family intervention" of senior White House staff. George Stephanopoulos recalls the
incident in his book, *All Too Human*:

> [Treasury Secretary Robert] Rubin was using creative financing to
> forestall the day of reckoning but if Congress didn't grant the gov-
> ernment authority to issue more bonds, the United States was, at
> most, weeks away from defaulting on its debt for the first time in
> history—on Clinton's watch. Publicly, the president was resolute;
> privately he was wavering. "I'm not comfortable being this hard-
> line," he said at a Morris residence meeting. . . . So when Gingrich
> called Clinton to discuss the debt limit, we intercepted the message
> and had Rubin return the call instead—joking that to keep him
> from calling Newt and trading away the store we would disconnect
> Clinton's phones, "like they did to Gorbachev during the coup."
> But the Speaker, correctly, would only deal with the president.
> An Oval Office meeting was scheduled for Wednesday, Novem-
> ber 1. . . . As Gingrich and Dole drove down from the Capitol, our
> Oval Office prep group had the feel of a family intervention. All of
> us . . . surrounded the president, bucking him up, telling him how
> strong he looked when he stood on principle and reminding him
> of the consequences of retreat.

At no time did Newt Gingrich, Bob Dole, or any other top Republican
involved in the budget negotiations require a "family intervention." Their
course was set, their goal clear. Politics be damned (at least at this stage).
The portrait that emerges of Clinton during this time from those who stood
with him in the White House is of a leader besieged by the unceasing will of
Republicans to balance the budget and of a White House desperately looking for a tactical way to achieve political victory while giving ground almost
daily on the underlying policy. It is not the portrait consistent with the deftly
spun version of events now so deeply ingrained in the public mind.

Of course, Clinton's moments of weakness occurred behind the
scenes. As Dick Morris's polling revealed, the president was doing better
with the American public. In a memo dated November 1, 1995—the day of
the White House staff's "family intervention"—Morris reported that Clinton had pulled ahead of his likely GOP challenger in the 1996 race, Dole,

and that the Republicans were facing rising public disapproval. The memo stated:

> (A) Approval is now 58–37—up from 57 two weeks ago 55 a month ago. Highest we have ever recorded. (B) Clinton v. Dole 46–36. Budget Strategy (A). Republicans will plead for negotiations—they are "withering on the vine."

And the Democrats used this information to formulate a political strategy—the one thing the Republicans sorely lacked. Former House majority leader Dick Gephardt told me in rich detail about how that strategy evolved, underlining how vulnerable Democrats felt even before the shutdown saga began.

"I'll never forget as long as I live the [November] meeting in the White House with Newt and Dole and me and [Senate Minority Leader Tom] Daschle, Clinton, and Gore, and this was when we were disagreeing on the budget. It was right before the shutdown. Clinton was disagreeing with Newt about what to do. Newt looked at him and said, 'You know, the problem here is you've got a gun to my head. It's called the veto. But what you don't understand is that I've got a gun to your head and I'm going to use it. I'm going to shut the government down. We are coequal branches of government, and I'm going to use my veto, which is shutting the government down.' The meeting broke up and Clinton asked Daschle and me to stay behind. They left and Clinton looked at me and said, 'Jesus Christ, is he going to do this? Do you really think he's going to do this?' And I said, 'Yes, I've been trying to tell you this for days. They're going to do this. This is what they came to do.' And he said, 'I don't see how he can do it.' And I said, 'Well, I'll tell you this, if he does it, I think we get blamed. I don't think the people are going to understand what's going on here. We're responsible. You're the president. You're a Democrat. And people are going to say if the government shuts down it's your fault, it's our fault.' And he said, 'I guess, maybe you're right.' We were all worried that that's what was going to happen. So then we came back in a day and we put together a public relations plan that if he did this that we could get across to the public that it was the Republicans' fault. That they didn't have to shut the government down. The press overall got the idea across that they didn't have to do it."

That was the strategy: Blame the Republicans for the shutdown. And it was within this narrowly defined tactical question that most of Washington and much of the country would come to judge the shutdown. The operative question became *So, America, who do you think is to blame?* The shutdown became a vessel for the laziest forms of reportage and analysis. After all, it's far easier to comprehend the trend lines of public opinion on whether the shutdown is the Republicans' fault or Clinton's fault than to ask the far more complex question of whether there are actually two specific, competing visions of balancing the budget. Had that question been asked or played as prominently as the blame question, a far different conclusion might have been reached about what precisely was at stake here. Through it all, there never were two competing visions of balancing the budget without raising taxes. There was the Republican plan, which was laid out in raw, declarative, and politically injurious specificity, and then there was Clinton's window dressing. The president never had a specific, competing budget. But he had the strategy, and that proved more valuable than a goal or a budget.

The best Republican thinkers knew this long before the fight had really been joined. Republicans would pursue their goal because they knew in a game of pure political strategy they were outgunned.

"We had a brief moment of opportunity when we pushed Clinton back on his heels," Gingrich's former press secretary Tony Blankley told me. "He was too good of a politician to give much time to adjust, because as soon as he figured out what he was going to do he was going to beat us. Because one thing Newt believed and I believed was that he's better than we are tactically, he will beat us at tap dancing every day of the week, he will beat us in every news cycle. But we have a strategic vision and he has no strategic vision. There was only so long that you could play out that game. A guy who can hit you twenty-seven times a day while you're taking one or two swings, you can't take that for very long. Clinton being the best politician since Roosevelt, he wasn't going to sit on his ass for six months. He paused, like a smart guy, he went down for the count, he took the count, and [at] nine and nine and a half he's going to look for something to do. We were getting weaker every day, so we had to use the extraordinary energy we got from the election and the explosive coverage of Newt to move as far as we could as fast as we could."

But Republicans also gave the White House the cudgel with which to beat them. They gave the nation ample reason to believe they were the instigators, the provocateurs, the agents of doom.

"I'll tell you what killed us," former House majority leader Dick Armey told me. "In '93 and '94 the Democrats killed themselves because they were too full of themselves, and [in] '95 and '96 we killed ourselves because we were too full of ourselves. And here I'll give credit to Newt and [House Budget Committee chairman John] Kasich. We spent the whole summer of '95 walking around this town saying, 'If he doesn't come to his milk on the budget, we're just going to shut the damn government down.' The presumption was when governments get shut down, the president gets the blame. The newfound stars on the block on center stage—Kasich and Gingrich—are threatening to every reporter they see, 'We'll shut the government down.' Why isn't it therefore perfectly credible for that reporter to say, 'The Republicans shut the government down'? You will not find any time during that summer where I said that was even possible. The lexicon was [a] train wreck. And I kept saying, 'That's not necessary. We can work that out.'

"Intuitively, we knew it was wrong. We were setting ourselves up. The best thing they [the Democrats] had going for them was the perception that we shut the government down. So if Newt and Kasich hadn't been so full of eagerness to tell everyone, 'I'm going to hit him with a right hook'— I mean, talk about telegraphing—even if you had it in your game plan to purposely shut down the government, why would you say it? But I think this was just a matter of strutting, thoughtless strutting—you know, 'We're big shots now, we're in power, we can do these things.' I talked about it a couple of times. It was very hard to challenge Newt's enthusiasm. The fact of the matter is, we set it up to be blamed. We gave Clinton just that much edge. If Clinton had been feeling the wrath of the public for the government being shut down, he'd have thrown in the towel."

Even Gingrich's closest friend in politics, former representative Bob Walker of Pennsylvania, the floor manager for the Contract and Gingrich's closest personal adviser outside the elected GOP leadership, agrees with Armey's biting assessment. Except Walker points out that he, too, spoke freely of the GOP's take-it-or-shut-down-the-government approach.

"What we made a mistake on is that we were pretty open and honest about how we were going to do this," Walker says. "That was a mistake, because I was one of the people out there telegraphing it. We created a dynamic that got us on the wrong side of the perception of it. We probably should not have talked as openly and telegraphed the fact that we were going to create a debt crisis, because that gave time to prepare and gave Rubin an opportunity to set up a scenario to defeat us on that front. And we probably shouldn't have been as open about using the shutdown as the way to do it, because again they kind of steeled themselves for it."

The Republicans made still other tactical errors. Just days after the government shutdown began, Newt Gingrich made his infamous (and misinterpreted) complaint that during a twenty-five-hour round-trip flight aboard Air Force One for the funeral of assassinated Israeli prime minister Yitzhak Rabin, Clinton made no effort to negotiate a budget compromise. The House Speaker said that this was one reason he had become so confrontational on the government shutdown. It wasn't true; Gingrich had been confrontational from the beginning, as had the entire Republican leadership. Worse for the Republicans, the White House wisely released a photo of Clinton sitting with Gingrich in the Air Force One conference room. The story now had a tantrum-throwing Speaker and a grieving, inclusive president—or so it seemed.

But Clinton *did* snub Gingrich. Why? This important dimension of the story was unknown and unknowable at the time, but the White House staff kept Clinton away from Gingrich during the flight home, fearing that he would, as Stephanopoulos later recalled, "concede too much in private negotiations with Gingrich or Dole." A historic opportunity to achieve an amicable breakthrough was passed up because Clinton's palace guard considered him too weak, too starved for public approval, too detached from his supposedly rock-solid political moorings to be left to his own devices. Principles indeed. Still, the damage inflicted on Gingrich was substantial, and he was soon mocked on the House floor as a crybaby in diapers (courtesy of a devastating cartoon on the front page of the New York *Daily News*).

"It could have all just fallen apart at that point if more and more [Republican] members rebelled," recalls Ed Gillespie, at the time Majority Leader Dick Armey's press secretary and later the chairman of the RNC. "But they didn't, even through the shutdown period. There was a remarkable unity through some extremely tough times, and even when Newt started making some of his more public gaffes, people hung in there."

Indeed, despite the tactical errors, the Republicans still had a chance to break the Clinton White House during the budget showdown. According to Stephanopoulos, after the government shutdown began in November, the White House was reeling and in danger of making huge concessions to the GOP. Even after Gingrich's and others' gaffes, Stephanopoulos writes in *All Too Human,*

> the Republicans were still in a strong position. On Sunday, November 19, six days into the shutdown, the White House was functioning with a skeletal staff, and our coalition was cracking. Forty-eight Democrats had voted for a new Republican CR [continuing resolution, a bill to reopen the government while negotiations continued on a final compromise].... With Thanksgiving approaching, Democrats were bailing out on us by the hour. In the House, we couldn't hold enough Democrats to sustain a veto. To ward off that disaster, our budget team drove to the Capitol with an offer to meet the Republicans' demand for a balanced budget in seven years "if and only if" they agreed to provide "adequate funding for" the president's priorities: Medicare, Medicaid, education and the environment.

The White House considered the offer internally self-defeating. A dullard would know that no one could balance the budget over seven years by protecting these Clinton priorities and making good on the GOP's one unshakable spending demand, protecting defense spending. Stephanopoulos writes, "In our minds, the two halves of the resolution canceled each other out; nothing would be agreed to until everything was agreed to."

The White House felt sure Republicans would see through its flimsy offer. But they did not. Again, Stephanopoulos:

> Certain the Republicans would reject it, we returned to the White House and waited. . . . Clinton was grumpy; the rest of us were grim—until Betty [Currie, Clinton's chief secretary] cracked the door and handed Leon [Panetta] the Republican counterproposal, fresh from the fax machine. Reading over Leon's shoulder, I saw that the only changes were cosmetic, replacing "if and only if" with "and," and adding language praising veterans and citing the need for a strong national defense. "This is it!" Panetta exclaimed.

"Yes!" I screamed in his ear. The president high-fived the whole room. Our fellow Democrats back on the Hill immediately agreed to accept the amendments, and the government was back in business. We Democrats emerged from the first shutdown more unified, while the Republicans fractured. Whether the cause was hubris, naiveté, or failure of nerve, the Republicans *had blown their best chance to splinter our party; from that point on, everything started breaking our way* [emphasis added].

Dick Morris agrees with Stephanopoulos's analysis. In *Against All Odds* he writes, "We were greatly surprised when the Republicans surrendered by offering to reopen the government without getting a budget deal and without any commitments from us other than to balance the budget in seven years based on CBO numbers. We all knew this was GOP surrender but to be sure the press interpreted it in that light we insisted that the Republicans confirm that we intended to protect Medicare, Medicaid, education and the environment."

Republicans read the agreement exactly backwards. They felt they had won by forcing Clinton to accept virtually all of their core demands— a balanced budget that fit within the conservative estimates of spending and taxing provided by the CBO. They had pulled Clinton from opposing a balanced budget at all to accepting one in ten years, as he did in June 1995, and finally to agreeing to balance the budget in seven years—and with a GOP-controlled agency, the CBO, keeping score.

According to Ed Gillespie, everyone in the GOP leadership saw victory in the Clinton commitment to balance the budget on the GOP's long-established terms: seven years and with CBO numbers. Everyone, that is, except Armey.

"What was frustrating about it is, is that we were this close," Gillespie told me, drawing his thumb and forefinger to within less than an inch of each other, "to winning the government shutdown fight. In my estimation, if we'd have hung in there forty-eight hours more, the worm was about to turn when we had the fax exchange. Armey didn't want to accept it. He said, 'This is a mistake.' I agreed with him. He picked up something. Armey picked up the weasel words that others didn't. Others may have seen them but didn't want to pick them up. They were ready to cut the deal. And Armey didn't want to. And I remember saying to him, 'Everybody else is in, we've just got to be in too.' We were wrong. If we'd had the strength to hang in there another two days, we would have done it on our terms. But we didn't."

So the Republicans accepted the terms of the deal that would allow the government to reopen while budget negotiations continued. The first shutdown was over, but they had a problem: Republican leaders defined victory in terms of how far they had moved Clinton; Clinton defined victory in terms of how far he was moving Republicans from the public. And by this time, polls showed that the public viewed President Clinton's reluctance to embrace Republican spending "cuts" as courageous and strong. By accepting the deal, the GOP essentially ended the shutdown on terms Clinton had successfully defined. As Dick Morris has written, Bill Clinton's skillful maneuvering allowed him "to have his cake and eat it too—to propose to eliminate the deficit but also to avoid the harsh cuts proposed by the Republicans."

### Battle's End

But the temporary agreement the congressional Republicans and the Clinton White House reached in November did not resolve the budget dispute. Talks collapsed in mid-December, and the government shut down once again.

The stakes were even higher now. At the apex of the budget drama, it was as if the entire Democratic Party, past, present, and future, lived within Bill Clinton, and the entire Republican Party—not the doddering, pliant, feeble legislative weakling of yore, but the rippling, youthful, proud, and intemperate majority of today—lived and breathed through Newt Gingrich. Clinton fought to protect, preserve, and bequeath an order, a philosophy that dated back to Andrew Jackson and flowed through Woodrow Wilson, Franklin Roosevelt, Harry Truman, and Lyndon Johnson. Gingrich fought for something new, a Republican legislative juggernaut, to remake the New Deal and Great Society through the mandated constitutional prerogatives of taxing and spending now controlled by a conservative majority with philosophical bloodlines that ran through Ronald Reagan and Barry Goldwater.

Behind the scenes, the strain showed, as key players both in the White House and in Congress were hysterical. Even when all the polling data showed President Clinton riding high, division among senior administration officials was rife. The whiff of capitulation was everywhere, and liberals were appalled. Clinton may have been winning the PR war with Republicans, but Republicans were winning the substantive battle. Clinton while in retreat was picking the most politically advantageous fights but substantively the least defensible ones. Clinton's own secretary of labor, Robert Reich, was disturbed by the president's actions. In the book *Locked in the Cabinet*, Reich writes:

> December 29 Washington: "B continues to cave. Now he's agreeing to balance the budget in *seven* years. Of course, Gingrich still isn't satisfied. In public, B demonstrates indignation only about Gingrich's threat to slow the growth of Medicare spending. Yet this is the *least* offensive part of the Republican plan. Medicare *is* out of control and too many of its beneficiaries are wealthy enough not to need it. The Republicans deserve credit for saying that something has to be done."

For the Republicans, the gaffes were much more public. With their noncompromising attitude, they played right into the Democrats' strategy of blaming the GOP for the government shutdown. Just before Christmas, Bob Livingston took the floor and bellowed on and on about the GOP's absolute determination to stare down Clinton come Hell or Armageddon: "We will never, never, never give in. . . . We will stay here till Doomsday."

Looking back, Livingston acknowledges that he and his fellow Republicans made a severe political miscalculation. "The shutdown in retrospect was a mistake, and I heavily contributed to that by giving one of the worst speeches of my life," he told me. "It was kind of a Howard Dean speech. At the time the federal employees thought I was crazy and my mother thought I was crazy. She called me and said, 'Don't ever give those speeches again.' We handled it badly. It was not a mistake at all in concept. The concept is better used as a threat than in implementation."

Finally the congressional Republicans' struggles in the war of perceptions caught up with them. By the end of December, the Senate Republicans, led by Bob Dole—who was never a part of the revolution—could no longer abide the House leadership's win-at-all-costs approach.

The breaking point occurred on Saturday morning, December 30, when Dole, Gingrich, and Armey met in the Senate majority leader's office.

All three were exhausted and beaten down by the Clinton White House. All three felt that Clinton had negotiated in bad faith and used the bully pulpit to shift the focus of the debate to the government shutdown and away from the overarching goal of balancing the budget. They were also furious about little slights from Clinton. Particularly galling was a picture in *Time* magazine that showed the president and assembled Republican leaders in the White House with Clinton pointing at an easel with budget numbers. Armey told me that it appeared as if "the president was giving a lesson and we were a bunch of school kids." The picture angered all three, but no one took it more personally than Armey. "I was furious because I had a long-standing requirement that my picture not be taken at the White House. I knew what Clinton did. They just used us as a bunch of props for Clinton."

At one point in the meeting, Clinton called. The president asked Dole if he and Gingrich and Armey were coming to the White House for further talks. A dispirited Dole said he didn't think it would do anybody any good. When Dole mentioned to the president that the picture in *Time* had irked Armey, Clinton asked to speak to Armey. According to Armey, "the president said, 'Dick, you can't hold me responsible,' and I said, 'What do you mean, Mr. President? It's your White House. You're the one who promised me they wouldn't be released. Who else am I to hold responsible for it?' "

What transpired next marked a watershed in the shutdown and a new low in the relationship between the Republican congressional leadership and Clinton. Armey recollects the moment precisely: "At that point, Newt, who had been sort of sitting there, stewing, jumped up and grabbed the phone and said, 'Give me the damn phone.' And I heard the most profane barrage out of his mouth at the loudest level of volume."

I have confirmed through others present that Gingrich said the following to the president of the United States: "You are a goddamn lying son of a bitch!"

When I asked Gingrich about the exchange, he responded, "I'm not sure how you maintain protocol with a man who is systematically lying to you. If I had to choose between telling the truth and adhering to protocol, I believe the American people want me to tell the truth."

Dole watched Gingrich and blanched. Armey considers it the moment when Dole gave up on the all-or-nothing strategy of confronting Clinton. "I think he was feeling the heat of the government shutdown and that exchange so offended Bob's sense of protocol that he thought, 'Look, we are not being responsible in our treatment, our demeanor is breaking down.' And I just think he was embarrassed. You know, we were losing control of ourselves. And I think Bob thought, 'This embarrassment might be private but the next one might be very public, and I'm just going to put an end to it.' "

Asked about Armey's theory, Gingrich says, "Dole told me he'd never heard a lawmaker speak to a president like that and I said we've never had a president of the United States like this. I said he is just a liar. Dole had been in the Army. He knew that kind of language. I don't think he changed his mind about the shutdown because of that language."

Even so, one day later, Dole effectively ended the shutdown by declaring, "I do not share the view of my colleagues that we ought to have a partial shutdown of the government or that the people should not be paid. But I do believe the we need to find some agreement. If we can get this done, we also would be willing to give some on what would happen if a balanced budget amendment were agreed to by the president, the Democratic leader, and the Republican leaders in the Senate and in the House, and we could move rather quickly if that were possible." The announcement caught everyone in the House Republican leadership except Gingrich flat-footed.

If Dole looks back on the shutdown battle as an example of how the House revolutionaries "didn't know anything about politics when it came to people," congressional Republicans are still bitter about Dole's capitulation.

"I will never forget that day as long as I live," says current House Majority Leader Tom DeLay. "I was cooking steaks in my apartment for a bunch of members. It was a Sunday evening. And we were watching the Senate floor. And Bob Dole went down there and opened the government." Technically, the Senate did not approve Dole's move to end the shutdown until two days later, Tuesday, January 2. The House rejected the Senate measure on Wednesday, but finally approved the measure that Friday.

Asked whom he blames for the failure, DeLay softly seethes before answering. "The Senate. Bob Dole had no backbone. If we would have held out one more day, we would have beaten them." DeLay's view is common among some conservative Republicans, but it is also a misconception: No doubt the Republicans had a chance to break the Clinton White House during the budget showdown, but as we have seen, that chance came much earlier, during the first shutdown. As George Stephanopoulos and other White House insiders have revealed, Clinton had been on the verge of breaking. But a political strategy turned out to be much more important than a substantive goal.

DeLay's acidic assessment is widely shared, even among those with whom he is no longer allies or even friends. DeLay's fellow Texan Dick Armey, who was House majority leader at the time of the budget showdown, was among those involved in the budget negotiations, and he too smolders with resentment at Dole.

"I believe Bob Dole was the most irresponsible person in that room," Armey told me. "He didn't want to be there. . . . And Newt's trying to get Dole's affection and to some extent attention. I think Bob Dole's attitude was 'This young upstart thinks he's going to come in here and create a revolution, by God I'm going to give him just enough rope to hang himself.' "

And in a sense, Gingrich did hang himself. Politically, the Speaker suffered enormously. By January, his personal approval rating had fallen under 25 percent, and he would never recover the political power he had had after the sweeping 1994 electoral victory. President Clinton, meanwhile, reaped enormous political credit for protecting vital programs such as Medicare, Medicaid, and welfare from alleged GOP budget savagery. That is an amazing tactical turnaround, a testament to Clinton's incredible powers of persuasion and agility.

Of course, tactical victories are not everything.

### Lasting Consequences

The true significance of the 1995 shutdown battle between President Bill Clinton and House Speaker Gingrich is that the argument occurred in the first place. It was an argument of almost unprecedented scope, ferocity, and duration. For the first time since America had been remade by the New Deal, the power to tax and spend was in the hands of Republicans. And the Republicans' power to legislate a balanced budget was far, far greater than Clinton's power to decide as the nation's chief executive that he wasn't quite ready for a balanced budget. The Republicans changed the dimensions of the debate. This was no longer about abstractions, rosy scenarios, somewhere-over-the-rainbow imaginings of a balanced budget; the

Republicans had a plan and it *forced* Clinton to respond. And respond he did. For those who cared to notice, it was perfectly clear that the president had made critical concessions to the Republicans. On January 9, 1996, the House formally received a "message from the president" that began, "I hereby submit to the Congress a plan to achieve a balanced budget not later than the fiscal year 2002 as certified by the Congressional Budget Office on January 6, 1996." There it was, in writing: President Clinton had accepted a seven-year balanced budget plan to be scored by the Republican-controlled CBO—exactly what the Republicans had sought.

The argument over the budget mattered immensely. Republicans put many of their most important policy changes in this budget, ideas that had little to do with tax dollars but everything to do with their vision of a center-right government. Those ideas died, with, as Mary Poppins might say, all their "little ciphers neatly in a row." But the ideas came back, and they reshaped the country in ways that Clinton's supposed centrism never envisioned. Clinton in the ensuing years would reform welfare more aggressively, fund the Defense Department more stoutly, and embrace larger middle-class tax cuts than he otherwise would have—all in the name of *Clintonian* centrism.

"I contend to this day the shutdown did not hurt us as a party," Bob Walker says. "It was in fact the thing that led to the balanced budget and was a huge win for us, not a defeat. Again, perceptually convincing people that's the case is very hard, including most of the Republicans on the Hill who were here. I've often been to dinner parties and I say, 'Did we lose an election as a result of it? No. Is there anything really bad that happened congressionally because of the fact that we shut down the government, really? No.' But for the first time, Clinton put down a balanced budget. It wasn't acceptable to us, but that's what led to the whole series of negotiations that ultimately led to a balanced budget. The reason I say it didn't make any difference is that ultimately we balanced the budget without a constitutional amendment, which is probably the preferable way of doing it."

Bob Livingston, who now believes that a government shutdown "is better used as a threat than in implementation," argues that political calculations after the 1995 showdown prohibited the Republicans from making all the changes they had originally envisioned. In part, he says, the problem was that they no longer could use the threat of a shutdown to effect change. "I was in favor of not imposing a ban on [government] closures," Livingston recalls. "That was Dick Armey pushing for a ban on closures. Every time we found ourselves delaying, it empowered Clinton, who wanted to spend more money. As we got closer to Thanksgiving, we'll just drag it out until after the holiday. And then you're in the Christmas season. How the hell are you going to make cuts in the holiday season? We would have been Scrooge. It's in timing and tactics, and I think by simply saying we're not going to shut the government down, that was giving away any clout and any stick we ever had. We made substantial cuts, and the cuts started to evaporate when we started saying, 'Well, we'll never close down the government—we're not going to do that again.' Clinton claimed victory when we won. I can remember telling Newt, and I said, 'Newt, we don't have a stick. You guys have traded it away.' "

But even with the rise in spending that would follow, the country was in far better shape to digest its coming prosperity than it would have been had the budget fight not occurred. In 1996, the year after the shutdown saga, the U.S. Treasury began seeing a flood of revenue from the lucrative but short-lived dot-com bubble—taxes paid on dot-com capital gains, dot-com stock options, dot-com salaries, dot-com sales, dot-com consultancies, dot-com legal fees, and dot-com incorporations. This influx gave the nation its first chance to durably balance the budget in a generation.

Consider just the revenue that came in from capital gains taxes applied to dot-com stocks, stock options, and 401(k) and mutual fund profits. The numbers are nothing short of staggering. In 1995, the Treasury collected $180 billion in capital gains taxes. This was an 18 percent increase over each of the previous two years (1993's take was $152 billion; 1994's, $153 billion), but capital gains taxes still accounted for only 6.8 percent of all individual federal tax receipts. In 1996, capital gains receipts rose to $261 billion, a 45 percent increase from the previous year; capital gains taxes now represented 8.3 percent of all individual federal tax receipts, the highest total in U.S. history. And the numbers kept rising. In 1997, capital gains receipts rose to $365 billion, or 9.8 percent of all individual federal tax receipts—again, a U.S. record. In 1998, the number was up to $455 billion—10.1 percent of all individual federal income taxes. In 1999, $553 billion—11.3 percent of all tax revenue. In 2000, at their zenith, capital gains receipts amounted to $644 billion, or 11.8 percent of all individual federal income taxes. In short, from 1995 to 2000, capital gains revenue increased by *357 percent*. And in the five years of the dot-com boom, the government collected well over *$2 trillion* from capital gains taxes alone.

The windfall was utterly unexpected. It gave the political classes the kind of revenue with which New Deals or Great Societies are made. Unless, of course, there is an alternative political reality, an alternative regimen. And so there was. Among the myriad choices Clinton had before him— including diverting this gusher of cash to innumerable federal programs— he and successive Republican Congresses chose deficit reduction and debt repayment. That is a testament to the hard-won political consensus reached at the end of the Republican Revolution's budget showdown. Yes, Clinton refused to sign many of the Republican tax cuts, but he also won less in annual spending increases than would have been achieved through a Democratic Congress. One cancels the other. The showdown defined destiny. No other conclusion is possible.

The argument of '95 created the essential political pretext to achieve just that result, to reach a deal to cut some spending and cut some taxes in 1997 and to spend the rest of the 1990s moving toward balance and paying down public debt. In light of all the cynicism about the puny effects of the Republican Revolution, it's worth asking ourselves how different America would have looked had there been no balanced-budget debate in 1995 and had Clinton not been required to make iron commitments *in public* to balance the budget in seven years (even if he did it differently from how House Republicans wanted). What, do you suppose, would have become of those hundreds of billions in dot-com tax revenue? Dedicated to deficit reduction? Funneled to paying down the debt? Clinton's own budgets and approach to the question of achieving balance throughout much of 1995 argue against it. So even as we celebrate the visceral political spectacle of the 1995 budget fight, even as we applaud its thumping good theatrics, let us also remember it was vitally important politics, and among the most consequential domestic debates of the twentieth century.

"We lost the battle but we're continuing to win the war," says Ed Gillespie, the head of the RNC through 2004. "I think we've passed good [economic] policies and enacted good policies, but think of what would have been enacted if we hadn't been in the majority too. . . . Is the balance more center or more right [today]? From my perspective we're more toward the center than the right, but we're center-right. We're not left, which is where we were. We can always do more, we can always do better. But the political process doesn't allow for perfection. I hate to think after twenty years in this town I'm a prag [in conservative circles the epithet for the hated compromiser is prag, short for pragmatist], but I am."

The question in the era of Clinton is not so much what it was but *what it would have been* had there not been an intervening force to change its direction, to fundamentally alter the terms of debate, to establish a new set of center-right parameters inside which Clinton was forced to operate to first resurrect and then maintain his own political viability. This question is most profound when it comes to the federal budget, the shutdown confrontation, and what it left behind.

"They give us a hard time with spending," DeLay says now, referring to restive conservatives unhappy with the growth in the federal budget. "Well, during the Clinton years we couldn't shut down the government anymore; that was obvious. We were still fighting and clawing not to be pulled into more spending. And that held spending down way below what it would have been with a Democratic Congress and a Bill Clinton as president. Yes, we had to give him more spending, but nowhere near what he would have gotten with a Democratic Congress."

The budget is the most political document in America. It is an exercise in zero-sum politics. Everything is played off against everything else—more money for this means less money for that. Even when it appears there are no limits and deficits be damned, the limits are real, and every White House and Congress feels them. This was acutely true during the Clinton years, when to survive the budget showdown with Republicans, the White House had to embrace and make much of the Republicans' fiscal discipline. This became the anchor that prevented Clinton from moving the country toward a more expansive, costly, and bureaucratic federal government. When Democrats and Clinton supporters sing the praises of Clinton's record of balancing budgets and retiring debt, they applaud the result without crediting the antecedent austerity that made it a political imperative.

The 1995 budget showdown radically altered the zero-sum politics of the budget and reshaped America's horizons, its vision of itself, its sense of fairness, and the sense of the proper size, scope, and ambitiousness of government. The argument left the nation stronger than before, left it more confident about the dos and don'ts of federalism than it had been at least since the 1960s and quite possibly since the Great Depression. And it all happened with only a degree of inconvenience. Yes, federal offices were closed; yes, National Parks were shuttered and monuments kept off-limits; yes, paychecks were delayed; yes, unemployment checks were delayed; yes, federal "services" were delayed. But remember, after the battle, there emerged a consensus on behalf of a tamer, less gluttonous federal leviathan. By any fair reading, the shutdown drama represents a seminal moment in America's search for definition and direction.

Yet Clinton sycophants to this day spin the budget battle as an anarchic assault on the tender, benevolent president. Consider this hysterical portrayal from Sidney Blumenthal's *The Clinton Wars:*

> For the first time ever—even including during the War of 1812, when Washington was burned and occupied—the federal government was shut down. All services stopped. National monuments and museums on the Independence Mall, as well as national parks and all federal facilities in all fifty states, were closed. The Republicans had achieved the dystopian goal of antipolitics—twice. These willful acts appeared as a strange, if nonviolent, reenactment of the belligerence toward government demonstrated at Oklahoma City.

And there you have it. Within the political spirit of the shutdown can be found the antigovernment malevolence that led to the slaughter of 168 innocents in the Alfred P. Murrah Federal Building in Oklahoma City on April 19, 1995. It's a classic Clintonian canard: If not for Bill Clinton's vigilance, the ideologues who made up the House Republican majority would have destroyed everything. This analysis-as-epithet has gained a degree of legitimacy and currency, since the politics of the shutdown has over the years become much more memorable than the substantive difference the argument made. Indeed, the shutdown fight illustrates an odious truth about contemporary American politics: Politicians, reporters, and political scientists gravitate to the ephemeral lessons taught by short-term tactical victories and losses as they shy away from the deeper, more complex analysis of altered trajectories. But then again, Sun Tzu never covered Congress.

# 6

# THE WELFARE REVOLUTION

On August 22, 1996, President Bill Clinton signed a sweeping welfare reform bill. Seven days later, as he accepted his party's renomination for president, Clinton hailed the bill as if it were his own and had been from the very beginning. "The welfare reform law I signed last week," he declared, "is a chance for America to have a new beginning—to strike a new social bargain with the poor."

It was a new beginning. Today, the welfare reform law that President Clinton signed is regarded as a landmark piece of legislation. And to many observers, it is one of Bill Clinton's great achievements as president.

But in fact, the impetus for the sweeping changes in welfare policy came from the Contract with America. Bill Clinton might have vowed to "end welfare as we know it" as a presidential candidate in 1992, but it took the Republican majority to effect the profound changes we have come to know. Numerous Clinton White House advisers have admitted that the final bill the president signed looked much more like the welfare reform bills contemplated in the Contract with America than it did Clinton's own welfare reform proposal from 1994. They have also confessed that the GOP version was much more popular than Clinton's and drove the president to where he had never been before on the issue—not to the center but to the right of center.

Yes, Clinton vetoed the GOP welfare bill twice, but he extracted only minor concessions from the Republicans before signing the final bill into law. Though long forgotten, Clinton's own welfare reform proposal sought to *increase* welfare spending by $9 billion, while the Contract-driven proposal aimed to *cut* welfare spending by $16 billion. The two proposals were miles apart. And once again, Clinton made the most concessions substantively, even if tactically he could claim victory.

Significantly, almost none of the horrors of welfare reform predicted by opponents of the GOP bill came to pass. Instead, millions of those who liberals were convinced could not and would not work—regardless of what government policies were in place—responded to the new two-year limit on welfare payments by seeking and finding work. Sometimes they used government-financed child care and transportation services, but more often they did not. As predicted by Republican welfare reform specialists (such a species does exist—some Republicans actually think long and hard and quite creatively about how government does and does not work), millions left the welfare rolls, entered the workforce, and began the gradual, arduous climb toward self-sufficiency.

Even after the initial success of welfare reform, critics promised with the same gruesome certainty that those who had left welfare and found jobs would be flushed out of the labor force during the first recession. But when a recession did come a few years later, in 2000–2001, welfare rolls continued to decline, dropping 70,000 from April 2001 to June 2003. The new workers tenaciously fought to keep their jobs, and in fact a fairly high percentage moved above entry-level work and into positions far less vulnerable to the last-hired-first-fired vicissitudes of the service economy where most found their first jobs. From 1996 to 2001, wages for employed workers previously on welfare rose from $466 per month in 1996 to $686 per month in 2001, a 49 percent increase. In their clinical condescension, the critics had ignored the power of both positive, free-market incentives (higher pay for better performance) and negative incentives (the threatened cutoff of benefits); they had also disregarded the universal spiritual affirmation a regular job provides. The recession only proved the permanence of the Republicans' ideas about welfare and the role government should play in the lives of those at the bottom.

"Welfare reform was the biggest success of the Republican majority to date, in my estimation," says former House majority leader Dick Armey.

It was another success of the Contract with America. But during some tense moments back in 1994, it had appeared that welfare reform might not even make it into the Contract.

### An Eleventh-Hour Deal

After months of internal debate, the Contract with America was almost ready to go to the printer. It was September 26, 1994, the day before 337

Republicans were to stand before the country on the steps of the U.S. Capitol, present the Contract, and sign their names.

But there was just one problem: The welfare plank was still unresolved.

Welfare reform was among the Republicans' highest priorities. Conservative think tanks had been working on the issue for more than a decade. Many conservatives were grievously disappointed by the results of the last attempt at welfare reform, the Family Support Act of 1988. That bill had been watered down, they believed, by the Democrat-controlled Congress and as a result only nibbled at the edges of what Republicans dubbed the "liberal welfare state." Republicans were appalled by the costs of welfare. According to a 1995 report by Robert Rector of the Heritage Foundation, the preeminent welfare reform advocate, total welfare spending since 1965 was $5.4 trillion. Annual welfare spending had seen a fivefold increase since 1965—from 1 percent of the gross domestic product that year to 5 percent in 1993. For every $1 spent on national defense, $1.17 was spent on welfare; for every $1 spent on education at the local, state, and federal levels *combined*, 91 cents was spent on welfare. And welfare spending was only projected to go up.

Republicans also knew that welfare reform divided Democrats. Three months earlier, President Clinton had unveiled his own welfare bill in Kansas City, proclaiming, "There's no greater gap between our good intentions and our misguided consequences than you see in the welfare system." But most congressional Democrats scorned this sentiment and dismissed Clinton's bill as stingy and cruel—a notion Republicans found absurd, since the White House proposal actually increased welfare spending by $9 billion. Democrats in Congress understood the politics—that speaking out for welfare reform could play well in election years. But in the real world, they had no intention of allowing Clinton to undermine welfare or to end direct cash payments through Aid to Families with Dependent Children (AFDC), an assistance program with Rooseveltian roots. In contrast, the president's centrist advisers were in favor of welfare reform, and some actually thought that Clinton's bill was not aggressive enough. Bruce Reed, Clinton's chief domestic policy adviser, told me that the Democratic leadership on Capitol Hill "pleaded with [Clinton] not to send them a welfare reform bill." The congressional Democrats, says Reed, "were terrified of welfare reform. The Republican caricature of Clinton has it all wrong. Clinton wanted to do welfare reform, but the Democratic congressional leadership wouldn't have it."

The public was with the Republicans on welfare reform, and the GOP leaders knew the issue was ripe. But the clock was ticking, and the Contract had to go to the printer that night.

Kerry Knott, Armey's chief of staff and policy guru for all Contract items, was checking and double-checking the Contract language before taking it all to the printer. This was not a matter of checking grammar and spelling; he knew that the Contract with America was a rigorous policy document, a detailed legislative agenda that the Republicans would immediately take to votes if they seized the majority. The legislative language would be binding.

Most of that language had come from much younger, more conservative House members, since most senior Republicans had ignored the Contract task force process. Jim Talent of Missouri, elected in 1992, and Nancy Johnson of Connecticut, elected in 1982, led the welfare task force. It was a rare instance when a senior Republican, Johnson, got involved in a Contract task force. But Johnson was an early supporter of Gingrich, voting for him in the crucial battle for the whip's position in 1989. Rare among senior Republicans, Johnson not only believed in the Contract but also jumped into the work of drafting the policy. Welfare reform was part of her jurisdiction on the Ways and Means Committee. (Interestingly, none of the four more senior Republicans on Ways and Means played any role in developing Contract items on welfare or tax cuts, a decision they would come to regret.) Talent was part of the new breed of conservative activists. He had served in the Missouri state legislature and opposed all tax increases, even a road tax proposed by Governor John Ashcroft, a conservative. When elected in 1992, he kept with the no-holds-barred attitude of the young Turks, plunging into welfare reform even though none of the committees he served on had any jurisdiction over the issue. Johnson and Talent wrote the underlying welfare legislation, which was far, far tougher than the Republican alternative to Clinton's bill produced by the Republican Ways and Means staff. "We essentially discarded our first welfare bill," Knott recalls. "The welfare reform bill that Republicans had been fighting for, well, most people thought was just a slightly lightweight version of what the Democrats had been doing, too milquetoast."

Knott had been in downtown D.C. late on the afternoon of September 26. Republicans were pouring into town for the next day's signing ceremony. Knott had instructed his staff to send the full Contract to the printer, where copies would be prepared for each lawmaker and candidate to hold after the event on the Capitol steps and for members of the media. He thought everything was buttoned down. Then his cell phone rang.

"I was told there were big problems with the welfare language, that Nancy and Jim couldn't agree on the language."

Knott returned to the Capitol and assembled some of the top welfare staff, as well as representatives from Johnson's and Talent's offices. Talent's emissary, chief of staff Mark Strand, made it clear that the Missouri congressman would not budge on the language dealing with work requirements. Johnson's staff sought softer language. The negotiations lasted long into the night. If Democrats knew such a thing was happening, they probably would have doubled over in hilarity. Here were two members of the *minority* party haggling over language in a bill that would be introduced *only if they were the majority*, which seemed exceedingly unlikely. Johnson and Talent fought over the language as if it was going to become the law of the land.

"We pushed ideas back and forth to try to find some way to resolve a couple of sticky issues," Knott recalls, "and finally we got Nancy Johnson to budge a little bit. And then we had to find Jim Talent." But it was now 1 A.M. on September 27, the day of the signing of the Contract. The document still was not at the printer. Knott relates what happened next:

"We had to find Talent. I mean we had to get this thing printed and copies made. And then I remembered that Jim Talent slept in his office." Knott and others hustled from the Capitol, crossed Independence Avenue, dashed into the Longworth House Office Building, passed through the magnetometers and by the perplexed U.S. Capitol Police, and trekked down the marble hallway to office number 1022, their footsteps still echoing when they knocked on the door.

"Talent comes to the door; his hair is all mussed up and he's putting on his glasses. We present the final compromise language to see if he would sign off. He read it over and signed off, standing in the doorway of his office with his pajamas on."

Talent remembers the encounter slightly differently, at least when it comes to the pajamas part. "I don't think I was in pajamas," Talent told me. "I might have been in casual clothes—you know, blue jeans and a rumpled shirt of some kind. Kerry Knott came over with the compromise language. We'd been working on it all night. It was the very final preparation for the Contract and lots of his people were involved—Nancy, [Michigan's] Dave

Camp, [Pennsylvania's] Rick Santorum, [Arkansas's] Tim Hutchinson. Tim and I were freshmen and we'd developed a tougher alternative to what most Republicans had been proposing. Our bill had come to represent what most conservative welfare scholars were pushing for. And there was an undercurrent that what we were doing was something that Newt and Armey had to deal with, and that through the task forces set up to draft Contract language we were empowered and we became a force the leadership and Nancy had to recognize."

At 1:30 A.M., the Contract with America finally headed off to the printer.

## The Call for Reform

The Contract with America called for fundamental changes to welfare policy. Among the key provisions: Discourage illegitimacy and teen pregnancy by prohibiting cash welfare benefits for mothers under eighteen with children born out of wedlock; deny AFDC payment increases for children born while recipients are on welfare; cap welfare spending; impose a state-sanctioned two-year limit on welfare benefits; deny welfare payments to legal immigrants who were not naturalized citizens.

President Clinton had hoped to address some of these same issues when he unveiled his own proposal in June 1994. For example, in his Kansas City speech, he zeroed in on the rising rate of illegitimacy, a central issue in the welfare debate: conservative Republicans argued that the existing system at best condoned and at worst encouraged illegitimacy. Clinton proclaimed, "The rate of illegitimacy has literally quadrupled since Daniel Patrick Moynihan, now a senator from New York, first called it to our attention thirty years ago." Republicans might have applauded this reference, but it sent shivers down the spines of liberal congressional Democrats. Back in 1965, as a member of Lyndon Johnson's domestic policy staff, Moynihan authored a study that pointed to the rising level of illegitimacy among black families and warned that it would sentence them to a permanent life of poverty. The government could do little to alleviate poverty, Moynihan argued, if poor families refused to raise children in two-parent households. Liberals denounced the treatise as racist, demeaning, and counterproductive to the then seemingly unstoppable movement toward full-scale federal intervention to abolish poverty.

Clinton had also proposed a two-year limit on welfare payments, but his version was decidedly different from the one the Republicans would put forward with the Contract. The president promised a federal parachute—a subsidized job if able-bodied recipients didn't find work within two years. Clinton even invoked a noun that was about to gain considerable political prominence. "We propose to offer people on welfare a simple contract. We will help you get the skills you need, but after two years, anyone who can go to work must go to work, in the private sector if possible, in a subsidized job if necessary."

If Clinton's bill was more liberal than some of his centrist advisers would have preferred, it was certainly more liberal than what the Republicans believed was necessary. Its proposed two-year limit on benefits would be slowly phased in and would apply only to those born after 1971. The Clinton bill also called for more money for job training and child care to meet a welfare caseload that was predominantly undereducated and would be more likely to take him up on the offer of a federally subsidized job at the end of the two-year window. Republicans criticized the plan's promise of a federally subsidized job after two years, decried the two-year-and-out requirements as hopelessly vague, and faulted Clinton for failing to cut welfare payments to legal immigrants. The White House bill was crafted to avoid public disputes on Capitol Hill. But since, as Bruce Reed points out, the congressional leadership was dead-set against welfare reform, the plan died a quiet death. A few perfunctory committee hearings were held, but nothing else.

At one of those hearings, conducted by the Ways and Means Subcommittee on Human Resources on August 9, 1994, a telling exchange occurred that highlighted the coming clash of welfare apologists and welfare reformers. When the Heritage Foundation's Robert Rector testified that he considered the Great Society's war on poverty a "failure," Tennessee Democrat Harold Ford, who chaired the hearing, reacted angrily. Ford had been working on welfare programs since 1981 and was in no mood to hear anyone declare thirty years of federal efforts to end poverty a failure. As Rector produced a chart that he said documented $5.3 trillion worth of failed programs, Ford repeatedly challenged him, asking questions like "Can you name the programs?" Rector continued discussing his data for a while before Ford had had enough.

> *Ford:* Let me say this. I am going to correct you now. With all due respect to you, and I appreciate your testimony, but you are not going to come before this subcommittee and give us these numbers.

*Rector:* Do you want me to finish my testimony?

*Ford:* You are going to finish it, but you are going to talk about AFDC [Aid to Families with Dependent Children]. When you are talking to the public like this, you are not going to talk about supplemental security income for the blind and the aged.

*Rector:* What about food stamps?

*Ford:* Hold on one minute! Let me finish. We are not going to deal with food stamps unless you break it out and talk about what the elderly population might receive under food stamps. . . .

*Rector:* I am talking about the aggregate welfare system, which is what President Clinton was talking about. I think if we are talking about welfare reform, you, Congressman, have to take cognizance that all of the Republican bills . . . deal with what I'm talking about today, which is a cap on the aggregate growth of welfare spending. If you don't want to debate that issue here in this subcommittee—

*Ford:* I don't have to debate that issue with you here. You are going to testify but you are going to talk about what is in the welfare bill we are discussing. You aren't going to set the debate on this table with the Heritage Foundation. You are going to testify, but you are not going to leave the public with the perception that we are spending billions of dollars on welfare.

*Rector:* On AFDC.

*Ford:* That is what this subject matter is about and that is what I anticipate you to testify on and nothing short of that.

*Rector:* Your remarks remind me of the famous line—

*Ford:* I don't need you to comment on what my remarks remind you of, Mr. Rector. I am asking that you complete your testimony.

For House Republicans this encounter revealed not only congressional Democrats' intense opposition to welfare reform (even Clinton's watered-down version) but also the enormous lengths some would go to silence debate about the fundamental question surrounding existing welfare policy—that is, was it a waste of tax dollars and could something different save more while also achieving better results?

As long as Republicans were in the minority, they would not be able to push through a substantive welfare reform bill. The Republicans had to make concessions to the Democrats on the 1988 Family Support Act, because the Reagan White House was playing out the string and the Democrats controlled both the House and Senate. Conservatives considered the compromises a defeat. This act focused on education and employment, and it also forced states to provide Medicaid (joint federal-state financed health care for the poor) and child care services to welfare recipients, even after the families (single mothers typically) found work. But it should be noted that the Family Support Act marked the "the first basic restructuring of the AFDC program since its enactment as part of the 1935 Social Security Act," as *Congressional Quarterly* points out. If some of the measures were only token gestures, the law was the first of its kind to wrestle with real-world problems in the nation's welfare system: recipients who never sought work, soaring illegitimacy, unpaid child support, holes in the health care safety net. Moynihan, at the time Congress's most innovative welfare thinker, had set this process in motion. Also spurring the 1988 act were recommendations from a special National Governors Association welfare task force led by the Republican governor of Delaware, Michael Castle, and the Democratic governor of Arkansas, Bill Clinton.

Ultimately, though, it would be the Contract with America that produced the most sweeping changes to welfare in U.S. history. It enabled those changes because it swept in a Republican congressional majority. In control at last, House Republicans intended to drive the welfare debate and force Clinton to cave. But their early efforts were sidetracked in the 1995 budget showdown with President Clinton. (Welfare reform had been wrapped up in the GOP budget that Clinton successfully vetoed.) In the end, House Republicans had to be rescued by Republican governors, who, after all, were the ones who would have to enforce the new federal welfare rules. And though House Republicans had no idea at the time, governors positioned themselves to be the rescue squad in January of 1995, just as the Republican Revolution was about to begin.

## A New Beginning

Soon after the Republicans' smashing victory in the 1994 elections, Republican National Committee chairman Haley Barbour decided that the victory was becoming too wrapped up in Beltway celebrity. It was all about Newt Gingrich and the House revolution and, to a lesser extent, about Bob Dole and the new Republican Senate. Barbour feared that the huge victories won by Republican governors were being overlooked and, worse, that

Washington Republicans were dashing off to write new laws on welfare, Medicare, Medicaid, and crime that governors would have to translate into real policy. (This was especially true on welfare and crime, since Republicans wanted to convert all federal funds to block grants that each governor could use as he or she saw fit to achieve a federally authorized goal—for example, smaller welfare rolls or more prisons for violent offenders.) The GOP's gains at the governor's level were enormous. Republicans had won eleven gubernatorial races. Not a single incumbent lost. It was the best Republican performance in any election since 1867, before the readmission of ten of eleven ex-Confederate states after the Civil War. Republicans now held thirty governorships, meaning that they ruled a majority of statehouses for the first time since 1970.

So Barbour wanted a gubernatorial face on the revolution. He knew Republican governors were among the ablest thinkers and politicians in the party: Tommy Thompson of Wisconsin, John Engler of Michigan, Pete Wilson of California, Arne Christenson of Minnesota, Mike Leavitt of Utah, George Voinovich of Ohio, and Jim Edgar of Illinois. There were bright newcomers elected in 1993 or 1994: George W. Bush of Texas, George Pataki of New York, Tom Ridge of Pennsylvania, and George Allen of Virginia. Barbour wanted these Republicans to share the spotlight. He also wanted to ground the revolution in the way federal politics interacts with state government. In other words, he didn't want Gingrich and the House Republicans to go off half-cocked. Barbour's plan was to establish the Republican Governors Association as the "swing" constituency between firebrand House Republicans and timid Senate Republicans. Barbour figured correctly that Senate Republicans would resist most of the House-driven revolution unless the governors gave the green light. The governors would become the Good Housekeeping seal for House bills. That was Barbour's dream. He began to realize it at the first Republican Governors Association meeting in Williamsburg, Virginia, in early January 1995.

Barbour assigned his top political aide, Don Fierce, the job of getting the governors in the game. Fierce tore a page from the House Republicans. He decided there needed to be governor-level task forces on all key issues: welfare, crime, Medicaid, unfunded mandates, education, health care, and so forth. Barbour okayed the idea and ordered Fierce to set the plan in motion. Fierce knew that both Gingrich and Dole were lined up to address the governors' meeting, but he knew the governors were in no position to propose this idea to the Capitol Hill leaders, who were, at the moment, riding as high as Republicans could ride. So Fierce decided to make the play himself. He checked the schedule and saw that Dole was scheduled to speak first. He had no idea what Dole's pitch was going to be. But he knew that whatever it was, he had to intercept it. Fierce called Dole at about 7:30 A.M., three hours before the senator was to speak.

"I told Dole he needed to propose the formation of task forces the governors could use to help shape policy," Fierce recalls.

The idea was ingenious and devious on many levels. Fierce knew the governors wanted to become players. He also knew they didn't know how to do it. He was aware that Dole valued Gingrich's newfound power, prestige, and publicity but also resented Gingrich's tactics and methods. Fierce suspected it would be easy to sell Dole on something that would appear to undercut Gingrich and place the governors on equal footing with the Senate, which would give the new Senate majority leader two negotiating partners instead of just one. Fierce also knew Dole was desperate for some policy guidance he was sure the governors could provide. Lastly, Fierce understood that if he sold Dole on the idea and Dole proposed it first, Gingrich would have to accept the idea. Quite possibly, Fierce theorized, Gingrich would one-up Dole just to stay ahead of the curve.

That's exactly what happened. Dole called for the task forces and Gingrich went one better, promising the governors that his committee chairmen would meet with the governors once a month to ensure their support and cooperation. The governors were now smack-dab in the middle of the revolution.

This proved particularly important on welfare, because, in the end, Republican governors saved Republicans on the Hill from themselves. The Republican Congress sent two welfare reform bills to Clinton in 1995. He vetoed both. In Clinton's veto message of January 9, 1996, he said, "I urge the Congress to work with me . . . to produce a welfare reform agreement that is tough on work and responsibility but not tough on children and on parents who are responsible and who want to work." Clinton pushed for guaranteed child care for working mothers and rewards to states for reducing welfare rolls. He also criticized cost-saving measures designed to save tax dollars, such as eliminating legal immigrants from welfare rolls (estimated to save $20 billion). This standoff lasted for all of 1995.

The Republican Governors Association broke the standoff by producing the template of compromise at its annual meeting in February 1996. This proposal established workable spending targets for welfare and Medicaid; ended cash welfare payments (AFDC) as a permanent entitlement for poor families; made the work requirements less restrictive than in earlier, vetoed bills; provided more federal funds for child care; and gave states control over foster-child programs through block grants. From this proposal the final bill emerged. But it took a while.

On May 22, 1996, Republicans unveiled their newest welfare bill, which was based almost entirely on the Republican Governors Association outline. Unlike previous bills that required states to pass new laws denying cash payments to children on welfare, this bill gave states the power to determine whether such cash assistance should be given or denied. The bill imposed a lifetime five-year limit on welfare benefits, increased money for child care, imposed a requirement that welfare recipients find a job after two years or lose benefits, and dropped welfare payments to legal immigrants. Through back-channel negotiations between new Senate majority leader Trent Lott and Clinton political adviser Dick Morris, Republicans learned that Clinton was unlikely to veto this third incarnation.

Lott became leader after Dole stepped down to concentrate on his bid for the presidency. Republicans had two options: hold welfare back and let it become a campaign issue, or send welfare reform to Clinton a third time knowing he would sign it and take the issue off the table. Republicans stewed on this question throughout the spring and summer of 1996.

"We knew Dole had no chance" in the 1996 presidential race, Fierce says. "We started polling on the generic ballot in March and it was about even (when the question was 'Who do you prefer as a congressional majority, the Republicans, or the Democrats?'). But when we asked voters who they preferred if they *knew* Bill Clinton would be president, we went up 12 points. The question on voters' minds was, 'How do you check him [Clinton]?' We knew Dole was dead, but we had to wait for a critical moment to pull the plug on him. Welfare reform was it. Haley wanted to send Clinton welfare reform. Armey was for it. Newt was against it. Dole, of course, was against it."

Republicans were still smarting from losing the budget confrontation with Clinton, and their own polling showed that if they achieved success on welfare reform, they would show the American public that they could restrain Clinton's liberalism *and* produce solid results. No polling data suggested that keeping the welfare reform issue alive would benefit Dole. They decided to send the bill to Clinton. And that meant they were throwing Dole over the side.

Gingrich's top political adviser, Joe Gaylord, remembers the moment well.

"When the third welfare bill was sent up and Clinton signed it, [Dole campaign manager] Scott Reed called me up and said, 'You asshole,' " Gaylord recalls. "That was a huge decision. That was a huge fight."

At the White House, the pressure to sign the bill was building among Clinton political advisers, especially Morris.

In his book *Locked in the Cabinet,* former Clinton labor secretary Robert Reich summarizes the debate and the anguish felt among Clinton's policy advisers as the day of decision on welfare loomed:

> Today [July 31] . . . he'll decide whether to sign the welfare bill. If he does, it will put a million more kids into poverty. Almost two and a half years ago, we debated B's *own* proposal for welfare in this same room. The idea was to spend $2 billion a year *more* than the nation was spending on welfare in order to help move welfare recipients into decent jobs. . . .
>
> I look around the table at the other members of the cabinet and the White House staffers who have assembled for this meeting. No one looks happy to be here. The mood is tense and somber. How did we come to this? We go around the table. Most of the cabinet is firmly against signing. Most of the political advisers are in favor. . . .
>
> What I don't say is this: *You're twenty points ahead, for chrissake. You don't need to hurt people this way. You don't need to settle for this piece of shit.* I am certain B has decided to sign the welfare bill and I feel sick to my stomach.

On August 1, Clinton announced he would sign the Republican bill.

In April 2004 I asked Dole about his reaction to Clinton's declaration: "Did you think (a) 'This is a great thing for the country, a major and long overdue reform of welfare' or (b) 'This is the end of my presidential campaign'?"

Dole's response was direct: "Well, I thought both. But I thought (b) before (a)." It came down to timing, he said. Clinton had a presidency to protect and Republicans had a majority to protect. Dole was the odd man out. It's all politics. No hard feelings.

"He knew when to sign it. . . . Let's face it, they knew we were in a weakened position; we had an uphill road to be elected. In politics you got to look at the whole deck, not just the one card. So you gotta save House seats and Senate seats, and if you look like you're trying to protect the presidential nominee, it doesn't work."

Others were equally disturbed by Clinton's decision to sign the bill, but for very different reasons.

One of Clinton's top welfare advisers at the Department of Health and Human Services, Peter Edelman (husband of Children's Defense Fund president Marian Wright Edelman), resigned in protest, sure the law would force millions of poor Americans into the streets.

The day of Clinton's announcement, Daniel Patrick Moynihan took the Senate floor. The architect of much of the nation's welfare policy for thirty years served up grave warnings. The bill, Moynihan said, "terminates the basic federal commitment of support for dependent children in hopes of altering the behavior of their mothers. The best available evidence is that this legislation would substantially increase poverty and destitution while doing too little to change the welfare system to one that provides greater opportunity for families in return for demanding greater responsibility." These moves, Moynihan said, amounted to "the most brutal act of social policy abuse since Reconstruction." He proclaimed that "those involved will take this disgrace to their graves."

The Children's Defense Fund said the bill would increase child poverty by 12 percent, "make children hungrier," and cut incomes for one-fifth of families with children. Marian Wright Edelman declared that the bill would "leave a moral blot on [Clinton's] presidency and on our nation."

The Urban Institute said the bill would shove 2.6 million people into poverty, 1.1 million of them children.

Senator Edward Kennedy of Massachusetts denounced the bill as "legislative child abuse."

Senator Frank Lautenberg of New Jersey said, "This is a peculiar time for the U.S. Senate. The body is on the verge of ending a sixty-year guarantee that poor children in this country might not go hungry. Women with children, many of them unwed—I do not approve of that condition, but that is life. The punishment should never exceed the deed, and that is what I fear. For sixty years, we could rest easier at night and be sure American children had a minimum safety net. The bill before us takes away this peace of mind and throws up to 1,100,000 children into poverty."

## *The Numbers Don't Lie*

The critics were exercised because the 1996 welfare reform act had completely transformed the welfare system that had been in place for decades. These were profound changes, and they closely resembled what House Republicans had originally envisioned. True, the act was not as tough as what Jim Talent had fought for when he and Nancy Johnson struggled over the fine print the night before the Contract with America was signed. But because Talent and Johnson fought so hard and reached a *durable compromise,* the GOP largely succeeded in pushing their program into law. The final product was far more aggressive than the 1988 bill or anything Clinton had ever proposed. In politics, where you finish depends entirely on where you begin.

What did the new law do? The details matter immensely, because each provision revolutionized the welfare system that just a few years earlier had seemed impossible to reform. The 1996 welfare reform act

- Eliminated a guaranteed check to every eligible mother and child and replaced it with state flexibility tied to federal guidelines for work and time limits.
- Created Temporary Assistance for Needy Families (TANF). TANF became a block grant that replaced AFDC, Emergency Assistance for Needy Families, and the Job Opportunities and Basic Skills Training (JOBS) program.
- Authorized $16.4 billion for the TANF block grant each fiscal year from 1996 to 2001.
- Created minimal work rates for all states. Under the new law, 50 percent of all families and 90 percent of two-parent families had to have at least one working parent. That parent was required to work at least thirty hours (nearly twice the 1988 requirement). The work requirement was twenty hours for parents with children under six, unless the mother was living with an adult. The law also forbade parents under age eighteen from receiving TANF funds.

- Required all adults receiving welfare under state-supervised block grants to find a job within two years.
- Set out specific goals for moving welfare families to work: states had to have 50 percent of families off the rolls by 2002.
- Defined work broadly as nonsubsidized employment, subsidized private-sector employment, public-sector employment, and community service.
- Limited cash aid to families with minor children and pregnant women.
- Imposed time limits: five years for the block grant to make cash payments to the head of household or spouse of the head of household. There were no time limits for children. A five-year limit was imposed for children as soon as they reached eighteen.
- Gave states permission to exempt 20 percent of "hard cases" (that is, homes where substance abuse, spousal abuse, child abuse, or other complications were prevalent) from the five-year federal time limit.
- Erected barriers for welfare recipients to receive disability benefits through Supplemental Security Income (SSI).
- Created state registries of newly hired workers to cross-reference names and payment histories, required states to withhold welfare payments of parents who were behind on child support payments, and expanded the federal program to locate "deadbeat dads."
- Imposed restrictions on legal and illegal immigrants' access to welfare. Illegal immigrants were denied all benefits except emergency Medicaid services and temporary noncash disaster assistance. Legal immigrants were forbidden from receiving SSI benefits through Social Security and from receiving direct cash food payments. Exceptions were made for immigrant refugees, veterans, and those who came to America before 1996. (Clinton and Congress restored SSI disability benefits and food stamps for legal immigrant children in 1997.)
- Created the Child Care and Development Block Grant, which folded most existing child care programs into block grants distributed to states on a needs-based formula.
- Cut food stamp benefits and imposed new work requirements. Specifically, the law reduced benefits based on the Agriculture Department's "Thrifty Food Plan" formula; made it more difficult for recipients to deduct elements of their income and still receive benefits; required eighteen- to fifty-year-olds without dependents to work for twenty hours each week (or lose food stamps nine months out of the year); disquali-

fied for one year applicants who committed fraud (the previous penalty was six months) and for two years applicants who committed a second offense; disqualified for life anyone convicted of selling food stamps of $500 or more; and disqualified anyone who refused to work in their state job or in state job-training programs.

- Provided $50 million annually for abstinence education, the first ever federal allocation of funds to teach abstinence as part of public school sex education.

All dry policy details? Hardly. These changes drastically reduced the number of families and individuals receiving public assistance. The numbers don't lie. The Department of Health and Human Services' Second Annual Report to Congress, issued in August 1998, reported that the 1996 welfare law had produced the following results:

- Welfare caseloads dropped nationally from 8.4 million in 1996 to just over 3 million in June 1998, a 64 percent decrease. By 2002, the caseload was down to 2 million—a 76 percent decrease from 1996.
- By October 1998, the average monthly number of welfare families (those receiving the new TANF benefits, not AFDC) had fallen in every state. In two years, welfare rolls fell 22 percent.
- From October 1996 to June 1997, 13 percent of welfare adults were working; by October 1998, 23 percent were working. Their average earnings increased from $500 a month to $553 a month, an 11 percent increase.

Other government reports offered further evidence of the 1996 act's dramatic influence:

- The number of individuals receiving TANF benefits dropped from 12.2 million in 1996 to 5.7 million in 2000, a 53 percent decrease in four years.
- In 1996, the number of families receiving federal welfare payments as a percentage of the U.S. population was 4.8 percent; in 2000, it was 2.1 percent.
- Figures from the 2000 census showed that 3.5 million fewer Americans lived in poverty than in 1995, the year before welfare reform (the

poverty rate dropping from 13.8 percent to 11.7 percent); 2.9 million fewer children lived in poverty than in 1995 (11.7 million in 2001, compared with 14.6 million in 1995); black child poverty dropped by more than 25 percent from 1995 to 2001, with 1.2 million black children lifted from poverty; the poverty rate for single mothers fell from 50.3 percent in 1995 to 39.8 percent in 2001 (it had hovered near 50 percent for the preceding *quarter of a century*); and 400,000 fewer children lived in hunger than in 1995, a drop of nearly 50 percent.

Most important, as noted, none of these trends reversed dramatically during the recession of 2000–2001. The slight increases in the adult poverty rate were far lower than in the recession of the early 1990s. What matters most is that the recession did not undermine work requirements or the ability of previous welfare recipients to find and keep work (again defying dire predictions of liberal critics).

The numbers prove the underlying validity of the GOP's indictment of the welfare system: that it condoned and encouraged dependency and did nothing to force welfare families to look for work. Given strict orders to find work or lose benefits, millions of impoverished Americans found work, increasing their wages, saving taxpayers tens of billions of dollars, and dramatically improving their sense of personal worth and responsibility.

Until the 1996 welfare reform act, the trends were exactly opposite. Welfare caseloads rose every year, starting at 150,000 in 1936 and reaching almost 5 million in 1994—the year of the Republican Revolution. From the 1960s forward, illegitimacy rates rose steadily, increasing the likelihood that poverty would spread among low-income families. The GOP welfare reform plan sought to reverse both trends and has succeeded.

Bill Clinton and his admirers are right to consider the Welfare and Medicaid Reform Act of 1996 a signal achievement, a law that improved millions of lives and reshaped the country. But they are wrong to seize credit for this landmark act. The law must be understood as part of the Republican Revolution.

# 7

# THE REVOLUTION AND 9/11

The Senate hearing room was packed with spectators, photographers, reporters, and Senate staff. Every member of the Senate Armed Services Committee was present for this critical hearing, one that would shed light on perhaps the biggest scandal to emerge out of the U.S. war in Iraq.

It was May 11, 2004, and the senators were assembled to look into the criminal abuse of Iraqi prisoners detained at the Abu Ghraib prison on the outskirts of Baghdad. The star witness was Major General Antonio Taguba, the Army general who had first documented what U.S. soldiers and private contractors working at Abu Ghraib had done—rape, sodomy, hideous forms of torture, humiliation, even murder. Taguba's searing fifty-seven-page report on the conduct of U.S. prison personnel—military and civilian—shocked and horrified the nation, drew justifiable scorn worldwide, and diminished America's moral authority, such as it was, throughout the Muslim and Arab-speaking world.

At the top of the hearing, Senate Armed Services Committee chairman John Warner of Virginia asked General Taguba this simple yet profound question, a question that crystallized the thoughts of tens of millions of despairing, disbelieving Americans: "In simple words—your own soldier's language—how did this happen?"

Taguba gave a direct response: "Failure in leadership, sir, from the brigade commander on down. Lack of discipline, no training whatsoever, and no supervision."

Warner and other senators nodded sadly. General Taguba later testified that confusion over who was in charge—military intelligence or military police—left soldiers and private contractors to run roughshod over prisoners and invent their own forms of sadistic and humiliating torture to extract information the military said it needed to prevent the roadside bombings, car bombings, and sniper attacks that were killing dozens of Iraqi civilians and U.S. military personnel in the Sunni Triangle.

But one Republican on the Senate panel, an active member of the revolution, discerned a different cause. Senator Jim Talent of Missouri, who occupied the same Senate seat once held by Harry Truman, leaned into the microphone, looked across the hearing room to General Taguba, and said the following:

> I'm going to make a statement and you can comment if you want. I was in the other body [the House of Representatives] all throughout the '90s, during which time the highest civilian authorities here and on the other side of Pennsylvania Avenue were cutting the size of the Army and in my judgment not funding adequately the end-strength we had remaining. And what I saw consistently was the Army, in order to keep the tip of the spear sharp, if you will, allowing some of the rest of the spear to go rusty. And you know, sooner or later those chickens come home to roost. You get a poor commander. You don't have enough people. The guys you've got are not trained up adequately because you don't have money for it. And something like this happens. And I'll just say I wish we had the interest nationally through the '90s about funding the Army adequately and maybe we wouldn't be sitting here.

Talent, uniquely among all senators on the panel, blamed chintzy Clinton-era defense budgets for the abuse of Iraqi prisoners at Abu Ghraib. General Taguba did not offer a comment, but he nodded in agreement when Talent referred to the sacrifices the Army had had to make to "keep the tip of the spear sharp." He nodded even more vigorously when Talent described the consequences that inevitably arise from not having "enough people."

Democrats, however, refused to sit still while a Republican tried to indict President Bill Clinton for a scandal of global proportions that occurred on President George W. Bush's watch and arose from his decision to invade and occupy Iraq as part of the U.S.-led War on Terror. Senator Ben Nelson of Nebraska, who was next in line to question the witnesses, yanked the microphone in his direction and practically barked this broadside: "I'm going to ignore some of the partisan sniping that has been going on from the other side today, because I don't think it's particularly helpful."

Talent's comments lay at the heart of Republican frustration with the revolution and the post-9/11 world. They knew the nation was better able to fight the War on Terror from the minute the jetliners pierced the two World Trade Center towers in Lower Manhattan because Republicans had controlled Congress for six years. They knew defense budgets were higher than they would have been under Clinton and a Democratic Congress. They knew they had shielded intelligence spending from budget cuts in their first year in control of Congress and set about boosting spending each year after in the face of nonstop Democratic efforts to decimate intelligence budgets. Even if most of that money, unhappily, paid for more satellites and interceptors instead of human intelligence—more spies— they at least maintained the nation's spy infrastructure.

The Republicans knew all of this was true, but in the fall of 2001 they also recognized that it went almost entirely unappreciated by grieving Americans who were beginning to wonder how America would respond to the terrorist atrocities. Republican revolutionaries still in Congress on 9/11 had no idea how President Bush would respond militarily, but they knew the fighting and spying force he would have to call upon would be readier to fight than if it had been left to what they regarded as the knee-jerk, cut-defense-first instincts of Bill Clinton and the Democrats in Congress.

The vast majority of Republicans I interviewed for this book believe the nation is better able to prosecute the War on Terror because the congressional Republican majorities first elected in 1994 forced President Clinton to increase spending on national defense and intelligence throughout the late 1990s. They believe that if Clinton had been able to work with a compliant and far more dovish Democratic congressional leadership, defense and intelligence budgets would have continued to shrink and the nation would not have had the resources necessary to fight the wars in Afghanistan and Iraq. What's more, they say the troop-strength problems U.S. forces encountered during the occupation of Iraq would have been far, far worse had Republicans not held the line on spending dedicated for troop strength, training, equipment, and maintenance. (Interestingly, many Democrats who advocated defense cuts in the Clinton years later ridiculed the occupation force in Iraq as too small.)

For the conservatives who now accuse House and Senate Republicans of wanton profligacy—domestic spending has risen steadily every year since 1997—there is at least one reasonable line of explanation: During the post-shutdown years of the Clinton administration, Republicans had to agree to domestic spending increases to secure defense and intelligence spending increases. After Clinton's political victory in the 1995–96 shutdown saga, the Republicans wielded a smaller stick on spending cuts, to borrow the imagery used by former Appropriations Committee chairman Bob Livingston. If Republicans had sent Clinton budgets that increased defense and intelligence spending but did not increase domestic spending by equivalent or greater amounts, they would have been vetoed, as the Clinton White House shrewdly threatened. So the GOP made deals with the Democrats. Sometimes the deals were overt, but on occasion, as we will see, they were covert. These were not always dollar-for-dollar transactions; domestic spending sometimes rose more than defense spending. But Republicans held the line on defense policy and in the latter stages of the Clinton administration began to rebuild a military weakened by deep cuts and strength-sapping peacekeeping deployments. Between 1992 and 1998, the Army and Marines conducted twenty-six operations, compared with ten from 1960 to 1991. Clinton deployed forces of 20,000 or larger in four noncombat operations from 1993 to 1998: Somalia (1993, started by George H. W. Bush, enlarged by Clinton), Haiti (1994), Bosnia (1996), and Iraq and Kuwait (1998).

"Clearly had we not been in power, they would not have funded the Defense Department to do what we did," recalls Livingston, among the strongest advocates of military spending within the Republican House. "There is a passivism strain in the Democratic Party that's just mind-boggling."

"Who controls the House is very important for setting the agenda," says Representative Mac Thornberry, Republican of Texas, who was elected in 1994 and has carved out a policy-making niche on defense and homeland security issues. "There were relatively few people who came to Congress in my class who had national security issues at the top of the agenda, but [without] Republican control of Congress, there's no telling what the Clinton White House would have done had we not been there to restrain them."

Many Democrats generally agree, but say the differences would have been far smaller than Republicans suggest. They argue that the advantages the nation enjoyed in the immediate aftermath of 9/11 in terms of troop strength, equipment, and intelligence capabilities were only minimally larger than what they would have been under Democratic control of Congress. The facts, as we will see, don't back them up. If left unchecked, Clinton's defense cuts would have left the military virtually incapable of waging a global war on terror by the year 2001 (there's no reason to believe that a President Al Gore would have immediately stepped up defense spending). And without GOP intervention in the late 1990s, the intelligence community would have been little more than a hollowed-out shell on 9/11. It was weak enough as it was, lacking linguists, spies, and operatives with Middle East contacts and savvy. But the technological capability remained, and the human intelligence corps was at least functioning at a sufficient level, meaning that the nation was not forced to start from scratch after 9/11.

Still, Republicans are plagued by questions to this day: Did they fight hard enough on behalf of defense and intelligence? Did they see the terrorist threat as clearly as they should have? Did they marshal the same political intensity to prepare America for war that they marshaled to dislodge the Democrats from power after forty years? Did the party of national defense take seriously enough the global perils, think creatively enough about how to anticipate them, or at least better prepare the nation to respond? In essence, did congressional Republicans do their duty?

For many conservative Republicans, there remains the frustration that Jim Talent voiced at the Abu Ghraib hearing in May 2004. As the United States embarked on a global war on terror, the nation was better off militarily because Republicans won control of Congress in 1994, but it was not nearly as strong or as ready to confront the scourge of jihadist Islamic terrorism as it should have been. Talent articulated the Republicans' frustration with the Clinton administration's willingness to undermine our own military and thus our national security. But if conservative Republicans can argue that they prevented Clinton and Democrats on Capitol Hill from completely gutting the military and intelligence apparatus, they must acknowledge now that they did not wage these fights as if the fate of the nation rested on the outcome.

### *"We Did Not Do Enough"*

In the Clinton years, Republicans pursued higher defense and intelligence budgets as a natural extension of their governing philosophy, not as vital national interests on which they could not and would not compromise. While they thought creatively about applying what small increases they won to improving operations and maintenance and nuts-and-bolts troop preparedness, they were not willing to face a presidential veto on these issues, particularly in the wake of the 1995 budget showdown. They simply did not foresee how important these issues would become to the nation.

In fact, as committed as Republicans were to a strong national defense, it was not a foregone conclusion that the Contract with America would include a plank calling for more spending on troop strength, weapons systems, and missile defense. It was widely reported and remains widely believed that every item in the Contract was a so-called 70/30 issue (70 percent of those surveyed supported it, while only 30 percent opposed it), but this was *not* true of the defense plank (which also called for reducing U.S. peacekeeping missions and abolishing any use of U.S. forces in any mission under United Nations command).

"Newt said all the time that we didn't put anything in the Contract that didn't have 70 percent or more," says Tony Blankley, Newt Gingrich's former press secretary and now editorial page editor for the *Washington Times.* "That was true, except for defense, because in 1994 nobody wanted to spend any more on defense. This was the golden era of the peace dividend."

Gingrich and Bob Livingston, who drafted the defense section of the Contract, demanded more military spending, and at times had a tough time selling the concept to fellow Republicans far more interested in cutting the deficit. Representative John Kasich of Ohio, who drafted the alternative GOP budgets in 1993 and 1994, cut the defense budget each time to prove that the GOP was willing to sacrifice all sacred cows in pursuit of a balanced budget. In the early days of the revolution, defense spending was higher than Clinton proposed but did not grow nearly as fast as the most hawkish Republicans would have preferred. Spending on intelligence lagged even farther behind. Both would prove vital after 9/11.

"We did fight Clinton's disdain for the military and for the CIA," recalls Tom DeLay. "I think we should have fought harder. It was a battle and a fight, but the tone of the time didn't lend itself to fight this fight. We had so many fights, so we allowed him to decimate our military and decimate our intelligence capabilities to the point where we had no human intelligence worldwide. None! Knowing what I know now, if I could do it all over again, I would fight to the death his just hollowing out the CIA and completely redesigning our defense. Within the constraints of our budgets, we did the best we could."

Like DeLay, many Republicans to this day brood over what could have been, what they should have done differently before 9/11. The list of failures feels tragic: Why didn't they see the threat more clearly? Why didn't they comprehend and confront the mounting threat of jihadist Islamic terror? Why didn't they press for more spending on spies to infiltrate the Islamic world? Why didn't they challenge Clinton's decision to place the Justice Department instead of the Pentagon in charge of fighting terrorism? And most of all, why didn't they work as hard to develop a strategic vision to defeat terrorism as they did to defeat congressional Democrats?

Over dinner, Blankley grows quickly despondent as he gropes for answers that never come. A mask of melancholy descends as he ruminates aloud, apologetic to the point of despair that history must judge the GOP congressional majority guilty of negligence on the greatest issue of our time. It starts with Blankley's reminiscences of the revolution's headiest times, when the man for whom he spun, Gingrich, was the center of America's political universe.

"I have an odd feeling about it," Blankley says, the words coming slowly, achingly. "I loved it all. I loved that time. It was the best professional time I've ever had, but it all seemed pointless since September 11 in a certain regard. It doesn't in the American political process, but I got so emotionally sucked into what 9/11 meant to my kids [two teenage boys]."

Like almost everyone who has ever worked for Gingrich, Blankley was drawn to the Speaker's ability to analyze history, filter its important conclusions, and apply them to the needs of the country and explain in a politically plausible manner how the solution, informed by history, fit the times. But this prescience proved illusive when it came to terrorism, a realization that haunts to this day.

"We did not make a decisive enough difference on intelligence and the military. We were clearly better than Clinton, but we were both on the wrong side of being seized with a sense of urgency," Blankley recalls. "We could have stood forth on fighting terrorism and we didn't. What we did with it was minimal. We tried to goose up the [defense and intelligence] budgets a little, [but that] was derivative of our desire to be more supportive of those issues. Given that what we were able to accomplish was insufficient to avoid the catastrophe, it's hard to argue we made a strategic difference. We made an incremental difference, but the incremental difference was not enough to protect us, and so we all failed. We missed that strategic perception as much as Clinton did. We had lots of technical arguments, but we never put in a strategic argument. Did Newt ever give a set-piece speech on terrorism? I don't think he did. We all failed. None of us was Winston Churchill [who foresaw Hitler's menace and unsuccessfully warned England and the world]. We never made that a strategic point. I got briefings on bin Laden. We all did. We did not do enough and we didn't say enough between '94 and '98 to claim strategic advantage."

Gingrich doesn't disagree, but he's nowhere near as despondent about the difference the Republican majority made in preparing the nation for the bleak realities of a post-9/11 world.

"We should have been more aggressive about defense and intelligence," Gingrich told me. "But the difference we made was substantial. We put stronger defense in the Contract with America. It would have been nice to have done more, but when you compare the McGovern-Carter-Clinton defense weakness with the Reagan–Contract with America defense approach, the difference is huge."

The 9/11 terrorists killed nearly 3,000 civilians. By that measure, the Republicans failed. By these lights, failure is self-evident. But it is wrong to conclude that Republican control of Congress made *no* difference. The GOP made vital contributions on defense and intelligence, some of which have gone almost completely unnoticed.

### A Behind-the-Scenes Victory

To argue that the Republicans were not willing to face a presidential veto on issues of defense and intelligence spending is not to say that there were no fights. One of the most significant fights occurred in the fall of 1998. Though almost no one recalls it now, it was a fight for more intelligence funding, and it just might have cost Newt Gingrich his job.

Republicans were negotiating a final budget with Clinton in the late fall, just before the midterm elections. Gingrich and others were sure the elections would produce huge gains and consolidate the GOP's grip on congressional power. The Speaker had engineered the release of Independent Counsel Kenneth Starr's sexually explicit investigative report on Clinton's affair with White House intern Monica Lewinsky. Gingrich was certain the Starr Report would spark moral outrage and incendiary hatred of Clinton among evangelical Christian voters (a sizable portion of the GOP base, particularly in low-turnout midterm elections) and propel the Republican Party to gains of as many as twenty-five to thirty House seats. But Republicans still had to negotiate a budget, and as he had since the shutdown fiasco, Clinton held all the cards. As much as Gingrich and other top GOP leaders thought they had Clinton on the defensive over the Lewinsky scandal, they did not dare shut down the government again.

The budget was nearly complete, but Gingrich—at the urging of Representative Porter Goss of Florida, a former CIA agent who was chairman of the House Select Committee on Intelligence, and former CIA director R. James Woolsey—inserted a last-minute demand into the budget negotiations. Gingrich told Clinton he wanted to boost intelligence funding by $20 billion. "It was Newt's initiative to pour more money into intelligence," recalls Bob Livingston. Clinton hesitated but said he would be willing to do so if and only if Gingrich would agree to boost domestic spending by the same amount. The clock was ticking, the election was drawing near, and rank-and-file Republicans as well as GOP strategists were eager to erase growing talk of a potential government shutdown.

"That is correct," Tom DeLay told me. "It was $20 billion in domestic spending or nothing. They had us over a barrel. We knew the Republican Senate would never have shut the government down again. Most definitely, that was the only deal we could make."

Gingrich reluctantly agreed to Clinton's demand.

"We were going to end up with a high budget number," Gingrich told me. "And like Reagan, I valued defense and intelligence more than [the lack of] deficits. George Tenet has testified that I was the only person in the 1990s to get extra money for intelligence. This is not something that's in dispute. But I will tell you, the minute I left office, [White House Chief of Staff] John Podesta reneged on that agreement."

I asked Podesta about Gingrich's accusation. He offered this blunt response: "That's bullshit, that's fucking bullshit. We lived up to the agreement in the first year. It was the Republicans who took the money out the next year. That's all on the record."

The truth is largely unknowable, because by custom and to protect national security, overall intelligence spending is classified. Numbers usually leak out after the money has been spent, but even then they are not officially confirmed. Details on specific intelligence programs are even more closely guarded secrets. Gingrich and Podesta agree that the increases sought cannot be publicly discussed. What is indisputable is that Gingrich sought the boost in intelligence spending but that to receive it he had to horse-trade for an equivalent boost in domestic spending, a bargain that would have far-reaching political consequences.

The announcement of a budget deal that included $20 billion in additional domestic spending was not accompanied by an announcement that intelligence spending would be increased by the same amount. Gingrich knew going in that intelligence funding could not and would not be discussed publicly and that neither he nor the GOP would reap any political benefit from this deal. But he believed that the increased spending would give the CIA and other U.S. intelligence outlets a much-needed boost. He also calculated that few people would notice or care that Clinton had won another round at the budget table.

But the perceived collapse of fiscal discipline infuriated conservatives. Many of them, in fact, sat out the election in protest of the Republicans' apparent obsession with Clinton's sex life but indifference to his spendthrift ways. Voter News Service exit polls showed turnout for self-identified conservatives dropped 6 percent from 1994 to 1998, and support for the GOP among self-identified independent voters dropped 7 percent from 1994 to 1998. Republicans alienated their base by raising spending, and alienated crucial swing voters by apparently abandoning principled policy positions to pursue what seemed to independent voters a morals-based vendetta against the president. As angry as they were with Clinton's ridiculously oafish sex life, conservatives were even more livid at a GOP majority that seemed to have no backbone when it came to spending. So instead of winning twenty-five to thirty House seats, the Republicans lost five, a historic and humiliating reversal that sealed Gingrich's fate. He resigned three days later. He appeared an utterly defeated, marginalized figure, a revolutionary who had seemingly become obsessed with the president's sex life but had failed to defend a bedrock principle of the Contract with America, reducing spending.

That was the perception. The reality was different, as Gingrich's behind-the-scenes maneuvering on the intelligence funding revealed.

"Gingrich sacrificed his position as Speaker to get that money," says John Feehery, spokesman for current Speaker Dennis Hastert. "There's no way we would have gotten that intelligence money without that deal. And nobody knew about it. And most people don't know about it now. They just assumed we caved for no reason."

## A Quiet Revolution

Gingrich achieved an important victory when he secured the boost in intelligence spending in 1998, but the Republicans made other valuable contributions as well. Consider defense spending:

The simplest way to understand the effect the Republican Revolution had on defense spending is to ask how much Clinton would have spent if proposals he made starting with his first full-fledged budget in 1994 had been carried out over his entire presidency. A straight-line extrapolation is fair here, because Clinton almost never enlarged his defense spending requests to increase the size of U.S. forces or to improve training, equipment, or maintenance. When he did propose an increase (surprise, the first one occurred *one month after* the 1994 election), the additional funds barely compensated for the costs associated with various peacekeeping missions. In other words, Clinton's first budget cut defense spending, and subsequent budgets sought still more real cuts—with funding levels that did not keep up with inflation or provide military personnel with pay increases that kept up with inflation.

Clinton's defense proposals cut tens of billions from projected defense budgets of President George H. W. Bush. In 1993, Bush signed a defense budget of $281 billion and projected gradual increases in defense spending that would result in a 1997 Pentagon budget of roughly $290 billion. These projections did not allow spending to keep pace with inflation, but they did maintain much of the Cold War force structure and weapons systems that Bush had inherited from Reagan. While the Bush White House was eager to create a "peace dividend," it also feared that dramatic defense cuts could undermine readiness, morale, and mobility. The Bush administration gave considerable thought to reforming and reshaping the U.S. military to reduce spending but preserve readiness. On balance, Bush sought budgets that would allow these reassessments to proceed and not use forced budget cuts to determine which forces to keep or shrink, which weapons systems to scrap or ramp up. Bush wanted policy to drive the numbers, not the other way around.

Clinton had a different approach. He wanted fresh thinking about the

Pentagon, but he also wanted to use it as a cash cow to finance other domestic priorities and help reduce the deficit. Clinton's first Pentagon budget, for 1994, cut spending from Bush's projection of $282 billion for 1994 to $263 billion, a $19 billion cut from Bush's projection and an $18 billion cut from Bush's last defense budget. The Democratic Congress passed this budget, which became the baseline from which all future defense budgets grew. Over time, baselines have a cumulative effect: Each and every year Clinton's budgets were considerably smaller than Bush's projections. Driving a baseline lower can profoundly affect an agency's ability to carry out programs and policies it assumed would be funded at the previously projected levels. Nowhere in government is this more true than the Pentagon, where weapons development and acquisition can take upwards of twenty years; where plans to recruit, train, station, and maintain Army and Navy forces operate on five-, ten-, fifteen-, and sometimes twenty-year horizons; where decisions about how many ships, tanks, bullets, nuts, bolts, spare parts, and myriad other components of war are made on similarly long time horizons (while room is always left for sudden, unexpected needs).

By 1997, Clinton's revised baseline would have produced a staggering cumulative reduction in Pentagon spending compared with what Bush had projected—roughly $80 billion. If the Republican majority elected in 1994 had not intervened, the military funding problems would have grown progressively worse, and readiness, training, and maintenance would have suffered severely.

The Republicans took over Congress in 1995 intent on reversing Clinton's accelerated defense cuts. Defense spending had been declining since 1985, but Republicans were alarmed by the fact that Clinton sought most of his quickest budget savings from the defense accounts even as he agreed to more and more peacekeeping deployments. The Clinton White House argued that the United States no longer needed the same force structure and weapons inventory that had been necessary to defeat the Soviet empire. To be sure, this argument reflected the general political consensus in the post–Cold War world, that the Pentagon could and probably should make do with less. But from the time he entered the White House, Clinton was extremely aggressive in looking to slash the defense budget. Upon taking office, he ordered a "bottom-up review" of defense spending that sought tens of billions in rapid defense cuts. Above all else he wanted to reduce the size of the fighting force, because that opened up other avenues of savings. After all, a smaller military would need fewer weapons and less money for training, basing, and overall maintenance.

In 1994, Clinton said in his State of the Union address that his defense budget "maintains our post–Cold War security at a lower cost." But throughout the year, various reports indicated that troop readiness was in decline and that the Pentagon was having to cannibalize its vital operations and maintenance accounts to finance peacekeeping operations. Republicans attacked Clinton for failing to keep the military in fighting shape and denounced extended (and at times limitless) peacekeeping commitments that further gnawed away at readiness. Because of these concerns, the Republicans ultimately decided to include the National Security Restoration Act as part of the Contract with America.

Less than a month after the stupendous Republican victory in November 1994, Clinton announced that he would add $25 billion to the six-year defense budget. It was a pittance, really—barely $4 billion extra per year. But it was an important political concession: Clinton was tacitly acknowledging what Republicans had said throughout the 1994 campaign—that he had cut defense too much and sapped readiness by agreeing to deployments without increasing funding. Clinton knew that, tactically, he had to get ahead of the coming GOP effort to boost defense spending.

"Secretary [of Defense William] Perry and I have repeatedly stated that our number-one commitment is to the readiness and well-being of our men and women in uniform," Clinton said on December 1. When asked if he had cut defense too much since being elected, Clinton referred to "unanticipated costs" and "unanticipated challenges" that had stretched defense spending thin and hurt military personnel's quality of life. These were euphemisms for peacekeeping and other military deployments that Clinton had ordered and had consistently paid for by pulling funds from other defense accounts and undermining short-term fighting readiness.

Extracting that concession from President Clinton was just the beginning of the Republicans' fight to protect the military and intelligence communities. As Tony Blankley points out, increasing defense spending was unpopular in the mid- to late 1990s. The Republicans did not have an easy fight. As the Pentagon struggled to adjust from the Cold War strategic thinking that had governed for two generations, lawmakers wanted to know why they should pour billions more into a defense establishment that didn't even know who its enemy was, let alone how to realign its forces, fighting doctrine, and weapons acquisition to fight that enemy. At a time when leaner defense budgets were the norm, Republicans did as much as if not more than could be expected to address military readiness.

The evidence can be found in the raw numbers. The first defense budget Republicans negotiated with President Clinton, for fiscal year 1996, totaled $266.1 billion—$7 billion more than Clinton had requested. Out of the overall budget, $93.6 billion, or 35 percent, was allocated for operations and maintenance accounts—that is, for the critical aspects of training, maintenance, and fighting fitness. The following year, 1997, the total Pentagon budget rose to $270.3 billion—$11.2 billion more than Clinton had requested. This time, the budget set aside $92.3 billion for operations and maintenance—a small decline from 1996 but a budget that made room for higher personnel costs and increased weapons research and testing. Though it was still far below Bush projections, the 1997 budget represented the first increase in defense spending since Clinton took office. What's more, President Clinton's requested figures reflected that the boost in defense spending he announced after the 1994 election rout was to be spread thinly over the early years and laid on thicker at some point in the distant future. This approach, largely thwarted by congressional Republicans, would have worsened the corrosive effects of shrinking defense budgets on preparedness and readiness. Further, the shifting of money toward military readiness, even as the overall Defense Department budget remained relatively constant, reflected Republican priorities that Clinton's budget requests simply did not share.

The Republicans moved even more aggressively to boost operations and maintenance spending in subsequent budget years. The 1998 defense budget of $271.3 billion set aside $97.2 billion, or 36 percent, for operations and maintenance spending. The $97.2 billion represented an increase of nearly $5 billion over the 1997 budget. No other part of the defense budget grew by even half this much in 1998. This budget was enshrined in the balanced-budget compromise Clinton struck with congressional Republicans in 1997. In other words, in the first budget that Republicans and Clinton agreed upon, defense spending increased, and operations and maintenance spending grew by a larger amount in real dollars and as a percentage of increases than any other part of the defense budget. Clinton had not pushed for such increases when he won the presidency or in his first two confrontations with Republicans over federal spending. The '98 defense numbers represented a significant policy victory for the Republicans. They were the first concrete proof that Republicans could not only resist Clinton's defense cuts but also require him to embrace increases.

In 1999, congressional Republicans passed and Clinton signed a $292.3 billion defense budget, which represented a one-year Pentagon spending increase of $21 billion. The operations-and-maintenance budget rose to $104.9 billion, a $7.7 billion increase over the 1998 budget. That $7.7 billion represented 37 percent of the entire budget increase, which maintained the operations-and-maintenance budget at 36 percent of the whole.

In 2000, the defense budget increased to $304.1 billion, a $9.1 billion jump. The operations-and-maintenance budget rose to $108.7 billion, meaning that it received 42 percent of that year's increased spending and maintained its 36 percent allocation of the entire defense budget.

In 2001 (the last Clinton budget), total defense spending increased to $329 billion. Readiness spending hit $117.7 billion, meaning that operations and maintenance held firm at 36 percent of the overall budget; the $9 billion increase in readiness also represented 36 percent of that year's overall defense spending boost.

In short, in five budget years, Republicans increased readiness allocations to 36 percent of the overall Pentagon budget and gave operations and maintenance a significant chunk of the new defense spending. And all this occurred as Clinton succeeded in reducing overall defense spending by *$50 billion* in inflation-adjusted dollars from 1992 to 2000.

In this little-known but vital approach to defense spending, Republicans made a decisive difference. By prioritizing readiness over all else, they gave soldiers usable equipment, deployable battlefield assets, flight-ready aircraft, seaworthy ships, and all the nuts-and-bolts essentials a military needs to shift from peacetime to wartime with a minimum of disruption. They gave President George W. Bush the kind of fighting speed, flexibility, and endurance he would need to call upon to fight the global War on Terror. This is the invisible, laborious work of governing. Silently and in the face of President Clinton's resistance every step of the way, Republicans helped provide for a fit and ready fighting force that was more lethal and better equipped to carry out the mission than it otherwise would have been. In this, Republicans also saved the lives of countless U.S. troops.

## *Holding the Line on Intelligence*

The Republicans achieved the same sort of quiet victories in protecting the intelligence community as they did on defense spending. The $20 billion increase in intelligence spending that Gingrich secured in 1998 was the most notable victory after the Republicans took control of Congress, but it was not the only one. At the time of the GOP takeover, the CIA and the intelligence community in general faced many questions about their role in the post–Cold War era. Making matters worse, scrutiny had increased with the fallout from the Aldrich Ames scandal in 1994, when a top CIA official was convicted of espionage.

Although it's difficult to determine precise numbers regarding the intelligence budget, because it is classified, it is clear that in the mid-1990s Democrats were looking to reduce expenditures on intelligence. For fiscal year 1994, President Clinton requested an estimated $28 billion for the intelligence community (which includes the CIA, the Defense Intelligence Agency, and the National Security Agency). Congressional Democrats cut Clinton's request by $1 billion, squeezing it, House Select Committee on Intelligence chairman Dan Glickman of Kansas said, in pursuit of deficit reduction and because of unanswered questions about the intelligence community's future mission. Clinton and CIA Director R. James Woolsey resisted these cuts. The next year's intelligence budget, for fiscal year 1995, was, according to Glickman's later announcement, 2 percent smaller than Clinton's request. The actual figure was later determined to be $27.4 billion, again reflecting the desire of congressional Democrats to reduce intelligence spending.

When the Republican majority came into power in 1995, it tried to reverse this trend. In its first intelligence budget, for fiscal year 1996, the GOP boosted intelligence spending back to $28 billion, and the next year intelligence spending jumped to $30 billion—a 9 percent increase in just two budgets. *Congressional Quarterly* said these intelligence budgets "protected much of the overall spending for the nation's spy agencies from the budget ax, a reflection of the new Republican majority's desire for robust spending on national security–related issues." It appears the intelligence budget rose again in 1998, to $30.5 billion. All figures on intelligence spending since 1998 remain classified, but it is widely believed that the budgets have gradually built on the increases Republicans pushed through upon taking power in 1995.

The final report of the National Commission on Terrorist Attacks Upon the United States, commonly known as the 9/11 Commission, took careful note of this reversal of fortunes: "The nadir for the Clandestine Service was in 1995, when only 25 trainees became new officers. In 1998, the DCI [Director of Central Intelligence] was able to persuade the administration and the Congress to endorse a long-range rebuilding program. It takes five to seven years of training, language study, and experience to bring a recruit up to full performance." As the budget figures above indicate and as *Congressional Quarterly* and the 9/11 Commission have verified, Republicans stopped the rapid decline in intelligence spending and gave the CIA and other intelligence agencies tools to collect and analyze data in the War on Terror that they otherwise would not have had.

The Republicans faced significant obstacles when they took control of Congress in 1995. On September 13, 1995, Representative Larry Combest, the chairman of the House Select Committee on Intelligence, summed up the problems in the intelligence community as the Republicans saw them:

> Fact one: In real terms, the intelligence budget has been cut in all but one of the last seven years. Fact two: The intelligence community is being reduced at twice the rate recommended by the President's national performance review program. Fact three: President Clinton proposed a few years ago to cut $7 billion from intelligence by 1997. That was accomplished over a year ago—two years early. We will probably come very close to doubling those cuts by 1997. Fact four: We have, until this year, been on a glide slope of intelligence cuts that would by the end of this decade put intelligence spending in constant dollars at about 65 percent of the 1989 level. Fact five: The intelligence community continues to reduce its personnel at a rate that will, by 1999, cut more than one of every five positions.

Combest and other Republicans were trying to revamp the intelligence system. They had "an excellent opportunity to take a fresh, open-eyed look at intelligence," Combest said. The key, to the Republicans, was breaking with the "past practice of concentrating on the short-term effect of our budgetary decisions" and instead taking "a longer view," examining "future needs and requirements for intelligence."

But Democrats pushed for even deeper intelligence cuts. Representative Barney Frank, Massachusetts Democrat, offered an amendment to cut funding an additional 3 percent—a measure that was supported by, among others, Representative Nancy Pelosi of California, the current House minority leader. Frank defended his amendment:

> The proposed authorization is 1.7 percent higher than last year's appropriation. It is 1.2 percent higher than what the President asked for. That seems to me a very grave error. Of course, we want to be protected, but there has been a more substantial drop in the task of the intelligence community than in virtually any other area of government. Yes, we have Iran and Libya and North Korea to worry about. But the argument that we cannot reduce our spending on intelligence, now that the Soviet Union's threat to our very physical survival has collapsed, must assume that Libya, North Korea, and Iran did not exist ten years ago. Yes, we still have these other threats, but we had them five and ten years ago. The CIA gets a 5 percent increase. Mr. Chairman, any other agency that had behaved disastrously, we would be talking about having to cut it.

Republicans defeated Frank's amendment, and they continued to push, at the margins, for more intelligence funding, or at least to keep spending cuts to a bare minimum. As Representative Combest said during the following year's debate over the intelligence budget, "We continue to believe that intelligence, more than ever, must be our first line of defense, of warning, and of analysis. Dollars well spent on intelligence are, I believe, fewer than dollars we would be forced to spend elsewhere if our intelligence capabilities decreased."

Some Democrats agreed. Representative Bill Richardson of New Mexico praised the 1997 bill for its emphasis on human intelligence. Presciently, he remarked, "It is critically important we beef up our intelligence capabilities, our human intelligence capabilities. It is critically important that we understand Islamic fundamentalism. That is going to take more linguists. To be perfectly candid, it will take more spies. It is going to take more James Bonds."

Of course, the Republicans' efforts on intelligence did not prevent 9/11, but they did leave the intelligence community in a far stronger position than it would have been in had the steep decline in spending won by the Democrats in Clinton's first years in office remained unchecked.

### Endemic Problems

Despite the real differences the GOP made by protecting military readiness and staving off deep cuts to the intelligence budget, the Republicans, like everyone else, failed to perceive the magnitude of the emerging terrorist threat. They did not, therefore, radically transform the strategic outlook of the American military or the nation's approach to counterterrorism. As it happened, the Pentagon's transition away from the Cold War strategic doctrine and toward a more agile, mobile, and easily deployable fighting force with complementary training and weapons systems would remain largely in the theoretical stages until 9/11, and it would take those attacks to prompt serious calls for reforming the U.S. intelligence apparatus.

But even if Republicans had seen the threat more clearly, it's hard to imagine how much difference it would have made. Given the Democrats' attitude toward the intelligence community and the military, the congressional Republicans could hardly have had much success pushing for a new strategic military doctrine to fight terrorism—which would have required billions in additional spending.

Some of the problems were so endemic that a Republican Congress would have found it impossible to correct them in a pre-9/11 world. One of the biggest problems was that the intelligence community in the 1990s established new rules that enforced an overly cautious, risk-averse approach to intelligence gathering. Then–CIA director John Deutch established the still-classified rules in 1995, during the fallout from House Intelligence Committee member Robert Torricelli's revelation that the CIA had paid an informant who had murdered two people in Guatemala, including one American. In making this disclosure, Torricelli, a New Jersey Democrat, violated congressional rules swearing all members of the Intelligence Committees to secrecy. But Democrats and Republicans were furious with the CIA, which had withheld this information for three years and, worse, had failed to disclose its connections to the Guatemalan military, one of the more vicious in a region rife with vicious militaries. The case highlighted concerns about the intelligence community's culture of secrecy and how U.S. tax dollars were going to known lawbreakers, human rights violators, and other unsavory characters. In the wake of the Aldrich

Ames scandal, the case was a national sensation. So Deutch established cumbersome regulations for dealing with intelligence sources associated with human rights violations, drug smuggling, terrorist groups, and so forth.

It should be noted that in the post-9/11 world, America's biggest intelligence gaps are the result of lack of contact with unsavory types throughout the shadowy world of Islamic jihadism. In fact, in 2001 Congress ordered the infiltration of potentially dangerous terrorist groups through recruitment of sources with questionable criminal and human rights backgrounds: "It is the sense of Congress that officers and employees of the intelligence community of the Federal Government . . . should be encouraged, and should make every effort, to establish and maintain intelligence relationships with any person, entity, or group for the purpose of engaging in lawful intelligence activities, including the acquisition of information on the identity, location, finances, affiliations, capabilities, plans, or information on any other person, entity, or group." But back in 1995, though the CIA noted the threat Islamic jihadists posed to America, it hamstrung U.S. efforts to penetrate their ranks.

The Clinton administration, too, created deeper problems that the Republican Revolution could not have overcome in the pre-9/11 climate. The biggest issue was that the Clinton White House was stubbornly, some would now argue heedlessly, committed to a law enforcement approach.

The Clinton administration placed the Justice Department, not the Pentagon, in charge of all counterterrorism efforts and resisted advice to more fully engage the military and the intelligence community in its terror-fighting efforts. Indeed, the administration went out of its way to place greater distance between the lead antiterrorism agency, the FBI, and the CIA than what the law already required. Since the late 1970s, Congress had prohibited the CIA and other intelligence agencies from conducting domestic spying. But in limited circumstances the FBI could conduct electronic eavesdropping and physical searches as part of foreign intelligence or foreign counterintelligence investigations, and by law it was prohibited from sharing this information with the CIA or other intelligence agencies. In 1995, Deputy Attorney General Jamie Gorelick established another separation, issuing a classified memorandum ordering the FBI not to contact U.S. attorneys' offices even if they had developed reasonable leads on potential terrorists or potential acts of terrorism through foreign intelligence or foreign counterintelligence investigations. In the memo, Gorelick wrote, "We believe that it is prudent to establish a set of instructions that will more clearly separate the counterintelligence investigation from the more limited, but continued, criminal investigations."

These new rules drew the ire of the nation's top counterterrorism prosecutor, Mary Jo White, U.S. attorney for the Southern District of New York. White prosecuted the al Qaeda figures behind the 1993 bombing of the World Trade Center, the first act of Islamist terrorism carried out on U.S. soil. She successfully prosecuted Egyptian cleric Sheik Omar Abdel Rahman for his plot to destroy numerous New York City landmarks. She also indicted Osama bin Laden for the twin 1998 bombings of U.S. embassies in East Africa that killed 224 people. If the CIA and other intelligence agencies were going to be kept in the dark, White certainly didn't want the frontline prosecutors at the U.S. attorneys' offices—especially ones such as hers, with vast experience in developing and analyzing terrorism evidence—to be taken out of the loop.

On June 13, 1995, White wrote Attorney General Janet Reno about Gorelick's new rules:

> You have asked whether I am generally comfortable with the instructions. It is hard to be totally comfortable with instructions to the FBI prohibiting contact with the United States Attorneys' Offices when such prohibitions are not legally required. . . . While I understand the need for centralization and control, this mechanism cuts out the U.S. Attorneys until the criminal division decides with FBI headquarters to open up a criminal investigation. Our experience has been that the FBI labels of an investigation as intelligence or law enforcement can be quite arbitrary depending on the personnel involved and that the most effective way to combat terrorism is with *as few labels and walls as possible so that wherever permissible, the right and left hands are communicating.* . . . I understand not wanting to have the FBI automatically contact all affected U.S. Attorneys' Offices whenever they contact the Criminal Division. But there should be that obligation on the Criminal Division so that U.S. Attorneys are made aware of *potential criminal activity in their districts at the earliest possible—and permissible—time* [emphasis added].

Gorelick rejected White's arguments and suggested revisions in a handwritten note to Reno in late July. "To the AG—I have reviewed and concur," Gorelick wrote, elevating a wall of separation between the FBI and U.S. attorneys' offices.

Gorelick's activities led prominent Republicans in 2004 to seek her ouster as a member of the 9/11 Commission. During his testimony before the commission, Attorney General John Ashcroft declassified the documents disclosing Gorelick's role in blocking intra–Justice Department cooperation on counterterrorism investigations. He said the Clinton Justice Department had "embraced flawed legal reasoning" in imposing the restrictions, which, he argued, had a "debilitating impact" on investigations into 9/11 conspirators. Specifically, he said, after the FBI arrested Zacarias Moussaoui, the so-called twentieth hijacker, agents were denied a criminal warrant to search his computer "because FBI officials feared breaching the wall." And when, in late August 2001, the CIA finally informed the FBI that 9/11 hijackers Khalid al-Midhar and Nawaf al-Hazmi were in the United States, "FBI headquarters refused to allow criminal investigators who knew the most about the most recent al Qaeda attack to join the hunt for the suspected terrorists." Ashcroft then revealed in his 9/11 testimony:

At that time, a frustrated FBI investigator wrote headquarters, quote, "Whatever has happened to this—someday someone will die—and wall or not—the public will not understand why we were not more effective and throwing every resource we had at certain 'problems.' Let's hope the national security law unit [NSLU] will stand behind their decision then, especially since the biggest threat to us, UBL [Usama bin Laden], is getting the most protection."

FBI headquarters responded, quote: "We are all frustrated with this issue. . . . These are the rules. NSLU does not make them up."

But as Ashcroft said, "Somebody did make these rules. Someone built this wall." The person who erected the wall was 9/11 commissioner and Clinton deputy attorney general Jamie Gorelick.

The 9/11 Commission's final report said that the Clinton-era "procedures—while requiring the sharing of intelligence information with prosecutors—regulated the manner in which such information could be shared from the intelligence side of the house to the criminal side. These procedures were almost immediately misunderstood and misapplied. As a result, there was far less information sharing and coordination between the FBI and the Criminal Division in practice than was allowed under the department's procedures." The commission said that FBI agents came to believe that they "could not share *any* intelligence information with criminal investigators. . . . Thus relevant information from the National Security Agency and the CIA often failed to make its way to criminal investigators."

The information that Ashcroft declassified exposed how the Clinton administration, already adamantly opposed to using the military to combat terrorism, hindered the efforts of the domestic law enforcement agencies that were supposedly at the forefront of counterterrorism efforts. In this context, the GOP's hard-fought victories in securing funds for military readiness and intelligence seem more impressive. To be sure, Tom DeLay, Tony Blankley, and other Republicans wish now that they *had* articulated a coherent counterterrorism strategy and fought to implement a new strategic military doctrine, but even if they had, it's hard to see it fundamentally altering the pre-9/11 reality.

### The Real Victory

So what did the Republicans accomplish on these vital issues affecting our national security? They bequeathed to the nation on September 12, 2001, a military better equipped, trained, and prepared *than it otherwise would have been* to fight a new, unimagined global war on terror. They made a similar difference in the intelligence world, even as the Clinton administration hindered the intelligence community's ability to deal with terrorist threats. The defense and intelligence budgets did not grow nearly as much or as fast as the GOP would have preferred, but the Republicans reversed the trends Clinton had set in motion.

To some Republicans, these quiet victories do not feel revolutionary—or, perhaps more accurately stated, sufficiently revolutionary. But to frontline troops whose supply lines are solid because the trucks work, to the pilot who knows his jet fighter is in razor-sharp condition, and to the Marine who knows his helicopter transport isn't hovering with makeshift parts, it doesn't matter if there was a revolution or not. All they care about is having what they need to succeed.

The Republican majority spared the military and intelligence agencies from the hollowness that would have made the War on Terror far more difficult to start and continue at anywhere near its present level. By whatever name, the election of 1994, the Contract with America's commitment to increased defense spending, and GOP ingenuity to prioritize military readiness and intelligence spending even in a time of tight Pentagon and intelligence budgets made a decisive difference.

# 8

# THE PATH TO WAR

There is one thing upon which Republicans Newt Gingrich, Dick Armey, Tom DeLay, and Bob Livingston as well as Democrats Tom Foley, Richard Gephardt, and Harry Reid all agree: If Republicans had not controlled Congress from 1995 forward, there would not have been an Iraq Liberation Act. And waging war in Iraq in 2003 would have been much harder without that 1998 law.

This does not diminish the tragic and painful role the 9/11 atrocities played in the decision to invade, conquer, and occupy Iraq. But as the nation has learned since Operation Iraqi Freedom was launched, there were no direct connections between the 9/11 terrorist attacks and Saddam Hussein's regime. What's more, many voters have wondered how Congress so easily followed President George W. Bush when he asked for a resolution authorizing war against Iraq in October of 2002. One of the most important reasons Congress granted Bush this power is that years before, back in 1998, it had thoroughly debated the concept of overthrowing Saddam *and voted affirmatively to do so.*

Though little noticed at the time, the Iraq Liberation Act established that it was the policy of the United States to overthrow the Iraqi government. The law stipulated that the preferred method of achieving this objective was through the support of outside dissident groups like the Iraqi National Congress, which received most of the $64 million in the U.S. Congress's annual appropriations designed to foster revolt and overthrow of Saddam. But as we will see, during the debate on the Iraq Liberation Act and companion resolutions, Congress openly debated and ultimately embraced the use of unilateral military action as an option to force Iraq to comply with underlying United Nations resolutions. The record clearly shows that Congress was on the side of unilateral confrontation with Iraq long before Bush was elected.

The driving force beyond this muscular, some might say bellicose, policy toward Saddam Hussein was the congressional Republican leadership. The Republicans made sure bills and resolutions seeking confrontation with Saddam received ample floor time and debate. And in the course of floor debate, all the issues that have divided America after Operation Iraqi Freedom divided members of Congress: the extent to which Saddam posed a real threat; what role, if any, the United States should play in creating a tribunal to punish Saddam for his war crimes; Saddam's relationship to Islamist terrorism; Saddam's pursuit of weapons of mass destruction; whether Saddam's barbarity justified U.S. or multilateral military intervention; and whether the United States should assume the responsibility of enforcing UN resolutions when other nations appeared reluctant to join the effort. By and large, at the end of these debates, Congress approved the most aggressive option. Every piece of hard-charging legislation against Iraq was bipartisan, but make no mistake, Republicans stoked the debate and kept it hot until President Clinton signed the Iraq Liberation Act in 1998. And that law laid the groundwork for the 2003 Iraq war. In fact, much of the language in the 2002 congressional resolution giving President Bush the power to initiate Operation Iraqi Freedom was drawn *directly* from the Iraq Liberation Act that the Republican majority drafted and pushed.

"It doesn't happen without us," DeLay says.

### Foreshadowing

Our story begins on November 13, 1997, when the House of Representatives passed a resolution expressing the "sense of Congress" that the United States should take action to ensure that Iraq complied with all UN Security Council resolutions ordering the Iraqis to destroy any capabilities for weapons of mass destruction. Iraq had repeatedly and routinely stonewalled the United Nations Special Commission (UNSCOM), the inspection agency created at the end of the Gulf War to find and destroy "Iraq's capability to produce chemical, biological, and nuclear weapons and its ability to produce missiles capable of delivering such weapons of mass destruction." Representative Tom Lantos, California Democrat, introduced the resolution because Saddam had refused to allow U.S. weapons inspections experts to participate in UNSCOM searches. The resolution sought compliance via diplomatic means first, but it made clear that the use of military force—unilateral, if necessary—was the second option. When Lantos introduced the measure on the House floor, he declared, "We must be certain that we eliminate Saddam Hussein's ability to produce weapons of mass destruction and the missiles which deliver them. If we can do that peacefully through active diplomacy, that clearly is the course we should take. If diplomacy fails, however, we should use force—through multilateral cooperation with our allies, if that can be done, but *unilaterally if that is our only remaining option* [emphasis added]."

The measure had nineteen cosponsors, both Democrats and Republicans, but Republican leaders made sure the Lantos resolution made it to the House floor. The House agreed to it without objection. Though the Lantos resolution never became law—a companion resolution was not introduced in the Senate—it established House policy on Iraq, compliance with UN resolutions, and the possible use of multinational or unilateral military force to compel compliance.

The same day it passed the Lantos resolution, the House also passed a resolution calling for the creation of a war-crimes tribunal to punish Saddam for multiple crimes against humanity, among them invading Iran and Kuwait and using chemical weapons to slaughter Kurds in northern Iraq. Some of the language in this resolution would carry over into the Iraq Liberation Act that Congress would pass one year later, in 1998.

Many representatives were emphatic that the Iraqi dictator must be brought to justice for his crimes against humanity. For example, one of the resolution's cosponsors, House International Relations Committee chairman Benjamin Gilman, New York Republican, spoke of Saddam's use of chemical weapons against Kurdish villages and declared that "the United States cannot allow such atrocities to go unpunished if we want to prevent the proliferation of these weapons of mass destruction." On the day of the vote, another cosponsor, Representative John Porter, Illinois Republican, articulated a case that would be widely heard before, during, and after Operation Iraqi Freedom: "Once again, Saddam Hussein is showing his true colors as a ruthless dictator who will attempt to do anything to manipulate his way out of sanctions and weapons monitoring through whatever means he can. We must stop Saddam Hussein now. We must isolate him and make certain that the world understands the nature of his ruthless regime. . . . If there is any individual in the world who deserves to be brought to justice today, it is Saddam Hussein."

No one questioned Saddam Hussein's human rights abuses, but at least one congressman wondered aloud whether it was America's place to try to bring Saddam to justice. Texas Republican Ron Paul, a libertarian skeptical of U.S. military interventions, questioned the constitutional legitimacy of the resolution. In language that critics of the Iraq war would later echo, Paul proclaimed, "I agree certainly with the sharp criticism against the government and the leaders of Iraq . . . but I do not see that we have the authority to all of a sudden impose our system of justice across the entire world. I think it drums up anti-American hostility more than it achieves justice."

At that point, hawkish California Republican Dana Rohrabacher, a former Reagan White House aide, challenged Paul's reasoning, arguing that Saddam's abuses were so profound, the threat he posed to neighbors so great that tougher U.S. policy was justified. The Paul-Rohrabacher colloquy foreshadowed a debate that would rage in America six years later:

*Rohrabacher:* Would the gentleman suggest that there is not a relationship between freedom and peace?
*Paul:* Mr. Speaker, I am not sure what the gentleman is getting at. I know the most important thing for freedom and peace is for me to obey the Constitution. Where is it the authority of the Constitution for us to police the world?
*Rohrabacher:* The gentleman is suggesting, then, that this body should not have condemned Adolf Hitler until he actually attacked the United States, is that what he would suggest? Is that his foreign policy?
*Paul:* I think that is not the debate on the floor right now. I think when our national security is threatened, the American people have a right to vote through their Congressmen for a declaration of war. This is the kind of thing that leads to Vietnam War–type wars and UN sanctions. This is the kind of thing that leads to Koreas, Vietnams and useless wars. This is why we did not win the war in the Persian Gulf and why we are still faced with this problem.

Paul's objection drew little notice, however, as the measure passed by a vote of 396–2.

The following spring, the Senate passed a similar bill, which would become another foundation document for the Iraq Liberation Act. The Senate measure sought a UN-led commission responsible for "indicting, prosecuting, and imprisoning Saddam Hussein." The debate over this bill revealed that a bipartisan consensus, similarly pushed by Republicans, was forming in the Senate. Pennsylvania Republican Arlen Specter introduced the measure, but prominent Democrats spoke out on behalf of the resolution. For instance, Senator Byron Dorgan, a North Dakota Democrat, stated, "A tribunal for Iraq should be constituted by the United Nations, and war-crimes trials should begin. . . . The list of war crimes during the Persian Gulf is a lengthy one. However, Iraq's criminal record goes back further than that. . . . Name another leader on the face of this Earth who has decided, not once but on numerous occasions, to use weapons of mass destruction against his own people and his neighbors." Moreover, Senator Joseph R. Biden Jr. of Delaware, a prominent member of the Senate Foreign Relations Committee, declared, "The weak international response that followed [the chemical weapons attacks at] Halabja emboldened Saddam. It is time to systematically compile the evidence of Saddam Hussein's atrocities and undertake criminal proceedings to deliver the punishment that he so richly deserves. Our action in passing this resolution presents a challenge to the international community to join the United States in putting the wheels of justice into motion. We should not underestimate the difficulty of physically delivering Saddam Hussein to a tribunal, but it would be unconscionable to abandon the quest for justice. Silence and inaction would be a grave injustice to the hundreds upon thousands of his victims."

But Senate passage of the war-crimes tribunal resolution obscured a deeper split over how aggressive U.S. policy against Iraq should be. Back in January, a much tougher resolution had been introduced but had been shelved despite the measure's high-profile sponsors from both parties, including Republicans like Senate Majority Leader Trent Lott of Mississippi and Senators John McCain of Arizona and Jesse Helms of North Carolina, and Democrats like Senate Minority Leader Tom Daschle of South Dakota and Senators John Kerry of Massachusetts, Robert Byrd of West Virginia, and Daniel Patrick Moynihan of New York. The two sides could not agree on the exact terms of the resolution. Hawkish Republicans demanded a clear statement that the resolution's purpose was to indicate that the United States supported efforts to overthrow Saddam. They insisted that the measure include these statements: "[The resolution] condemns in the strongest possible terms the continued threat to international peace and security posed by Iraq's refusal to meet its international obligations and end its weapons of mass destruction programs" and "urges the President to take all necessary and appropriate actions to respond to the threat posed by Iraq's refusal to end its weapons of mass destruction programs." Democrats weren't willing to go that far—not just yet, anyway. The bill stalled.

Though the resolution failed to get through the Senate, it indicated growing GOP insistence on toughening U.S. policy against Iraq. Some high-profile Democrats showed interest but weren't prepared to interpret the language as broadly as Republicans insisted. The Republicans obviously intended to turn up the heat on Saddam, and they were also trying to get the attention of the Clinton White House. These moves would pay off in the not-too-distant future.

### Tightening the Screws on Saddam

On February 25, 1998, Representative Benjamin Gilman invited Paul Wolfowitz, then dean of the Paul H. Nitze School of Advanced International Studies at Johns Hopkins University, to testify before the House International Relations Committee on the subject of U.S. policy options with Iraq. Wolfowitz was well known in GOP circles as a hawk on Iraq, and his testimony was part of Republican leaders' systematic effort to place Saddam Hussein's crimes in the congressional record and build support for some type of confrontation. Wolfowitz's testimony did not call for a U.S. land war against Iraq. In fact, it appeared to ridicule the very notion of using U.S. forces to overthrow Saddam. Instead, Wolfowitz tried to reassure lawmakers that dissident groups could topple the Iraqi dictator. Wolfowitz would, of course, become deputy defense secretary in George W. Bush's Pentagon and play a pivotal role in developing the U.S. military attack on Iraq.

During his testimony before the International Relations Committee, Wolfowitz stated:

> If we must act militarily in Iraq, it should be in support of a serious effort to help Iraqis to liberate their country from Saddam Hussein's tyrannical grasp. That is the only way to rescue the region

and the world from the threat that will continue to be posed by
Saddam's unrelenting effort to acquire weapons of mass destruction and to exact vengeance for the defeat he suffered in the Persian Gulf War. What is needed is not the "major land campaign"
that top [Clinton] Administration officials falsely suggest is the
only effective way to remove Saddam from power. The real option
is to support the many Iraqis who desperately want to overthrow
this tyrant, but who have so far found the U.S. stinting and unreli-
able in the support we have provided them.

Wolfowitz would later be blamed for relying too heavily on the advice
and counsel of these very same dissident groups. According to critics, this
failure cost hundreds of American lives and dramatically complicated
efforts to develop a coherent postwar strategy to rebuild, pacify, and
democratize Iraq.

In his 1998 testimony, Wolfowitz also pressed for a more confrontational approach, criticizing the Clinton administration's limited goal of
restoring UN-sanctioned weapons inspections:

Saddam has been rewarded by the repeated statements by top U.S.
officials—not to mention those of other countries—that our goal
is limited merely to getting the UN inspections restored. That is to
say, or rather as President Clinton said, "Would the Iraqi people be
better off if there were a change in leadership? I certainly think
they would be. But that is not what the United Nations has authorized us to do; that is not what our immediate interest is about." Or
in the words of the Secretary of Defense [William Cohen]: "What
we are seeking to do is not to topple Saddam Hussein, not to
destroy his country, but to do what the United Nations has said in
its declarations."

Wolfowitz then turned to the question of U.S. military action. Clev-
erly, he framed the issue from the perspective of an unnamed veteran:

Which brings us to the question asked by the elderly veteran in
Columbus, Ohio: "If push comes to shove and Saddam will not back
down, will not allow or keep his word, are we ready and willing to

send the troops . . . and finish this job, or are we going to do it half-assed, the way we did before?" . . . I am sorry to say that the single best opportunity to support the Iraqi opposition was during the [George H. W.] Bush Administration. . . . Where the Clinton Administration came to office promising to do more, they in fact have done less.

Wolfowitz pressed Congress to allot $100 million for something he called an Iraqi provisional government, a sort of government-in-exile that would plot Saddam's ouster. Little did anyone realize how important the phrase "Iraqi provisional government" would become.

What we should be doing now is preparing for the time when we face another crisis with Saddam Hussein or another opportunity to act to help the Iraqi people liberate themselves. For that purpose, I would urge the Congress to:

- Urge the United States government to recognize, and assist in all practicable ways, a provisional government of free Iraq. . . .
- Appropriate $100 million for the purpose of assisting the provisional government. . . .
- Press for the United States to seek an indictment of Saddam Hussein for war crimes and crimes against humanity.

That summer, the effort to put pressure on Saddam Hussein picked up steam. On June 25, Lott, the Senate majority leader, and House Speaker Newt Gingrich introduced companion resolutions that found Iraq in "material breach" of existing UN resolutions. "Material breach" was a phrase the UN had used repeatedly over the course of a decade to chastise Saddam for various violations of international law. It is the closest the UN ever gets to fighting words. Though designating someone in "material breach" doesn't guarantee or even explicitly threaten military reprisal, it does suggest that the UN is at least leaning in that direction. That is why Lott and Gingrich insisted that "material breach" appear in the resolutions. Lott even proposed an amendment to drive home the point: "The Government of Iraq is in material and unacceptable breach of its international obligations, and therefore the President is urged to take appropriate action, in accordance with the Constitution and relevant laws of the United States, to bring Iraq into compliance with its international obligations."

The Senate passed the resolution with *no debate* and by unanimous consent on July 31, 1998, reflecting the mounting concern about Saddam Hussein. On the House side, the debate was formulaic. Representative Gilman, a cosponsor of the resolution, reminded his fellow House members of "Iraq's record of continued evasion and obstruction of UN resolutions" and "the fact that Saddam Hussein's behavior has not improved and that he remains in material and unacceptable breach of his international obligations."

But Indiana Democrat Lee Hamilton, ranking Democrat on the House International Relations Committee, voiced concerns about the resolution. Hamilton, a cosponsor of the 1997 Lantos resolution, readily acknowledged that "Iraq is violating UN Security Council resolutions, it is engaging in unacceptable behavior." But he warned that the use of the phrase "material breach" would set the United States on a more hostile course with Iraq and would unnecessarily complicate negotiations with other nations about future steps against Saddam Hussein, since some countries might prefer a less aggressive posture toward Iraq. Hamilton also argued that most members of the UN Security Council thought only the Security Council itself could find a nation in material breach of its international obligations. For Congress to make such a finding, he warned, would be taking a "a unilateral position" that "strains U.S. relations with other UN Security Council members and jeopardizes a solid UN Security Council front against Iraq." In short, Hamilton feared that by creating resentment at the UN, the United States would make it more rather than less difficult "to win international support for the use of force against Iraq." Last, Hamilton faulted the resolution for referring to U.S. military force as an option but not stating the conditions under which force would be used, the goals to be achieved, or the military methods to achieve them.

Despite his reservations, Hamilton voted for the resolution, in part because he saw no viable alternative. "I am uncomfortable voting for this resolution, principally because I think it does not measure up to the way a responsible Congress should engage in foreign policy making," he stated. "I am even less comfortable, however, voting against it. I do not want to go on record against the use of force."

On August 3, 1998, the resolution passed overwhelmingly in the

House, by a vote of 407–6. President Clinton signed it on August 14. The contours of a more aggressive U.S. policy toward Iraq were taking shape. Of course, in the lead-up to the 2003 Iraq war, Lee Hamilton's warnings would seem particularly prescient.

## To Overthrow Saddam

The yearlong push for a tougher policy against Iraq hit the jackpot in October 1998, when Congress passed and Clinton signed the Iraq Liberation Act.

This law stands as the legal linkage between the congressional resolution authorizing President George H. W. Bush to prosecute Operation Desert Storm in 1991 and the congressional resolution that President George W. Bush would use in 2003 as legal authority to launch Operation Iraqi Freedom. In the prelude to Operation Iraqi Freedom, the White House, State Department, and Pentagon routinely cited this law as establishing a U.S. legal mandate to overthrow Saddam's regime. White House spokesman Ari Fleischer invoked the law dozens of times to justify Bush's active consideration of invading Iraq to compel compliance with UN disarmament resolutions. Though it's certainly possible that Congress would have followed Bush's lead in 2002 without this law, it's hard to see how. The Iraq Liberation Act was the culmination of more than a year of steady GOP pressure on the Clinton White House, which not incidentally was fighting against impeachment arising from the Lewinsky scandal, to intensify pressure on Saddam and place U.S. military invasion squarely on the table— not merely as saber rattling but as a matter of federal law.

The law established a long indictment against Saddam. Among the charges: From the 1980 invasion of Iran through its decision in 1998 to throw UNSCOM and International Atomic Energy Agency inspectors out of the country (in violation of the Gulf War cease-fire agreement), Iraq had been an aggressor state; and Saddam was intent on developing weapons of mass destruction to use against Iraq's neighbors. The law also recounted Saddam's acts of war: his use of chemical weapons in Halabja, the 1993 assassination attempt on former president Bush, and repeated rebuffs of UN inspectors.

The Iraq Liberation Act established a new U.S. policy to respond to these acts of aggression and disregard for international law and the threats they posed to the United States:

Section 3: It should be the policy of the United States to support efforts to remove the regime headed by Saddam Hussein from power in Iraq and to promote the emergence of a democratic government to replace that regime.

The law also called for direct U.S. assistance to dissident groups to topple Saddam. Section 4 called for up to $99 million in communications, humanitarian, and military aid that the president "may provide to the Iraqi democratic opposition organizations designated" by Congress. Building on earlier resolutions, the Iraq Liberation Act established procedures to create a war-crimes tribunal, an open declaration that the intent of the law was to see Saddam overthrown. The UN was to use the law's language as guideposts for creating a Nuremberg-style tribunal for Saddam and his henchmen. In addition, the law promised that the United States would deliver humanitarian aid to Iraq once dissident forces removed Saddam from power, in order to smooth the transition to democracy.

The law was not a declaration of war, and it did not provide explicit warmaking powers against Iraq. But in style and substance, it shifted U.S. law from a position of neutrality and deference to UN procedures to one directly advocating the overthrow of a foreign government. And though lawmakers pointed to the fact that the law didn't require any U.S. military action, a question hung in the air: If dissidents failed to topple Saddam, who would? The law thus marked a major transition in the United States, establishing a legal and political predicate for Congress to side with Bush in 2002 to authorize the use of force against Iraq. Although critics accuse Bush of misleading Congress or dragging the United States into war, the record throughout 1997 and 1998 clearly shows that Congress wrestled with these issues and agreed that Saddam's transgressions posed a threat to the region. What's more, hawks and doves alike considered it important to defend and uphold the UN resolutions that the Iraqi dictator had repeatedly flouted.

Amazingly, the Senate bill passed by unanimous consent. That means *no dissent at all*. During the limited debate, senators affirmed the need to oust Saddam Hussein. Trent Lott, for instance, argued that the United States needed this new policy "that overtly seeks the replacement of Saddam Hussein's regime through military and political support for the Iraq opposition." The Clinton administration, he said, was "beginning to understand the strategic argument in favor of moving beyond containment to a policy of 'rollback.' Containment is not sustainable." Similarly, Senator Jesse Helms, North Carolina Republican and chairman of the Foreign Relations Committee, declared, "Saddam Hussein is a threat to the United States and a threat to our friends in the Middle East. . . . For nearly eight years the United States has stood by and allowed the UN weapons inspection process to proceed in defanging Saddam. That process is now in the final stages of collapse, warning that the U.S. cannot stand idly by hoping against hope that everything will work itself out. . . . For as long as he and his regime are in power, Iraq will remain a mortal threat."

Senator Bob Kerrey, Nebraska Democrat, took a slightly different approach, insisting that "it is for Iraqis, not Americans, to organize themselves to put Saddam Hussein out of power" and that "this bill is not a device to involve the U.S. military in operations in or near Iraq." But he embraced the bill, proclaiming that it was "a clear commitment to a U.S. policy replacing the Saddam Hussein regime and replacing it with a transition to democracy." America, Kerrey said, "refuses to coexist with a regime which has used chemical weapons on its own citizens and on neighboring countries, which has invaded its neighbors twice without provocation, which has still not accounted for its atrocities committed in Kuwait, which has fired ballistic missiles into the cities of three of its neighbors, which is attempting to develop nuclear and biological weapons, and which has brutalized and terrorized its own citizens for thirty years. I don't see how any democratic country could accept the existence of such a regime, but this bill says America will not."

The House, too, approved the resolution in an overwhelming, bipartisan vote (360–38). But the debate in the House mirrored earlier Iraq debates. Representative Gilman, a driving force all year in the Iraq debate, reached a different conclusion from Kerrey's about the possible need for U.S. military forces to do the job this bill laid before Iraqi dissidents. "The purpose of this legislation," he declared, "is to finally and irrevocably commit the United States to the removal of the regime headed by Saddam Hussein. The time has come to let Saddam know—to let the whole world know—that the United States will not tolerate this regime's continued grip on power. Simply put, Saddam must go." He made clear that although the bill did not mandate the use of the U.S. military to oust Saddam, military force might be ultimately the only workable option: "Some suggest that our nation should go to war and rid the Persian Gulf of the threat posed by Saddam. We may yet be compelled to do so."

Democrat Lee Hamilton announced his support for the bill but identified two problems: a newly aggressive U.S. policy about to be enshrined in law, and a vague, low-level commitment of U.S. resources to achieve the stated goals. Hamilton wondered aloud where such a policy would lead if dissidents failed to overthrow Saddam's government. "My understanding is that U.S. policy toward Iraq since the Gulf War has been a policy of containment," he said. "That policy has been reasonably successful at a price that we are willing to pay. Having rejected an invasion of Iraq, but still seeking to get rid of Saddam, we now come to this bill. The policy message that Congress sends with this bill is different than the stated policy of the United States." Hamilton was concerned that the bill did not "spell out very carefully and in writing what the United States is prepared and not prepared to do," and had provided "modest means to achieve what has proven to be a very difficult objective." He concluded, "When you have a gap between goals and means, that often leads to trouble in the conduct of American foreign policy."

The House debate over the Iraq Liberation Act brought another confrontation between Ron Paul, the Texas libertarian, and Dana Rohrabacher, the hawkish Californian. Paul challenged statements from supporters that the bill didn't alter U.S. policy or raise expectations of a newly confrontational policy. He also said that in proclaiming it the policy of the United States to "support efforts to remove the regime headed by Saddam Hussein from power," the bill essentially advocated killing Saddam. "That sounds pretty clear to me," Paul declared. "As a matter of fact, I think it sounds so clear that it contradicts U.S. law. How do you remove somebody without killing them? . . . So we are talking about killing Saddam Hussein, a ruthless dictator. But how many ruthless dictators do we have? We have plenty. So how many more should we go after?"

Rohrabacher rose to Paul's challenge and minced no words about the stakes: "The only thing coming back to haunt us now is that when the Gulf War was going on, we did not dispatch Saddam Hussein from this planet. We did not finish the job. Saddam Hussein now has a blood feud with us, and he will murder if we give him the opportunity to do so with weapons of mass destruction. He will murder millions of Americans. So like it or not, America's safety is now tied to events in Iraq and in the Persian Gulf."

On October 31, 1998, Clinton signed the Iraq Liberation Act. There was no elaborate Rose Garden signing ceremony, with pens as mementos and handshakes for the cameras; instead, the White House simply released a statement. But Clinton's signing of the Iraq Liberation Act was extremely significant, placing U.S. law on the side of overthrowing a foreign government. It was indirect unilateralism, but unilateralism just the same. It was pushed by congressional Republicans, yes. But it was codified in federal law by a president who prided himself on collective security and multinational cooperation.

Just two weeks later, Saddam Hussein said, again, that he would comply with United Nations weapons inspections—this after he had thrown UN inspectors out of Iraq. (In reality, UN inspectors would be barred from Iraq until 2002.) At a November 15 press conference, addressing the issue of Saddam's noncompliance, Clinton spoke overtly about U.S. support for efforts to overthrow the Iraqi regime. In fact, a close inspection of his statement reveals language remarkably similar to Bush's in the days leading up to Operation Iraqi Freedom:

> This crisis also demonstrates, unfortunately, once again, that *Saddam Hussein remains an impediment to the well-being of his people and a threat to the peace of his region and security of the world.* We will continue to contain the threat that he poses by working for the elimination of Iraq's weapons of mass destruction capability under UNSCOM, enforcing the sanctions and the no-fly zone, responding firmly to any Iraqi provocations. However, *over the long term, the best way to address that threat is through a Government in Baghdad—a new Government—that is committed to represent and respect its people, not repress them, that is committed to peace in the region* [emphasis added].

### The Path to War

In October of 2002, Congress debated President George W. Bush's request for authorization to use force to compel Iraqi compliance with all existing UN resolutions, especially those dealing with disarmament. The debate followed political, intellectual, ideological, and legal logic laid down four and five years before, when congressional Republicans began pressing for a tougher policy. Democrats who opposed Bush's request for warmaking powers in 2002 had a chance in those years to raise questions about, debate, and even vote against substantive changes in U.S. policy that Republicans were aggressively pursuing. But they did not. Remember, the Iraq Liberation Act passed the Senate with almost no debate and *zero opposition.*

While it's true the situation in 2002 was far different from that in 1998, an examination of the debate back in 1997 and 1998 clearly shows that some lawmakers feared or at least anticipated where these new policies were headed: military confrontation with Iraq. And yet Democrats had done nothing. Significant portions of the 1998 Iraq Liberation Act were incorporated into the 2002 Authorization for Use of Military Force Against Iraq. Both bills cite Iraq's repeated violations of UN resolutions, the threat it posed to neighboring countries, its continuing attempts to violate no-fly zones, its past use of chemical weapons, and its pursuit of weapons of mass destruction. Fully six clauses in both bills are virtually identical and, of course, the 2002 Authorization of Force cites the precedent established by the Iraq Liberation Act and earlier congressional actions regarding Iraq. Past was prologue. Democrats who spoke out in 2002 had abdicated a policy-making role many years earlier. Give Republicans credit, they were consistent. They put their policy positions into law and used that law to justify the fight when the time came.

Sure enough, during the October 2002 debate on the resolution authorizing the use of force in Iraq, Senator Trent Lott cited the Iraq Liberation Act:

> In 1998, at the request of President Clinton, I moved aggressively, in a bipartisan way, to pass the Iraqi Liberation Act. . . . We passed that resolution, which also called for a regime change unanimously. . . . I hope we can get inspectors in there, that they can find the weapons of mass destruction, and they are destroyed. But I don't trust Saddam Hussein. In the end, he will try to block this. Some people say, why now? Well, because the threat is not going to lessen. It has been four years since we passed the Iraqi Liberation Act in 1998. We want to see action from the UN. We need to act to show our commitment, and we need to show our determination to get them to act in a way that has real force.

Senator John Warner of Virginia, chairman of the Armed Services Committee, seconded Lott, saying that "the United Nations has done nothing for

four years" and that this resolution would "put in place the tools for our president and our secretary of state to get the strongest possible resolution in the
United Nations."

Two prominent Democrats, Ted Kennedy of Massachusetts and Robert
Byrd of West Virginia, rose in opposition, seeking a broader UN role. "We
cannot go it alone on Iraq and expect our allies to support us," Kennedy
said. "We cannot go it alone and expect the world to stand with us in the
urgent and ongoing war against terrorism and al Qaeda. . . . We should
approve a strong resolution today calling on the United Nations to require
Iraq to submit to unfettered UN weapons inspections or face [a] UN-backed
international force. If such option fails, and Saddam refuses to cooperate,
the president could then come to the Congress and request Congress to provide him with authorization to wage war against Iraq." Senator Warner had
pointed out, however, that President Bush had already "taken the initiative
to go not only to the American people, but to the whole world, and very carefully and methodically tell the world we should be on alert."

Senator Byrd condemned Congress for failing to stand up against
Bush's "rush to war." "This is my fiftieth year in Congress," Byrd said. "I
never would have thought I would find a Senate which would lack the backbone to stand up against the stampede, this rush to war, this rush to give to
the president of the United States, whatever president he is, whatever
party, this rush to . . . to let him determine alone when he will send the
sons and daughters of the American people into war, let him have control
of the military forces. He will not only make war, but he will declare war."
But antiwar Democrats might ask where Byrd was during the Iraq debate of
the late 1990s, when Iraq policy was being changed and when military
force was explicitly referred to as an option in an eventual U.S. confrontation with Iraq.

The House debate, meanwhile, echoed a not-so-distant and not-so-
unimportant past. California Democrat Tom Lantos, who had introduced
the 1997 measure saying that the United States should ensure that Iraq
complied with UN Security Council resolutions, urged his colleagues to
join him in supporting "this historic resolution." He stated, "Against such
an implacable foe as Saddam Hussein, peace can only be achieved through
strength, the strength of conviction as much as the strength of arms. . . . If
the costs of war are great, the costs of inaction and appeasement are
greater still."

Representative Henry Hyde, Illinois Republican and chairman of the International Relations Committee (having replaced Benjamin Gilman in 2001), declared, "We are faced today with a situation whose analogies to 1936 seem all too clear. An aggressive dictator has once again willfully and repeatedly defied the basic norms of international law. . . . We have tried diplomacy. We have tried sanctions. We have tried inspections. We have established no-fly zones. We have run out of options. . . . We cannot entrust our fate to others, for others may never come."

Democrats who opposed the resolution spoke out against President Bush's failure to demonstrate that Iraq posed an "imminent threat" to the United States and against the costs of a war—in human life, in dollars, and in America's relations with the rest of the world. For instance, Representative Donald Payne of New Jersey proclaimed, "First of all, let me say from the outset that I oppose a unilateral first-strike attack by the United States without a clearly demonstrated and imminent threat of attack on our soil. . . . A unilateral first strike would be codified in this resolution. House Joint Resolution 114 is not a declaration of war, but it is a blank check to use force without moral or political authority of the declaration of war."

Former House minority whip David Bonior of Michigan said, "We have to be cognizant of what this war will unleash upon the world. . . . If we strike first, what kind of message does that send to the tinderboxes of Pakistan and India, China and Taiwan, North and South Korea? By rushing into war, we alone will bear the burden of seeing this conflict to its bloody end, most likely in the streets of Baghdad among innocent families and U.S. troops engaged in door-to-door combat. It will strain our military. It will cost us tens and tens, if not hundreds of millions of dollars, and it will erode any cooperation from Arab and Muslim nations in tracking down and neutralizing the remaining al Qaeda cells."

Just as the debate was more heated this time around, the votes were more split. Yet both the Senate and the House passed the resolution authorizing war—the Senate by a vote of 77–23, the House by a vote of 296–133. And five months later, on March 19, 2003, President Bush launched Operation Iraqi Freedom.

## *Majorities Matter*

The Iraq war deeply divided the country. When some politicians who had supported the 2002 resolution authorizing the use of military force in Iraq later spoke out against the war, many observers naturally turned their attention to the debate that occurred in October 2002. But as we have seen, the terms of that debate were set much earlier—and they were set by the Republican majority that came to power on the back of the Contract with America.

Iraq policy had nothing to do with the Contract per se, but it was a direct outgrowth of two things the Contract called for: a GOP majority in Congress and a more assertive U.S. foreign policy. The Contract could not have been more explicit about either goal. Republican majorities drove the Iraq debate in Congress in the late 1990s, persuading a self-proclaimed mulitlateralist president to sign the first law in U.S. history to publicly advocate overthrowing a foreign government. The long-standing U.S. policy of "regime change" was used as a rhetorical palliative in the prelude to the war, and quite shrewdly so, by a Republican White House that inherited the policy from Clinton. But there would have been no "regime change" policy to inherit had not Republicans demanded it.

When I asked former Clinton political adviser Paul Begala whether he agreed that the Republicans had made the 2003 Iraq invasion possible as far back as the late 1990s, he responded, "I've never thought of the Iraq Liberation Act as a GOP strategy to set the table for war before—but now that you lay out your theory, I think you're right. Who wouldn't be for regime change in Iraq? Just as I'd be for regime change in Communist China and Castro's Cuba and North Korea and Syria and Iran and any number of other countries. It was not seen at the time as a precursor to war, but in hindsight I think you're right, it was. Ingenious. Tragic, but ingenious."

Depending on your perspective on Operation Iraqi Freedom, either Saddam was a casualty of the Contract, or U.S. national security policy was. Either way, the world is a far different place because of it.

# 9

# THE UNHERALDED
# VICTORY ON BALLISTIC
# MISSILE DEFENSE

For the cynics who suggest that the Contract with America was merely a concoction of poll-tested bromides that had little transformative value, let me cite one of the astounding ideas from the Contract that received almost no attention at the time, was shorn from the Contract during the celebrated first hundred days, but returned in later years to establish a new global consensus on nuclear deterrence. This example may be the most important of all in demonstrating the profound importance of ideas first conceived by the Republican minority, given voice in the Contract with America, and then allowed to work their way through the political system to literally change the world.

The idea: ballistic missile defense.

No one remembers this, but ballistic missile defense was part of the Contract with America's National Security Revitalization Act. The language, crisp and clear:

> Renewed Commitment to a National Missile Defense: Protecting against rogue nuclear states like North Korea by providing adequate funding for effective national missile defense to be deployed as soon as possible. It also instructs the Clinton administration not to foreclose the Strategic Defense Initiative in its ongoing Anti-Ballistic Missile Treaty negotiations with the Russians.

This policy was included in a comprehensive list of national security reforms, among them: restricting the use of U.S. forces under command of the United Nations and requiring U.S. command of all forces operating in peacekeeping zones; commissioning a so-called bottom-up review of U.S. military needs, force readiness, and modernization; restoring budget rules that prevent cuts in defense spending in order to fund "social spending programs"; and urging swift expansion of NATO to include Poland, Hungary, the Czech Republic, and "other Central European nations that are striving to meet the criteria of democratic elections, free market economies and civilian control of the military."

Each of these defense planks of the Contract is now law. But none has had as profound an effect as the provision dealing with ballistic missile defense, because none of the others touched as many other nations. The ballistic missile defense plank reversed a generation of global nuclear deterrence policy and reshaped assumptions about the threat posed by ballistic missiles in the hands of rogue nations or terrorists. This change was slow in coming. It didn't manifest itself in the first hundred days. It didn't become law in the first year of the GOP majority, or the second, or the third, or even the four or fifth or sixth. By the standard measurements, it's been quite easy for scorekeepers to leave ballistic missile defense off the list of the Republican Revolution's accomplishments and assume the idea was one George W. Bush latched on to during the 2000 campaign and made the centerpiece of his national security strategy upon taking office. But ballistic missile defense is like so many component parts of the Contract, an idea that was nurtured for years within conservative think tanks before becoming a part of the Contract and ultimately being pushed by the '94 majority.

Of course, the concept of ballistic missile defense was not unique to the Contract. It began with President Ronald Reagan's Strategic Defense Initiative (SDI) in 1983. But that system was conceived to thwart a different threat, a massive Soviet first strike of ballistic missiles with multiple-warhead payloads capable of hitting different targets. The original thinking behind SDI was to create a defensive system with interceptors orbiting in space, patrolling the seas, and in entrenched land-based positions. Although skeptics dubbed SDI "Star Wars" and doubted its efficacy, Reagan won approval for tens of billions of dollars for research and development throughout the 1980s. But the Soviet Union's demise in 1989 reduced the threat of a massive first-strike launch, and many began to question the utility of continued research and development. Many early tests of the underlying technology raised questions too. The concept of shooting a small projectile into the path of an oncoming missile was daunting enough on paper. In the real world it proved extremely difficult. Most early tests failed, even when the tests were dumbed down to increase the opportunities for success. Operation Desert Storm revived interest in some form of ballistic missile defense, but that was short-lived. The Clinton years witnessed numerous efforts to diminish the role of ballistic missile defense.

Congressional Republicans resisted those efforts as best they could and were often portrayed as the starry-eyed dupes of defense contractors for pushing an idea that not only was costly but also seemed utterly unhinged from the hard realities of nuclear deterrence. The conventional (though diabolical) wisdom held that mutually assured destruction (MAD) was the safest path to deterrence—that is, both sides needed large supplies of nuclear warheads that could be launched from land, sea, or air so that if any nation launched a first strike, the targeted country could pulverize the aggressor with a second-strike response. (As President George W. Bush would later put it, "Security of both the United States and the Soviet Union was based on a grim premise: that neither side would fire nuclear weapons at each other, because doing so would mean the end of both nations.") Under this theory, ballistic missile defense presented a more grave strategic threat than the missiles themselves. The nation that pursued ballistic missile defense would be advertising its interest in surviving a retaliatory second strike, which would suggest to other nuclear nations that their existing stockpiles had to be enlarged to increase the probability of delivering a retaliatory strike of sufficient magnitude to overwhelm the attacking nation's ballistic missile defense systems.

Republicans who learned at the feet of Ronald Reagan had long since rejected MAD as an unworkable nuclear national security policy. And with the dissolution of the Soviet Union came fears about the proliferation of nuclear material to rogue nations or terrorist groups eager to strike or blackmail the United States or its allies. Those fears multiplied when deliverable warheads tipped with biological or chemical agents were added to the equation. Congressional Republicans tried to force the Clinton White House to respond to this threat, but Clinton offered only delaying tactics, staking his nuclear strategy on MAD-induced dogmas. The Contract with America revived the concept of ballistic missile defense, and muscular GOP support for the idea, from that point forward, pushed it ever higher on the national security agenda.

Conservatives who specialize in national defense issues regard ballistic missile defense as a signal achievement of the Contract. Most other conservatives have forgotten that ballistic missile defense was even in the Contract. Critics consider this victory nothing less than appalling: a wasteful, destabilizing obsession that diverted countless billions from other military priorities (troop strength, equipment, training) and gave the nation a false sense of security that it was doing something to confront the terrorist menace. Still, whatever one thinks of ballistic missile defense, it is undeniable that it was a startling change to America's national security strategy—indeed, a change that was utterly unimaginable before the Contract was written or the GOP won its first combined congressional majority in 1994.

### The Patriot Push

The 1991 Gulf War spurred renewed debate over the feasibility and desirability of ballistic missile defense. The political impetus behind SDI had waned as the Soviet threat had diminished. But then came Operation Desert Storm, when Patriot antimissile batteries appeared to successfully intercept Iraq's Scud missiles. (The Patriots, later analysis would reveal, performed poorly, failing to intercept a single missile. Iraqi Scuds that appeared to have been downed often blew apart in flight because they malfunctioned; Patriots that did engage the target missed their proper flight trajectory and blew up in the neighborhood of incoming Scuds, thus knocking them accidentally off course. But this information would not be confirmed for quite some time.) Proponents of SDI technology used the apparent success of the Patriots to galvanize public support for an antimissile system and congressional interest in a new burst of funding. They also argued that the demise of the Soviet Union had not erased the threat of a ballistic missile attack but merely changed the nature of the threat, since terrorists or rogue states could illicitly procure weapons technology.

George H. W. Bush's administration was looking toward a technology known as GPALS (Global Protection Against Limited Strikes), a space-based system employing so-called Brilliant Pebbles to intercept missiles high above the planet, and also ground-based technology to intercept any missiles that evaded GPALS. In his State of the Union Address on January 29, 1991, President Bush urged Congress to pursue a more vigorous SDI program:

Most Americans know instinctively why we are in the Gulf. They know we need to build a new, enduring peace—based not on arms races and confrontation, but on shared principles and the rule of law. Our progress in this great struggle is the result of years of vigilance and a steadfast commitment to a strong defense. Now, with remarkable technological advances like the Patriot missile, we can defend against ballistic missile attacks aimed at innocent civilians. Looking forward, I have directed that the SDI program be refocused on providing protection from limited ballistic missile strikes—whatever their source. Let us pursue an SDI program that can deal with any future threat to the United States, to our forces overseas, and to our friends and allies. The quality of American technology, thanks to the American worker, has enabled us to successfully deal with difficult military conditions and help minimize loss of precious life.

The president's speech generated considerable debate, much of it turning on the age-old questions of cost, technological feasibility, and whether pursuing such a system would mean that the United States would be violating the Anti-Ballistic Missile (ABM) Treaty of 1972, which forbade both the United States and the Soviet Union from deploying a national ballistic missile defense. Also generating debate was Bush's budget request for $4.7 billion for SDI. Many Democrats denounced Bush's plan. For example, on February 5, 1991, Senator John Kerry of Massachusetts said the space-based Brilliant Pebbles Program "has not proceeded much beyond the view-graph state" and "will threaten the ABM Treaty long before it threatens the Iraqi Scuds that the Patriots have handled so successfully." Pointing out that the Patriot system was ground-based, not space-based, Kerry argued, "The success of the Patriot in the Gulf has demonstrated only that we can defeat a limited, short-range, decoy-free, nonnuclear, surface-to-surface Scud attack. This success should not be used as a justification for the grandiose, costly, and destabilizing SDI Program—most recently reincarnated under the name Global Protection Against Limited Strikes—which the Bush administration continues to pursue."

Two months later, Senator Joseph Lieberman of Connecticut applauded the Patriot technology (the lead Patriot contractor, Raytheon, was based in Connecticut), but he disputed the need or desirability of moving beyond its capabilities. "It is important to keep the Patriot in perspective," he said. "If there is a more immediate Third World threat, it probably comes from countries or terrorist groups that may smuggle weapons of mass destruction into the United States. . . . Counterterrorism methods and devices are the antidote to this, of course, not an ambitious antiballistic missile system. The success of the Patriot also does not mean that we should abrogate the Anti-Ballistic Missile Treaty, which already allows for 100 ground-based antiballistic missiles."

Democrats in the House also questioned the necessity or advisability of spending billions more for a system that, to date, had produced so few technological breakthroughs. During one hearing on SDI in May 1991, Representative John Conyers of Michigan argued, "The administration has been successful in convincing Congress to give it billions of dollars for Star Wars, but the program has proved remarkably unsuccessful in producing much of anything with these funds. SDI has pulled, in effect, a 'reverse Rumpelstiltskin'; it has spun gold into straw."

The Republicans were, of course, in the minority in both the Senate and the House, but they defended the push for a reinvigorated SDI, citing the Patriots' apparent success, the demise of the Soviet Union, and the need to confront newer threats. In February, Senator Dan Coats of Indiana proclaimed, "The American people have seen the evidence—ballistic missile defense works. . . . Despite this clear evidence that ballistic missile defenses are becoming more necessary and technically feasible, there have been numerous complaints that GPALS will violate the ABM Treaty—that it is more important to preserve the ABM Treaty as ratified in 1972 than to defend American citizens and friends. The point should be added, however, that the ABM Treaty was intended to be a living document that can be amended to meet changing conditions. . . . The ABM Treaty was negotiated and ratified in a very different strategic and international political environment. It is in the mutual interest of the United States and the Soviet Union to proceed with a cooperative transition away from the existing ABM Treaty."

In the House, Representative Jon Kyl, Arizona Republican, took to the floor to express his frustration with the Democratic majority, which had whittled President Bush's SDI budget request down to $2.66 billion, 44 percent below the request: "Up until this year, SDI, the strategic defense initiative, sometimes called Star Wars, was an abstract concept. But on one night during this war, we saw film footage of Israel, part of Haifa being destroyed by the debris from falling Scud missiles. And then, breathlessly, the people on CNN broke away to live coverage of an American Patriot missile actually intercepting a Scud missile and destroying it. So the whole world saw it, number one, that if you are under attack by ballistic missiles, you want something to defend you. Second, they saw that ballistic missile defenses can work. . . . Apparently some of our colleagues were sleeping through the war."

Coats's and Kyl's remarks encapsulated conservatives' key complaints: that Democrats were standing in the way of a program that could prove vital to America' national defense because of their nickel-and-diming and because they were unnecessarily clinging to the ABM Treaty. Conservative defense analyst Frank Gaffney—who would advise House Republicans on the defense component of the Contract with America—addressed these and other issues in a June 10, 1991, op-ed in the *Washington Times.* Arguing that the Democratic Congress had "consistently provided less funding for SDI than was needed and requested," Gaffney said that "congressional Democrats have taken the lead in imposing legislative restrictions intended to inhibit—if not prevent—the SDI program." Feasibility was not the problem, he claimed; politics was. "The real issue is not whether near-term space-based defenses can be made to work; testing to date inspires high confidence that they can. . . . Instead, the impetus seems to stem from a theological attachment to the ABM Treaty, which precludes the United States from obtaining effective territorial defenses."

The delicacy of the ABM Treaty was a major stumbling block at this time. Skeptics of SDI could always cite cost problems in holding back funding, but the politically more potent argument was that moving on SDI could undermine long-standing arms control agreements with the new Russian Federation. Polls showed that most voters were willing to spend billions to create a national ballistic missile defense system but that they were reluctant to pursue this if it appeared doing so could ruin the delicate arms control balance struck with the Russians. Combining the two arguments (high cost and fouling up arms control treaties) gave the Democrats a strong countervailing argument. Even within the Bush administration, the question of violating or subverting the ABM Treaty was by no means settled. In fact, the administration skirted the issue, as revealed by this question-and-answer session between Senator Carl Levin, Michigan Democrat, and Colin Powell, then chairman of the Joint Chiefs of Staff, during a September 29, 1991, hearing before the Senate Armed Services Committee:

> *Senator Levin:* I gather the administration has decided that they're going to seek a change in the Anti-Ballistic Missile Treaty, to seek amendments in that treaty. . . . Have you decided whether or not it is in our interest to withdraw from the Anti-Ballistic Missile Treaty if we are unsuccessful in negotiating modifications to it? . . .
>
> *General Powell:* The Joint Chiefs of Staff have not made a judgment on that question, nor have we been asked to yet.
>
> *Senator Levin:* Okay. Is the reason you haven't made a judgment only because you haven't been asked or you think it's premature to make that judgment?
>
> *General Powell:* One, we haven't been asked, and two, we haven't self-generated the question yet. I think it's much more appropriate at this point to enter discussions with the Soviet Union to see what their thinking is in light of recent developments with respect to strategic defenses, and if there are ways to modify the ABM Treaty or change the ABM Treaty or do something to the ABM Treaty that is acceptable to both sides then it is in the interest of strategic stability. And I look forward to seeing those negotiations begin and I hope they produce a result.
>
> *Senator Levin:* Is it fair to say that it's your position that the wiser course is to first pursue the negotiations and then make a decision following those negotiations what is in our best interests relative to any withdrawal from the ABM Treaty?
>
> *General Powell:* I wouldn't prejudge what the Secretary of Defense, the President, or other advisers to the President might wish to do in the course of the negotiation.

Without a Republican majority in Congress—and because it did not take a strong stand on such fundamental issues as the ABM Treaty—the Bush administration was hamstrung in its efforts to push for a strong ballistic missile defense. Then George H. W. Bush was replaced by a new president, who, it became clear, saw little need for national missile defense.

### *"We're Going to Deploy Them, End of Argument!"*

On May, 13, 1993, precisely 113 days into the new administration, Bill Clinton's defense secretary, Les Aspin, announced the death of SDI as President Reagan had envisioned it and as Republicans had fought for it. The Clinton administration, he said, was "renaming and refocusing the Strategic Defense Initiative Office to reflect the Clinton Administration's changes in the priorities." The office would be renamed the Ballistic Missile Defense Organization and, more significantly, would have a diminished bureaucratic status, as it would no longer report directly to the secretary of defense. "The fate of Star Wars was sealed by the collapse of the Soviet Union," Aspin said. Instead, the Clinton administration would focus on so-called theater ballistic missile defense—"not the massive program of space-based weapons that Ronald Reagan envisioned" but a defense that could provide protection for our troops on any given battlefield.

This shift may sound subtle, but it effectively halted the push for a system that could provide defenses for the entire country. The new Clinton emphasis on theater systems built on the apparent success of Patriots in the Gulf War and turned away from the heretofore unsuccessful pursuit of a national or regional ballistic missile defense capability. And while Republicans favored deploying a theater defense system as well as a ballistic missile system, they feared that the elevation of theater defense within a small overall SDI budget gave them virtually no hope of achieving the technologically daunting and expensive task of deploying a national missile defense program. This was bureaucratic starvation: The Clinton administration said publicly that it hadn't ruled out a national system but continued to point to problems with technology and cost overruns. When it came time for the 1994 fiscal year budget, President Clinton signed without complaint the Democratic Congress's $2.6 billion allocation for the newly minted Ballistic Missile Defense program, even though this amount was $1.2 billion less than he had requested and $2.5 billion less than the Bush budgets had projected costs to be.

The Clinton administration also precluded any prospect of creating or deploying a national ballistic missile defense system by demanding strict adherence to the ABM Treaty. When asked whether the United States would "honor or amend existing ABM treaties" with the former

Soviet Union (then known as the Commonwealth of Independent States), Defense Secretary Aspin replied, "If we have a missile defense of the United States that goes beyond the current limit of one site, we're going to have to get an amendment to the ABM Treaty. What we're doing now is developing theater missile defenses and that's fine, we don't have any problem with the ABM Treaty. If we go to the next stage, which is to protect the continental United States against ballistic missile attacks from a terrorist state, and to do that well, I think will require some changes in the ABM Treaty. But we would do that working with Russia and with the other nuclear states to make sure that it's consistent with what they want to do too."

It was in this context that the Republicans decided to include a provision in the defense section of the Contract with America calling for deployment of a national ballistic missile defense system as soon as technologically feasible. The Democrats had control of the White House and both houses of Congress, and they had effectively killed national missile defense. "The Democrats were doing everything they could to tie our hands on ballistic missile defense," recalls Bob Livingston, the former chairman of the Appropriations Committee. Livingston wrote the national security section of the Contract. "It was my initiative. There was no discussion about getting ballistic missile defense into the Contract. It was totally logical. It was like Reagan and the Pershing missiles in the '80s: We're going to deploy them, end of argument!"

Significantly, the policy laid out in the Contract went beyond what the first Bush administration had done, since it dismissed the potential harm deployment of a system would have on the ABM Treaty. In essence, SDI hawks argued that the ABM Treaty was a relic of the Cold War, an agreement reached with a country that no longer existed, and that the United States had every right—indeed, every obligation—to deploy a ballistic missile defense system. Under this policy, Republicans were attempting to commit the nation to investing tens of billions of dollars on SDI-related research, development, and deployment as well as a confrontational arms control strategy vis-à-vis the Russian Federation. The Clinton administration wanted nothing of the kind. Republicans knew this was a long-term project (costs remained high and the politics were, to put it mildly, unsettled), but the GOP revolutionaries had tenacity.

## *The Long Fight Begins*

The Republicans began their fight immediately upon seizing the majority. On the day they took control of the House, January 4, 1995, House Speaker Newt Gingrich and other GOP House leaders sent President Clinton a letter outlining their intention to block any negotiations with the Russian Federation that might preclude accelerated development and deployment of a ballistic missile defense system:

> Dear Mr. President: We appreciate your letter of October 22, 1994 responding to the letter of September 19, 1994 signed by a bipartisan group of legislators regarding the 1972 Anti-Ballistic Missile (ABM) Treaty and constraints on theatre missile defenses. We welcome your assurances that your Administration is not going to rush the process of negotiating changes to the 1972 ABM Treaty. . . . We respectfully suggest that further negotiations on either the demarcation or multilateralization efforts, or any other efforts that bear on the viability of the ABM Treaty, be suspended until the new Congress has had an opportunity to examine these questions with care.

Clinton responded on January 26, addressing his letter to Majority Leader Dick Armey:

> The Administration is firmly committed to two fundamental objectives in the area of missile defenses. First, we believe it is critical to preserve the viability and integrity of the ABM Treaty. This important Treaty remains a cornerstone of U.S. security policy and our new relationship with Russia. Second, we are committed to deploying highly effective theater missile defense systems (TMDs).

Gingrich and other GOP leaders then sent a letter to all House Republicans outlining the dispute and providing the marching orders:

> One of the highest priority defense capabilities currently under development and being fielded by the Department of Defense is theater missile defense (TMD). The threat posed by the proliferation of ballistic missiles is expanding. Such proliferation underscores the

importance of fielding, at the earliest practicable date, advanced
TMD systems. . . . Unfortunately, the U.S. ability to field highly effective TMD systems is being jeopardized by the Clinton Administration. They have also proposed to "multilateralize" the ABM Treaty.

The debate was now fully joined, but progress on the issue slowed
considerably. In pursuit of a balanced budget, Republicans were willing to
cut everything, and cost estimates on ballistic missile defense now were
through the roof. As a result, Republicans dropped the ballistic missile
defense section from the National Security Revitalization Act, the bill that
it brought to the House floor to fulfill its obligations under the Contract.
This omission was one of the rare occasions when a Contract provision did
not make it to the floor during the first hundred days. It would return later.

Costs were not the only reason the Republicans lost momentum on
missile defense in 1995. That year, Clinton received a crucial piece of evidence that he and other SDI skeptics used to stall legislative movement
toward accelerated development and deployment: The National Intelligence Estimate, a classified summary of the U.S. intelligence community's
conclusions, projected that "no country, other than the major declared
nuclear powers, will develop or otherwise acquire a ballistic missile in the
next 15 years that could threaten the contiguous 48 states and Canada. Ballistic missile programs of other countries are focused on regional security
concerns and are not expected to evolve into threats to North America during the period of this estimate." (Though the report was classified when
Clinton received it, the Brookings Institution later obtained and published
the document.) The National Intelligence Estimate did not deny that rogue
nations like Iran and Iraq might want ballistic missiles, but it reaffirmed that
those regimes would need at least fifteen years to develop them. As for the
established nuclear powers, the intelligence report said that Russia and
China could hit the United States but weren't likely to do so.

Possessing this intelligence estimate, Clinton felt no need to accelerate development and deployment of a ballistic missile defense system. On
top of concerns about abrogating the ABM Treaty and disrupting relations
with Russia, and about the soaring cost estimates, the president now had
the nation's best intelligence estimate saying that the risk of ballistic missile
attack from major powers was small and from so-called rogue nations
almost negligible. In sum, Clinton's ballistic missile defense policy

appeared politically bulletproof. (Appearances can be deceiving, however. As would later become clear, the intelligence community based the National Intelligence Estimate on some misguided assumptions. The United States should not have been so dismissive of potential threats.)

Although the Republicans excluded missile defense from the National Security Revitalization Act they brought to the floor of the House, they would attempt to include Contract language on ballistic missile defense in the catchall budget bill, calling for deployment of a national defense system "as soon as possible." This was the budget bill that provoked two Clinton vetoes, two government shutdowns, and an eventual GOP capitulation. As with much of the policy shoehorned into the budget bill, the Republicans had to eliminate ballistic missile defense from the final spending bills negotiated with Clinton. But the debate over the budget gave Republicans a new opportunity to make their case for ballistic missile defense. Representative Duncan Hunter of California, for instance, urged his colleagues not to cling needlessly to the ABM Treaty: "There are two parties to the ABM Treaty, us and the Soviet Union, yet there are countries like Libya, North Korea, China, and others that are developing theater ballistic missiles that could be targeted on our troops. They are not signatories to the ABM agreement and they do not care what kind of restrictions we must put on. In fact, they would like us to put restrictions on our defensive systems."

And they would keep up the ballistic missile argument. In the spring of 1996, the Senate Armed Services Committee and the House National Security Committee approved stand-alone ballistic missile defense bills that set a goal of deploying a national missile defense system by 2003. But the bills, labeled the "Defend America Act," died before ever coming to the floor. Cost was a big reason. The Congressional Budget Office, now under Republican supervision, projected future costs of up to $60 billion to develop and deploy an SDI system, a figure that rattled deficit-conscious Republicans and made even ardent SDI advocates do a double take. Still, Republicans fought to increase funding for some system development to defend against short-range combat ballistic missiles, and in the defense authorization bill—the main policy bill on defense matters—they included language mirroring the Defend America bill's call for accelerated development and deployment of an antimissile system. But Clinton vetoed the bill over this dispute. When the GOP relented on ballistic missile defense, the bill proceeded.

## Turning Point

The battle took a crucial turn in 1997. Though no one could have foreseen it at the time, decisions taken on the ballistic missile defense issue not only dramatically altered the course of U.S. policy on this issue but also helped determine the future civilian leadership of the Pentagon and contributed in no small way toward the U.S. decision to invade and occupy Iraq in 2003.

The salient aspect of the 1997 debate on ballistic missile defense was the GOP Congress's decision to create a bipartisan blue-ribbon panel to evaluate the ballistic missile threat posed by other nations and terrorist organizations. Clinton agreed to the commission in hopes of slowing down GOP momentum on the issue, which had been building with each and every debate. The panel's nine members, nominated by the bipartisan congressional leadership and appointed by CIA Director George Tenet, included five Republicans and four Democrats: Donald H. Rumsfeld, chairman; Barry M. Blechman; Air Force General Lee Butler (retired); Richard L. Garwin; William R. Graham; William Schneider Jr.; Air Force General Larry D. Welch (retired); Paul D. Wolfowitz; and former CIA director R. James Woolsey. (In the Bush administration, Rumsfeld would become the secretary of defense, Wolfowitz would become the deputy secretary of defense, and the commission's staff director, Steven A. Cambone, would become deputy undersecretary for defense policy under Rumsfeld.)

The Rumsfeld Commission's mandate was clear: to "assess the nature and magnitude of the existing and emerging ballistic missile threat to the United States," including those missiles "deployed on the territory of a potentially hostile state," from a surface vessel, submarine, or aircraft off the U.S. coastline, or "by a potentially hostile nation on the territory of a third party to reduce the range required of its ballistic missiles to strike the United States." The commission had access to all relevant classified information and was allowed to reach its own conclusions about data collected by different analysts studying different regions and different threats. In other words, the commission intentionally cross-referenced "hard data" collected in one region or about one type of terrorist group against data from another region or another type of terrorist group, and also compared the intelligence with reports from outside experts. The goal was to see if intelligence analysts were missing or underestimating the possibility that rogue states or terrorist groups could obtain weapons technology or expertise from other nations. As a means to consider how serious the threat could actually be if intelligence had not correctly analyzed the situation, the commission also developed hypothetical scenarios in which known arms producers shared weapons technology, expertise, and delivery vehicles (ballistic missiles) with terrorists or rogue states.

Donald Rumsfeld and his fellow commissioners unanimously concluded that estimates of future threats from ballistic missiles were too passive, too bureaucratic, that they failed to assume a higher level of cooperation. The commission's 307-page report, issued in July 1998, was classified. But its key conclusions, reached unanimously and published in a 23-page executive summary, were not:

- The United States faced a "growing threat" from nations such as Iraq, Iran, and North Korea and a continued threat from states like Russia and China.
- The intelligence community had underestimated threats posed by these "emerging capabilities."
- Ballistic missile technologies were developing faster than policy-makers had been led to believe.
- The intelligence community's inability to properly assess the threat showed that the United States needed to make dramatic improvements in intelligence gathering and analysis "in terms of both resources and methodology."
- The United States should not expect advance warning—through intelligence intercepts or surveillance—of ballistic missile development or deployment by hostile nation states, rogue states, or terrorist groups.

The Rumsfeld Commission's central conclusion was that the 1995 National Intelligence Estimate, also classified, had been wrong when it predicted that the United States would not face a serious ballistic missile threat for at least fifteen years. The commission's executive summary did not name the 1995 National Intelligence Estimate specifically, but it clearly referred to that report's conclusions when it said the contemporary threat was more dangerous "than has been reported in estimates" and noticeably "differs from published intelligence estimates." The executive summary concluded, "As a result of our intensive study over the last six months we are unanimous in our assessment of the threat, an assessment which differs from published intelligence estimates."

The commission said that it had used a "somewhat more comprehensive methodology" than the intelligence community had employed to assess risks. It also reported that it had taken "more fully into account three crucial factors":

- "Newer ballistic missile and weapons of mass destruction (WMD) development programs no longer follow the patterns initially set by the U.S. and the Soviet Union"—that is, a nation or terrorist group did not need much time to develop a weapons program because it did not need to develop lots of missiles or even especially accurate missiles in order to pose a significant threat.
- "Foreign assistance is not a wild card. It is a fact." In other words, anyone trying to develop a missile program could get "extensive technical assistance from outside sources."
- "Nations are increasingly able to conceal important elements of their ballistic missile and associated WMD programs and are highly motivated to do so."

Having taken all these factors into account, the Rumsfeld Commission was "able to partially bridge a number of intelligence gaps." The commission concluded that despite the intelligence community's earlier estimates, the nations currently developing ballistic missile capabilities "would be able to inflict major destruction on the U.S. within about five years of a decision to acquire such a capability (10 years in the case of Iraq)." But the most important part of the report was not the assessment of what specific capabilities America's enemies might or might not have at the moment but rather the broader conclusion that the United States remained vulnerable because U.S. intelligence services could not accurately assess the threats. "The Intelligence Community's ability to provide timely and accurate estimates of ballistic missile threats to the U.S. is eroding," the executive summary said. Worse, the commission concluded that it was virtually impossible for America to develop credible estimates of ballistic missile threats in dictatorships or in nations where neither the United States nor international inspection agencies had regular or even intermittent access. Highlighting the intelligence community's struggles with monitoring current threats, the report cited recent instances in which nations had demonstrated significant progress on ballistic missiles. For example, Pakistan had test-launched a medium-range ballistic missile in April 1998, and North Korea had deployed a three-stage Taep'o dong 1 missile on August 31, 1998. The third-stage test failed, but the attempt to launch an armed satellite into orbit occurred well before the U.S. intelligence community anticipated.

The Rumsfeld Commission's report drew major coverage in the news and hit with the force of an earthquake. It fundamentally altered the political dynamic. Republicans now believed they had solid evidence to back up their stubborn pursuit of a national missile defense system to be deployed at the earliest practicable time. And they used this evidence to push their case in Congress for *deployment*, not just development, of a national ballistic missile defense.

In 1998, Senate Republicans were unable to defeat a Democratic filibuster on a bill, the American Missile Protection Act, which would have made it U.S. policy to deploy a national missile defense system as soon as feasible. But a similar bill was passed out of committee the following year. The full Senate approved it, 97–3, but only after an amendment was added certifying that the United States would continue negotiations with the Russian Federation to reduce offensive nuclear weapons and that deployment of any ballistic missile system had to be funded through the annual budget process (again, the ABM orthodoxy and cost concerns held sway). And in 1999, Representative Curt Weldon, Pennsylvania Republican, introduced deployment legislation that passed the full House by a vote of 317–105. The House and Senate bills were merged, and the Senate language on continuing U.S.-Russian negotiations and adhering to the annual budget process prevailed.

President Clinton signed this measure on July 23, 1999, but ballistic missile defense advocates immediately protested. Clinton made it clear that the "deployment" language was nonbinding because the annual budget process made no room for the tens of billions of dollars required to deploy a national system. In essence, Clinton said the bill called for deployment of a ballistic missile defense system, except when he decided it didn't.

### The Rumsfeld Effect

The Rumsfeld Commission's report had other profound, though less visible, consequences. Most notably, it revived Donald Rumsfeld's career. As Texas governor George W. Bush was putting together his campaign for the presidency in 1998 and 1999, he took careful note of the Rumsfeld Commission report. He saw its unanimous, bipartisan conclusions as proof that the United States was indeed vulnerable to ballistic missile threats, and he determined that he would be the Republican candidate to push for deployment of a national defense system to fulfill most of Ronald Reagan's unfinished SDI agenda. It would become the heart of the candidate's national security agenda. In calling for a strong missile defense during a speech at the National Press Club on May 23, 2000, Bush echoed the Rumsfeld Commission's conclusions:

> There's broad agreement that our nation needs a new approach to nuclear security that matches a new era. *When it comes to nuclear weapons, the world has changed faster than U.S. policy. The emerging security threats to the United States, to its friends and allies, and even to Russia, now come from rogue states, terrorist groups, and other adversaries seeking weapons of mass destruction.* It is time to leave the Cold War behind. America must build effective missile defenses based on the best available options at the earliest possible date. It is possible to build a missile defense and defuse confrontation with Russia. America should do both [emphasis added].

Rumsfeld's work on the commission, numerous GOP sources confirm, put him almost immediately on the short list of potential secretaries of defense should Bush win the presidency. "This put Rumsfeld in the thick of it," one top Republican familiar with national security policy told me. "It was a perfect entrée for him to move into the SecDef [Secretary of Defense] position," said another, adding that Rumsfeld was "one of the few prominent Republicans who understood that these [arms control] agreements don't work."

Sure enough, when he took over the Oval Office, Bush named Donald Rumsfeld his secretary of defense. He also appointed Paul Wolfowitz and Steven A. Cambone to senior Defense Department positions, and the three veterans of the Rumsfeld Commission formed a hard-driving policy troika within the Pentagon.

Like Rumsfeld, President Bush saw new threats in new places and fretted that U.S. policy was trapped in a Cold War time warp. The time had come for a complete review of Cold War assumptions about arms control and defense, he believed, and if that meant abrogating the ABM Treaty, so be it. He also committed his administration to building a national ballistic missile defense system. All of this occurred well before 9/11. In fact, Bush declared this new policy emphatically in the first major national security speech of his presidency, delivered at the National Defense University in Washington on May 1, 2001.

To emphasize the point of how radically the world had changed, he asked his audience to "think back some thirty years to a far different time in a far different world," to a time when "the United States and the Soviet Union were locked in a hostile rivalry." The tension between the two superpowers was so great, he said, that "we even went so far as to codify this relationship in a 1972 ABM Treaty, based on the doctrine that our very survival would best be insured by leaving both sides completely open and vulnerable to nuclear attack. The threat was real and vivid." But, the president pointed out, at that time "few other nations had nuclear weapons and most of those who did were responsible allies, such as Britain and France." Flashing forward to the present, Bush said that we were now in "a vastly different world" but "still a dangerous world, a less certain, a less predictable one." He recounted the growing threats:

> More nations have nuclear weapons and still more have nuclear aspirations. Many have chemical and biological weapons. Some already have developed the ballistic missile technology that would allow them to deliver weapons of mass destruction at long distances and at incredible speeds. And a number of these countries are spreading these technologies around the world.
>
> Most troubling of all, the list of these countries includes some of the world's least responsible states. Unlike the Cold War, today's most urgent threat stems not from thousands of ballistic missiles in the Soviet hands, but from a small number of missiles in the hands of these states, states for whom terror and blackmail are a way of life. They seek weapons of mass destruction to intimidate their neighbors, and to keep the United States and other responsible nations from helping allies and friends in strategic parts of the world.

Again the president was echoing the Rumsfeld Commission. The panel's report had argued that rogue states who had missiles were a threat to international security not so much because they could destroy America or Asia or Europe or the Middle East but rather because such weapons could destabilize these regions or give those who held them a dangerous new trump card to play in games of geopolitical intimidation.

In this new world, said Bush, "Cold War deterrence is no longer enough." He declared, "Today's world requires a new policy, a broad strategy of active nonproliferation, counterproliferation, and defenses. We must work together with other like-minded nations to deny weapons of terror from those seeking to acquire them. We must work with allies and friends who wish to join with us to defend against the harm they can inflict. And together we must deter anyone who would contemplate their use." But most important, the president maintained, the United States needed "a new framework that allows us to build missile defenses to counter the different threats of today's world." Bush made clear that he would not allow the ABM Treaty to block this necessary advance: "We must move beyond the constraints of the thirty-year-old ABM Treaty. This treaty does not recognize the present, or point us to the future. It enshrines the past. No treaty that prevents us from addressing today's threats, that prohibits us from pursuing promising technology to defend ourselves, our friends, and our allies, is in our interests or in the interests of world peace."

The president also called for reducing America's nuclear arsenal as a sign that the United States was interested in peace, but he quickly returned to the subject of missile defense, emphasizing that deployment was a priority for the new Bush administration. "Several months ago," Bush said, "I asked Secretary of Defense Rumsfeld to examine all available technologies and basing modes for effective missile defenses that could protect the United States, our deployed forces, our friends and our allies. The Secretary has explored a number of complementary and innovative approaches . . . [and] has identified near-term options that could allow us to deploy an initial capability against limited threats. In some cases, we can draw on already established technologies. . . . We have more work to do to determine the final form the defenses might take. . . . We will evaluate what works and what does not. We know that some approaches will not work. We also know that we will be able to build on our successes. When ready, and working with Congress, we will deploy missile defenses to strengthen global security and stability."

At the core of President Bush's speech at the National Defense University was concern about the issue on which the Rumsfeld Commission had focused: the intelligence community's struggles to assess risk accurately.

Since the Western world had an abysmal track record in stopping the flow of hardware and missile expertise, and only limited success in blocking the movement of fissile material or chemical and biological agents, the Rumsfeld Commission assumed that the quickest and most reliable way to remove the threat that crude ballistic missiles could be used to wreak havoc or intimidate was to rapidly develop and deploy ballistic missile defenses at home and abroad. The commission's highly critical appraisal of the 1995 National Intelligence Estimate had deeply affected President Bush's view of the intelligence system. And it wasn't just the commission's report. Rumsfeld, Wolfowitz, and Cambone, now at the Pentagon, continued to view the intelligence community with suspicion. After all, they felt, U.S. intelligence had missed the potential threat of ballistic missiles and thus left the country more vulnerable than it should have been.

Not incidentally, Rumsfeld's hostility toward the intelligence community would become an important factor during the run-up to Operation Iraqi Freedom. When CIA and Defense Intelligence Agency estimates arrived downplaying Iraq's ability to produce, procure, or possess weapons of mass destruction, Rumsfeld was afraid the intelligence community was making the same mistakes his commission had discovered regarding the ballistic missile threat back in 1995. Were analysts again unwilling to consider worst-case scenarios about concealment and outside financial or technical support? While it's ludicrous to suggest that Rumsfeld's commission work led him to propose going to war with Iraq, it's equally ludicrous to suggest that conclusions he had reached studying ballistic missile threats in no way shaped his view of the potential threat Iraq posed. Consider that in a post-9/11 world, Rumsfeld shared the president's view that the United States could not wait for a "wake-up call" when dealing with weapons of mass destruction policy and thus had a duty to assume the worst about potential foes.

Let there be no doubt, the Rumsfeld Commission of 1998 has had a profound effect on American national security and foreign policy.

### The Contract's Long Shadow

On December 13, 2001, President Bush appeared in the Rose Garden with his national security team to announce that the United States had formally withdrawn from the ABM Treaty, paving the way for accelerated work toward deployment of a ballistic missile defense system. "I have concluded the ABM Treaty hinders our government's ability to develop ways to protect our people from future terrorist or rogue state missile attacks," the president said. This momentous decision did not merely reflect the influence of the Rumsfeld Commission's work. It had been something that congressional Republicans had been fighting for tenaciously for nearly a decade.

That same day, in Moscow, Russian president Vladimir Putin responded with minimal disappointment, despite the fact that Bush's withdrawal from the ABM Treaty meant the death of an entire generation of U.S.-Russian arms control assumptions. He did say that "we believe this decision to be mistaken," but his response was gentle, the language understated. "As is known," Putin said, "Russia, like the United States and unlike other nuclear powers, has long possessed an effective system to overcome antimissile defense. So I can say with full confidence that the decision made by the President of the United States does not pose a threat to the national security of the Russian Federation." The Russian president acknowledged "that the world has been confronted with new threats" and called for continued negotiations over a new strategic framework, confirming that Russia's commitment to a new order was nearly as strong as Bush's.

On December 17, 2002, a year after withdrawing from the ABM Treaty, President Bush announced the culmination of a decade's worth of policy work on behalf of ballistic missile defense. He declared that the United States would begin "to field missile defense capabilities to protect the United States, as well as our friends and allies. . . . While modest, these capabilities will add to America's security and serve as a starting point for improved and expanded capabilities later, as further progress is made in researching and developing missile defense technologies and in light of changes in the threat." By deploying missile defenses, Bush said, the United States was taking action to deal with "the new strategic challenges of the twenty-first century."

In his first three years in office, President Bush spent $34.9 billion for ballistic missile defense development and deployment, nearly tripling the amount Clinton spent on the program in eight years. Congressional Republicans applauded each increase in spending on the project (the 2005 budget allocated $10.5 billion, compared with the 2002 budget's $7.8 billion). Bush and congressional Republicans walked lockstep on the path toward deploying a national ballistic missile defense system.

But as we have seen, for a while it had seemed that virtually any hope for national ballistic missile defense had died. The idea stayed alive only because congressional Republicans persistently advocated ballistic missile defense at a time when the president of the United States, Bill Clinton, wanted to kill it. When a GOP congressional majority emerged in 1994, the Republicans could confront Clinton more directly. That confrontation did not lead to large increases in spending or even dramatic shifts in policy. But it did lead to a gradual shift in the political climate in favor of swifter development and deployment of a national missile defense system. And ultimately it led to the creation of the Rumsfeld Commission, the most influential private commission created in the national security sphere in the post–Cold War era and quite possibly the most influential since the end of World War II.

According to the conventional wisdom, the Contract with America did not change Washington or the nation very much. Reporters' instant analysis focused almost entirely on the number of Contract items passed versus the number proposed in those first days of the Republican Revolution. In almost every piece of contemporary analysis, the Contract was dismissed as a political document useful for one election but of virtually no long-term historical importance. The story of anti–ballistic missile defense by itself reveals the falsity of this analysis and speaks to the indifference many reporters and commentators at the time showed to the Contract's intellectual heft.

If ballistic missile defense had been the only item in the entire document, the Contract would still stand as a critically important political document. Ballistic missile defense against rogue nuclear, chemical, or biological attack is now the global consensus on nuclear deterrence. It hasn't supplanted theories about comparative balance among major nuclear powers, but it has erased MAD as the only theory of nuclear deterrence and promises to alter the technological balance of power between developed nations and rogue states and terrorist organizations that seek to use mass murder or the threat of it to pursue their goals. Hence, an idea from the Contract with America has reshaped global nuclear deterrence, transformed classical arms control theories, and altered the strategic posture of armed forces from Beijing to Islamabad, from New Delhi to Moscow, and most important, from Pyongyang to Tehran.

# 10

# GOD, GUNS, AND GRADES

You can sift and sift the Contract with America and you will find no references to changing America's policies on abortion, gun control, or education. But after the Republicans took over Congress in the fateful election of 1994, they committed themselves to reversing the course America had followed on all three issues since the 1960s. Before Republicans took power in the mid-1990s, America had moved consistently toward a liberal position on each—legalizing abortion, limiting access to firearms, and expanding federal control over class sizes, textbooks, and curriculum. In that sense, the three issues, while not commonly associated with one another, were of a piece for the Republicans, for abortion, gun control, and education spoke to the decades-long clash between liberals and conservatives over cultural values, constitutional law, and centralized federal power. All three issues relate to precise, passionately held definitions of individual liberty—sexuality, self-defense, knowledge. At the same time, they are important to larger questions about how American society should operate: Should the state protect your right to have sexual intercourse even if that means it could lead to abortion? Does your constitutional right to own a firearm carry any limits to protect society from stolen weapons or children from accidental shootings? Does the guarantee of education for all (enshrined in 1954's *Brown v. Board of Education*) allow Washington to interfere with decisions left largely to state and local officials since the nation's founding?

Although the GOP leadership in 1994 made a conscious decision to exclude social issues from the Contract, conservative Republicans, upon taking power in the House of Representatives, were committed to pursuing reforms on abortion, gun control, and education with an unmatched zeal. On the first two issues, at least, their zeal reflected their commitment to the

Republican Party's most loyal and most organized grassroots groups, pro-life and pro-gun activists. But it also reflected their belief that they had the answers on the issues—and the answers weren't the ones the Democrats had been pushing for decades.

The abortion agenda was multipronged: outlaw partial-birth abortion (a late-term abortion procedure in which the unborn child is delivered feet first until the trunk is outside the womb and scissors are then used to puncture the base of the skull so that a medical technician or physician can use a suction tube to vacuum the brain out of the skull); press for parental consent for teen abortions; criminalize the transport of minors across state lines to obtain abortions elsewhere; and establish federally protected fetal rights by punishing anyone who harms a fetus while committing a crime against the mother.

With guns, the agenda was far simpler: halt all movement on expanding gun-control laws; reverse existing gun laws where possible; and shift federal law in favor of crime victims and away from criminals (the Contract contained numerous tough-on-crime measures, virtually all of which have become law).

On the education front, Republicans intended to uproot the D.C.-based bureaucracy and shift funds en masse to state and local governments along the model envisioned with welfare reform: broad federal goals, block-granted funds, and minimal federal interference in testing, curricula, and day-to-day operations.

What sets these three policy areas apart from so much of the rest of the GOP agenda is that President Clinton resisted Republican efforts on all three strenuously, giving no quarter on politics or policy—as he did almost everywhere else he clashed with the new GOP majorities (spending, taxes, budgets, defense, welfare, health care, and so on). These battles were by no means new, but the power of congressional majorities gave Republicans something they had never had before: the ability to establish the terms of debate and set the legislative agenda. This proved enormously valuable in all future abortion and gun-control battles; it proved ruinous in the education debate.

While Republicans have steadily achieved and in some cases enlarged their goals on gun control and abortion, they have been utterly defeated on education. The defeats have been so thorough, so overwhelming, that Republicans have been forced not only to retrench but also to completely redefine the field of battle. When they arrived in power, Republicans sought to reduce federal aid to education and reduce federal intrusiveness. They have done exactly the opposite. For most of the Clinton years, they merely acceded to Democrats' demands for more money without altering the structural relationship of the federal government to the classroom. Under President George W. Bush, Republicans have approved massive increases in federal support for education, tying those increases to rigorous testing standards that apply to all students and all schools. The end result is a complete repudiation of Republican aims: larger budgets, more intrusive rules, less local control and flexibility. Stouthearted Republicans still consider this a partial victory, because they believe tough performance standards will drive schools to reforms that improve basic math, reading, and writing skills. But the truth is, Republicans confronted immovable political realities on education and had to adapt to them in ways they never imagined or would have considered ludicrous when first catapulted into the majority.

These three issues reveal three separate and compelling case studies of aspects of Republican power wielded outside the context of the Contract. In the case of abortion, it's a story of how the steady application of congressional power through oversight hearings and legislation reshaped public debate and forged fundamentally different policy. In the case of gun control and crime, it's a story of using majority power to halt the steady advance of one idea and replace it with another (gun control versus crime control). In the case of education, it's a story of pushing for radical change (abolition of the Department of Education), discovering the political limits of such radicalism, suing for peace with the existing policy construct, and then acceding to a new policy even more hostile to the party's underlying philosophy. Each of these issues moves votes and decides elections. And yet none was part of the Contract. Together they form an essential portrait of the advantages and limits of power and reveal the ways in which the Republican Revolution succeeded or failed in creating subrevolutions in places where voters may have least expected them.

## The Pro-lifers' New Approach

From the earliest days of the emergence of a conservative component of the Republican Party, the party has had important pro-life and pro-gun constituencies. Those constituencies have grown ever larger as the Democratic Party has moved steadily leftward on cultural issues. When Republicans won control of Congress, these two core constituencies had, for the first time ever, real power to change the flow of events, to set the terms of debate on future policy. Rearguard legislative tactics no longer applied, as pro-life and pro-gun bills were now driving the debate. It was now the minority Democratic Party's hard-fought task to make pro-choice and pro-gun-control arguments from the sidelines, where Republicans in the House and Senate (with the exception of the six-year majority from 1981 to 1987) had been arguing for years.

The 1994 election ushered into Congress not only a Republican majority but also a conservative majority within the majority, meaning that even pro-choice and pro-gun-control Republicans (primarily from the Northeastern states) were marginalized and pro-life and pro-gun argumentation and legislation took center stage. The newfound visibility of pro-life and pro-gun arguments proved politically empowering. Republicans have steadily enlarged the ranks of pro-life and pro-gun members within the party. They have also forced Democrats in swing districts to stake out more aggressively pro-life and pro-gun positions to save their seats. This has led to a shift in public opinion away from the pro-choice, pro-gun-control ethos of the early 1990s. It's not that America has suddenly become a pro-life, pro-gun Republic, but in the past decade the GOP majority's countervailing arguments on gun control and abortion have had a profound influence, reversing a three-decade-long leftward shift.

On the surface, public attitudes toward abortion don't look all that different from how they did before the Republican Revolution, but a closer look at the polling data reveals that the public has moved in a more antiabortion direction. Consider these three numbers, the ones most closely watched by advocates on both sides of the issue: In September of 1994, two months before the GOP revolution rocked Capitol Hill and much of America, the CNN/*USA Today*/Gallup poll showed that 33 percent of the American people believed abortion should be legal under any circumstances, 52 percent believed it should be legal only under certain circumstances, and 13 percent believed it should be illegal in all circumstances. In January of 2003, as the nation marked the thirtieth anniversary of *Roe v. Wade,* the landmark Supreme Court decision legalizing abortion in all fifty states, 24 percent believed abortion should be legal under any circumstances, 57 percent believed it should be legal only under certain circumstances, and 18 percent believed it should be illegal in all circumstances. In just nine years, there had been a 9-point shift away from the "legal under any circumstances" ethos and a 10-point shift toward a sense that abortion should be either "legal only under certain circumstances" or "illegal in all circumstances."

And that snapshot actually captured glimmers of good news for prochoice Americans. During the most intense national debates on GOP-driven measures to limit certain abortion rights—partial-birth abortion chief among them—the polling was even more lopsidedly pro-life. In August 1997, for example, only 22 percent said abortion should be legal in all circumstances, while 61 percent said legal only in certain circumstances and 15 percent said illegal in all circumstances. This poll, taken two months before Clinton's second veto of the partial-birth abortion ban, recorded the lowest support for abortion "under any circumstances" since 1975 and the highest "legal only under certain circumstances" number in the history of Gallup polling.

A Zogby International poll from April 2004 revealed similar trends. According to the poll, 56 percent of Americans opposed abortion in all situations or favored an extremely narrow definition of abortion rights (legal only to save the life of the mother or in cases of rape or incest), while 42 percent supported a broader definition of abortion rights (legal for any reason during the first three months of pregnancy, legal for any reason during the first six months of pregnancy, or legal for any reason at any time). Certain demographic groups reflected even stronger pro-life tendencies. Among eighteen- to twenty-nine-year-olds, fully 60 percent of young adults favored a narrow definition of abortion rights, while only 39 percent approved of a more broadly defined set of rights. Among Hispanic Americans, 78 percent supported the narrow set of abortion rights, compared with 21 percent who supported broader rights. And among African-Americans, the ratio was 62 percent to 38 percent in favor of the narrower set of rights.

The Zogby poll also revealed how public attitudes have changed not just about the legality of abortion but also about the cultural/ethical advisability of abortion. These shifts in attitude reflect the Republican majority's emphasis on the intricacies of fetal health and its frequent discussion of breakthroughs in fetal medicine, which have dramatically broadened the scope of public debate on abortion. Zogby asked whether abortions "should not be permitted" after the fetal heartbeat has begun, and 61 percent said yes, while 34 percent said no. When Zogby asked whether abortions "should not be permitted" after fetal brainwaves have been detected, 65 percent said yes and 28 percent said no. Then Zogby asked this highly technical question about fetal pain as it relates to abortion—something pro-life Republicans had made a critical issue through their majority power of investigation and oversight—and found stunning results. The question was this: "There is a growing consensus among scientists that human fetuses can feel pain after 20 weeks in the womb. Do you favor or oppose laws requiring that women who are 20 weeks or more along in their pregnancy be given information about fetal pain before having an abortion?" In response, 77 percent said yes, while only 16 percent said no.

Ralph Reed, chief political strategist for the Christian Coalition in the early and mid-1990s, was the driving force behind the recruitment and mobilization of millions of evangelical Christian voters and the most important grassroots organizer in the post-Reagan era. Legally, the coalition operated as a nonpartisan voter information resource to social conservatives. Politically, it was the most potent GOP organizing force in the nation. Reed talked to me at length about the evolution of abortion politics in America and how GOP control of Congress changed the terms of debate.

"After the *Casey* decision in 1992 we had clearly hit a brick wall in terms of *Roe*," Reed said, referring to *Casey v. Planned Parenthood*, the case that upheld the landmark 1973 case, *Roe v. Wade*, that created a constitutional right to abortion. In *Casey*, the court ruled 5–4 against most state regulations impeding access to abortion, specifically those dealing with twenty-four-hour waiting periods and parental and spousal notification. The court said a state could not impose a restriction on abortion access if "its purpose or effect is to place substantial obstacles in the path of a woman seeking an abortion before the fetus attains viability."

Reed continues: "With Clinton's election, a pro-*Roe* court, and a minimum of four years of Clinton judicial appointments to the Supreme Court, we all realized that the 1980s strategy of trying to elect a Republican president and moving pro-life judges onto the high court—well, there was just no way to do that. We had to develop a Plan B, and as it turned out that Plan B was the partial-birth abortion issue. And the credit really goes to Douglas Johnson of the National Right to Life Committee. He developed the issue. And it moved the pro-life agenda from Hail Mary pass dealing with the high court to a ground game of incremental, gradual victory. And that has remained the strategy. You do what you can do. You seek common-sense restrictions, and as part of the debate the nation's opinion has gradually turned. A larger number of teens are now pro-life than were twenty years ago, and the number of abortions is down in absolute terms and per thousand pregnancies."

Reed has watched the evolution from the perspective of a political operative immersed in what have long been called the culture wars. He organized millions of voters around issues such as abortion, school prayer, pornography, and gay rights.

Another perspective comes from Haley Barbour, former chairman of the Republican National Committee and now governor of Mississippi. Barbour's perspective is one of a Republican who had to make the clichéd concept of the GOP "big tent" a practical, durable reality. It wasn't easy. And nothing has roiled those efforts through the years more than the abortion issue.

Barbour told me, "I said it when I was running for party chairman, I said it as chairman, and I say it now as a governor: If Republicans let abortion be the threshold issue of Republicanism, they need to have their head examined. There are millions of pro-choice Republicans who are just as good Republicans as I am. We worked very hard in the mid-'90s to find an issue about abortion that would demonstrate to the American people that the pro-abortion people were the absolutists. Partial-birth abortion turned out to be the issue."

The pro-life GOP majority has not only shifted public opinion on the legality and the advisability of abortion but has also attempted to codify these changes through its legislative agenda. For example, in May 2004, just a month after the Zogby poll was taken, Republicans introduced legislation called the Unborn Child Pain Awareness Act, which would require every medical professional performing an abortion twenty weeks or more after fertilization to provide the woman specific information about the pain the fetus is likely to feel during the abortion. After reviewing the information, the woman must either accept or refuse a pain-reducing injection directly into the fetus. The bill would apply to all abortions past twenty weeks, regardless of the method used. "There are numerous laws to prevent cruelty to domestic and wild animals," said National Right to Life

Committee legislative director Douglas Johnson, "but no law to prevent well-developed unborn children from suffering excruciating pain as they are torn limb from limb or crushed during abortions." Neither chamber held a vote on the measure in 2004.

The Republicans' most concerted legislative fight was for the Partial-Birth Abortion Act, which they began pushing in their first year in power. In fact, much of the shift in public opinion on abortion is traceable to the debate on this legislation. "Partial-birth abortion was in truth a fight with the courts over the place of religion in the public square," Senator Sam Brownback, Kansas Republican and key player on all abortion issues, told me. "Up until then we were just ceding ground to the court all the time, allowing them to create social changes foisted upon the country that simply don't have popular support. But with partial-birth abortion you had a set of the legislators [who] had in their hearts a different set of values than the ruling establishment had in Washington."

Thus, rather than seeking an end to all abortions—as they had for years, with no success—Republicans tried to outlaw one comparatively rare type of abortion. But their pursuit of more nuanced legislative goals limited the progress of pro-choice forces, established new terms for debate, and gradually reversed public opinion. There are only two issues that the Republican majority considered every year between 1995 and 2003 that it was not required to consider—that is, that weren't part of an annual spending bill. Those two issues are tax cuts and partial-birth abortion. Republicans suffered numerous defeats on both but persisted. Clinton vetoes killed the partial-birth abortion ban twice, but the attendant political controversy worked to the Democrats' and Clinton's disadvantage, as for the first time in post–*Roe v. Wade* history abortion rights advocates were routinely described as outside the mainstream, slavishly devoted to a limitless definition of abortion rights. As the process moved forward, the testimony about the partial-birth abortion ban was nearly as important as the legislative debate itself. For the first time in congressional history, voices questioning medical and ethical aspects of abortion were given center stage.

The House Judiciary Subcommittee on the Constitution convened on June 15, 1995, to take testimony on a bill introduced by Representative Charles Canady of Florida that would ban partial-birth abortion unless the life of the woman was in jeopardy, and would make it a crime punishable by two years in prison for any physician or medical technician to perform the procedure. The testimony established new parameters in the abortion debate. No longer would it be an antiseptic discussion of legal rights or an emotional discourse about the difficulties of obtaining an abortion before *Roe v. Wade*. It would now include precise medical evaluations of a method of abortion most Americans found abhorrent. And though the testimony was about one infrequently performed procedure (at least when compared with all abortions annually), it became a new marker in a larger national debate about the fundamentals of abortion. This has had, as the polling data has shown, a sizable effect on the public's evaluation of the abortion issue.

The subcommittee called numerous medical professionals to describe, often in graphic detail, the procedure and its effect on the fetus. For example, the first witness, neonatal specialist Mary Ellen Morton, a registered nurse, said of the partial-birth abortion procedure, "Here is the reality of what takes place, simply put. It requires that a baby who is moving . . . can be suddenly and brutally pulled down the birth canal using forceps with jaws clamped on his or her little limbs. The baby is pulled out of the mother's body until the trunk is delivered as in a breech delivery. Now the chest moves in and out in an attempt to breathe but the baby is struggling because the head is lodged in the vaginal tract unable to open its airway. This baby is reduced to human rubble in my opinion. Even the one-pound babies have distinct signs when they are in pain and resolve when treated. They possess a memory and a learned response. So what is the difference between a 21–40 week baby inside the womb suffering or outside the womb suffering? They both have the capability to perceive and experience excruciating pain when inflicted. However, the baby outside the womb has civil or human rights, and is required to be given humane care."

Another witness, Robert J. White, M.D., Ph.D, a professor of surgery at Case Western Reserve University, affirmed that a partial-birth abortion is "an extremely painful experience for the human fetus." He pointed out how he and many other doctors routinely operated on "children just a few weeks older than those that are undergoing this form of abortion" and in those operations did "everything possible to assure ourselves that these infants are painfree during operative procedures." The alarming inconsistency could well have been the result of widespread ignorance within the medical community about the partial-birth abortion procedure, an ignorance that obstetrician and gynecologist Pamela Smith highlighted in her testimony. "When I described the procedure of partial-birth abortion to physicians and laypersons who I knew to be pro-choice," Smith said, "many of them were horrified to learn that such a procedure was even legal." Even more troubling, she testified, the Accreditation Council for Graduate Medical Education "is requiring obstetrics and gynecology residency training programs to provide abortion training either in their own program or at another institution," meaning that individuals and institutions could be coerced into participating in "procedures that violate their moral conscience." Smith pointed out how "even under *Roe v. Wade*," partial-birth abortion "is literally seconds and inches away from being classified as a murder by every state in the union."

One month later, the full House Judiciary Committee debated the very first bill to restrict access to abortion since *Roe v. Wade*. Unlike debates many years earlier on a constitutional amendment banning abortion, the politics of partial-birth abortion was much less clear. Even some pro-choice lawmakers felt uncomfortable publicly defending the procedure. The pro-life Republican majority had begun the historic process of shifting public attitudes about abortion through this debate. All the parameters of the partial-birth abortion debate—and, by extension of the abortion debate— were established in 1995.

During the Judiciary Committee's debate, Representative Patricia Schroeder, Colorado Democrat, laid out an argument that would become a template for pro-choice lawmakers and President Clinton in speaking out against the partial-birth abortion ban. The bill, she said, "dresses up inflammatory political rhetoric and parades it around like a medical and legal standard." Using the standard pro-choice language of "parents' rights," she said, "The parents who have made the very difficult, heart-wrenching, and personal choice not to continue a pregnancy where the fetus is doomed to die are now mandated by the Canady bill to carry the fetus to term, never mind the emotional, physical, or financial cost to the families involved." She concluded, "It is clear that this bill is but one part of a concerted, multistep effort to effectively deprive women of their constitutional rights and access to abortion."

Pro-choice lawmakers who seized on Schroeder's line of argument trapped themselves in a self-defeating debate. By defending partial-birth abortion as a necessary and acceptable part of the entire matrix of abortion rights, Schroeder and others essentially equated this procedure with all other forms of abortion, defining them as morally equivalent when in the minds of most Americans they were not. Most Americans considered partial-birth abortions disgusting and horrific, and when medical evidence revealed that they were unnecessary and inflicted measurable pain on the fetus, the moral quandary only increased—even for pro-choice voters and politicians. Had pro-choice lawmakers compromised early, accepted the ban, and shifted the focus of debate to other elements of the pro-choice campaign to expand a woman's right to choose, the noticeable shifts in public opinion on abortion probably would not have occurred and pro-choice forces would find themselves in a far different place today. Over the years, pro-choice defense of the partial-birth abortion procedure came to be regarded as morally bankrupt and as politically indefensible as the gun lobby's absolutist stand against regulating cop-killer bullets.

At the same hearing, the bill's original author, Representative Charles Canady, laid down what would become the implacable argument for the partial-birth abortion ban: "While every abortion sadly takes a human life," he said, "the partial-birth abortion method takes that life as the baby emerges from the mother's womb . . . while the baby is only partially in the birth canal. The difference between the partial-birth abortion procedure and homicide is a mere three inches." Canady continued, "Our opponents' argument that the baby is already dead when these abortions are performed betrays their desperation. They support abortion anytime, in any manner, for any reason. But they know the American people do not." He put the issue in stark terms: "No baby's life should be taken in this manner. It does not matter whether that baby is perfectly healthy or suffers from the most tragic of disabilities."

Republican control of the House was absolutely vital to pushing the pro-life agenda not just because pro-life Republicans could set the debate but also because they controlled the legislative agenda. Before assuming the majority, pro-life Republicans (along with the three dozen or so pro-life Democrats) could move their position through the House only by means of amendments to other legislation. And the pro-choice House Democratic leadership often kept pro-life amendments off the floor and away from must-pass legislation. (In fact, during the only time when Democrats have controlled either the House or the Senate since the 1994 election—from June 2001 to January 2003—the Senate Democratic leadership refused to bring the partial-birth abortion ban bill to the floor.) Even when a pro-life amendment would pass in the House, the comparatively pro-choice Senate often ignored it entirely or watered down the language in the final legislation. This changed when the House Republican majority could send the Senate freestanding bills such as the partial-birth abortion ban. Pro-life legislation was no longer part of a convoluted debate on a larger spending bill but was the central issue in freestanding legislation.

The House passed the ban by a vote of 288–139—more than enough to override a presidential veto, and the highest vote total since *Roe v. Wade* for any legislation that limited access to abortions. The Senate had to respond. In November 1995, the Senate Judiciary Committee convened its own partial-birth abortion hearing. This was a seminal moment in the Senate's deliberations over abortion policy, because since *Roe v. Wade* it had defanged all previous types of pro-life legislation. Now, however, the Senate heard testimony on both sides of the issue. Just as they had in the House, opponents and proponents of partial-birth abortion gave powerful testimony, clashing over the procedure's medical efficacy and morality.

The Senate passed companion legislation on December 7, 1995, by a vote of 54–44, twelve votes short of an override majority. Clinton vetoed the bill on April 10, 1996, saying in his veto message to the GOP-controlled Congress that the bill "does not allow women to protect themselves from serious threats to their health." The president reported, "I told Congress that I would sign [the partial-birth abortion ban] if it were amended to add an exception for serious health consequences." Canady's bill did, of course, make an exception for when the life of the mother was in jeopardy, but Clinton insisted on further exceptions; pro-life supporters of the Canady bill argued that the phrase "serious health consequences" could even include psychological problems and would therefore allow nonemergency partial-birth abortions.

The debate would rage for the remainder of Bill Clinton's presidency. Clinton would veto the bill again in 1998. As a candidate, George W. Bush promised to sign the bill. He made good on that pledge in a ceremony at 1:40 P.M., November 5, 2003, in the Ronald Reagan Building, only blocks from the White House. It had been nine years since Republicans won control of the House and Senate, but now—after a debate they had initiated, directed, and driven into the center of America's political consciousness— the pro-life majority in Congress (mostly Republican but also some House Democrats) had achieved its first legislative breakthrough against universal abortion rights enshrined in *Roe v. Wade*.

The pursuit of a ban on partial-birth abortions was the leading edge of the Republicans' pro-life campaign, but it was not their only policy goal. Republicans also unsuccessfully sought medical discussions of alternatives to abortions, mandated waiting periods to obtain an abortion, and limits on teen access to abortion. These policy choices focused attention on particular dynamics of abortion access and required the public to consider how the pro-choice dogma played out in the real world. Once these issues were raised and the public evaluated a less draconian set of choices (legal abortion versus illegal abortion), the dynamics of the debate shifted. Pro-life positions generally carried the day in the court of public opinion, and laws were rewritten at the federal level. Though often overlooked, the changes were a signal achievement of the Republican Revolution.

## Fighting Crime

Republican success in reversing the national trends toward gun control was equally profound but manifested itself in different ways. Republicans did not inject a new line of debate into what had been a one-sided legislative and political argument (at least within the halls of Congress). Instead, they used their newfound clout to drive an alternative set of policies to replace what they had come to believe was a fraudulent acceptance of gun control as a means of reducing violent street crime. The Republican majority systematically shifted the emphasis away from gun control and toward legal reforms, redirected federal funding streams, and victims' rights laws. In so doing, Republicans stopped the gun-control movement in its tracks and eventually rendered it virtually obsolete in terms of the national debate on crime.

Gun control was not a part of the Contract with America, but crime control certainly was. The success of the latter drove a political stake through the heart of the former, and it stands as one of the most significant yet least appreciated consequences of the Republican Revolution. Support for generalized gun control has not faded—a 2004 Pew Research poll found, for instance, that 58 percent of Americans felt the right to gun control was more important than the right to own guns. But what's striking is the attitude toward alternatives to gun control. A Zogby poll taken in December 2003 asked this two-layered question: "Which of the following two statements regarding gun control comes closer to your opinion? Statement A: 'There needs to be new and tougher gun control legislation to help in the fight against gun crime.' Statement B: 'There are enough laws on the books. What is needed is better enforcement of current laws regarding gun control.' " The poll found that 66 percent of America favored Statement B while only 31 percent favored Statement A. Not surprisingly, most gun owners favored enforcement of existing laws over new ones (80 percent to 17 percent), but significantly, a majority of non–gun owners favored no new laws (54 percent to 42 percent). The poll also showed that 79 percent of Americans—and 73 percent of non–gun owners—supported state laws allowing residents to carry a gun in public for self-defense if they pass a criminal background check, pass a firearms safety course, and pay for all administrative fees. Thirty-eight states had such laws in 2004. Of those, twenty-one had passed the laws since 1994. More than two-thirds of the U.S. population now lives in states with so-called right-to-carry laws.

To understand the effect the Republican majority has had, consider these appraisals of the gun-control issue from two veteran Democrats, Senate Minority Leader Harry Reid of Nevada and former House Speaker Tom Foley, both pro-gun Democrats in a party with deep, abiding hostility to gun ownership. Reid, talking about gun control and the 2000 election, told me, "Gun control, being very realistic and candid, the 2000 election was a very, very bad vote for white men across America—it wasn't just the South, it was all across the country. It was an important issue, and surprisingly even women cared a lot about that issue, more than people thought. That was an issue that everyone thought that the gun-control folks would become more powerful all the time, but they've certainly lost ground, there's no question about that." Talking about how the Democratic Party's hard-line stance against guns did not reflect the wishes of constituents, Foley told me, "The *New York Times* gets it all wrong about the NRA. It's not the money. They do these crazy stories about how the NRA is buying votes. It's bullshit. The reason they are effective is that people believe. They have an enthusiastic membership. The great value of that endorsement was that it swung votes. They had a code: 'Another sportsman for Tom Foley.' It doesn't say, 'Endorsed by the NRA.' But that is the message."

In 1994, the last Democratic Congress of the twentieth century passed the last of its crime bills, one replete with gun control and initiatives to confront so-called root causes of crime. It cost $30 billion over six years and provided $8.8 billion for state and local governments to hire more police officers. (The only problem was it was a mandate to use the funds only for the hiring of police officers, even if they were not needed as much as equipment or other crime-fighting personnel.) The bill incorporated a federal version of the "three strikes and you're out" provision, extended the federal death penalty to more crimes, created harsher penalties for sex offenders, and in a highly controversial measure, banned nineteen types of semiautomatic firearms (so-called assault weapons).

This bill was indicative of President Clinton's anti-crime approach. While the White House felt it was innovative and centrist, in the hands of Democratic House and Senate majorities on Capitol Hill it took a hard turn toward liberalism. Similarly, the previous year Congress had passed and Clinton had signed the Brady Law, which required a five-day waiting period for the purchase of a handgun. It was named after James Brady, Ronald Reagan's press secretary who was paralyzed during the 1981 assassination attempt on Reagan's life. Pro-gun Republicans and Democrats had resisted passage of the Brady Bill for years but relented after persuading Clinton to accept and pay for a nationwide database of known criminals that could be reviewed to avoid handgun sales to criminals. The Brady Law represented the first anti-gun breakthrough in twenty-five years.

The 1994 crime bill was the logical next step. But the failure of the Democrats' efforts to pass the bill gave the clearest sign yet that House Democrats were losing control of the chamber. Conservative Democrats rebelling against Clinton liberalism on guns, health care, welfare, and taxes scuttled the procedural motion to bring the first crime bill to the floor. This dealt Clinton and the House Democratic leadership a humiliating defeat and forced them to negotiate a compromise with moderate Republican House members who, at Newt Gingrich's direction, slow-walked the talks for months.

Some senior White House aides worried that gun politics could be their undoing. Top West Wing staffer John Podesta, who would later rise to chief of staff, was not directly involved in the crime bill debate, but he harbored serious reservations about the legislation, reservations that were never seriously heeded. "I don't think we'd have lost the House if we hadn't pushed the gun vote [on the so-called assault-weapons ban]," Podesta told me. "If you look back at where the seats were lost, a lot of that had to do with the gun vote. I remember Rahm [Emanuel, Clinton's political director] was running the drill on the assault-weapons ban in the crime bill. I said, 'This is all fun and great and it's probably good for Clinton, just make sure you don't win the vote.' I think I was the only one who thought that back then."

Republicans sensed the political consequences too. That is why they didn't kill the crime bill altogether. By this time they were feeling optimistic about gaining either complete control of the House or effective control through alliances with pro-gun conservative Democrats, which would mean they could rewrite Clinton's bill in the next session. Also, they did not want to appear overtly obstructionist on crime. In essence, Clinton won a small victory on his crime agenda but at an enormous cost. Republicans rebelled against the crime bill's billions in social service spending, which to them carried the stench of failed Great Society antipoverty programs.

While the House Republicans grappled with the Clinton crime bill of 1994, they were setting forth their own program for fighting crime—in the Contract with America. The Contract called for numerous changes in federal crime legislation: expanding the death penalty and shortening death penalty appeals; reforming habeas corpus; requiring tougher mandatory minimum sentences for drug crimes; making assessment of restitution for crime victims mandatory; creating block grants for law enforcement needs, thereby abolishing the Clinton-era requirement that federal funds be used only to hire police officers; giving federal grants for new prison construction only to states that pass laws telling juries what a sentence for crime would mean in terms of actual prison time served (so-called truth-in-sentencing guidelines); loosening the exclusionary rule that forbade prosecutors from using evidence obtained in an unlawful search; setting new limits on prisoner lawsuits; and expediting deportation of illegal immigrants who commit crimes.

House debate on Contract crime items began in late January 1995, almost as soon as the GOP had taken control of the House. The tone of the debate was anything but Clinton-friendly. During a Judiciary Committee hearing on January 23, Georgia Republican Bob Barr spoke for many Republicans when he said, "There is an overwhelming sense in this country that violent crime has robbed the citizens of a sense of safety and security that they have a right to enjoy. After decades of one Democratic-controlled Congress after another jawboning the problem of crime with lots of taxpayer money but little in the way of results, we are finally on the way to passing a crime bill with real teeth."

Clinton tried gamely to reverse the GOP onslaught and appealed for comity in a speech to law enforcement personnel gathered in the Old Executive Office Building on February 8, 1995, after the House had already passed its Contract crime provisions. "I want to work with the new Congress to build on this crime bill, but we should not move backwards," the president said. "We shouldn't undermine our ability to implement the drug control commitment to provide 100,000 police officers. And we shouldn't let this become a partisan, political issue. The crime bill passed with bipartisan support; it should be maintained with bipartisan support."

The word from the Hill? *Not likely*. Although Clinton and many Democrats on Capitol Hill complained that the GOP was dismantling the achievements of the 1994 crime bill, the Republican majority forged ahead with the anti-crime initiatives in the Contract with America. The revolution brought a brand-new approach to crime. Republicans did not simply call for further federal intervention to "reduce crime," as Democratic Congresses had for decades (often in a backdoor attempt to impose gun control or to address so-called root causes of crime). The Contract's anti-crime initiatives overhauled the federal approach to searches and seizures, the death penalty, victims' rights, the length of prison time served, and prison construction. In every case, federal policy moved against the criminal and in favor of the victims of crime. Republicans also blocked all efforts at new gun control and established new parameters for the debate—for example, tougher laws against criminals versus more gun control. The tougher crime side prevailed to the point where after the 2000 election, Democrats fairly ran from the gun-control debate entirely.

How successful were the Republicans? Consider that virtually every anti-crime initiative in the Contract with America became law.

### The Education Setbacks

Initial Republican efforts to transform federal education policy can best be described with the adjectives Republicans often applied to the policy itself: wasteful, ineffective, inappropriate, and costly. For all the gains the revolution made standing against abortion and gun control, the Republican majority failed to make inroads into the federal education bureaucracy it so deplored.

Conservative Republicans have distrusted federal involvement in education since President Jimmy Carter created the Department of Education, which, in their minds, was little more than bureaucratic ransom paid to politically supportive teachers' unions. Ever since 1965, when President Lyndon Johnson signed the Elementary and Secondary Education Act, the federal government had been committed to providing funding to schools to close the gap between rich and poor school districts. Since then, the terms of debate had not changed. Surprisingly, however, the Republicans who seized the majority in 1994 had few big thinkers on education policy and focused on small subissues. To the degree Republicans possessed coherent thoughts about national education policy, they expressed enthusiasm for these three ideas: using taxpayer-subsidized vouchers to allow parents to move their children from poorly performing urban public schools to higher-quality private schools or academies, even ones with compulsory religious education and observances; support for home schooling, a concept that grew up as an alternative to all publicly financed and supervised education, a kind of education entrepreneurialism that produced pockets of impressive results all around the country and grew as a self-sufficient community; and support for increasing federal funding for special education.

But these did not amount to a real agenda. Many Republicans in the new majority were fairly obsessed with the idea of vouchers, but otherwise the GOP had no real program. Since there was no real "home school" policy to pursue, Republicans could merely offer praise from the sidelines and keep the tax code neutral to allow the movement to flourish. As for funding so-called special-needs education, this wasn't an idea so much as an accounting maneuver. The 1975 Individuals with Disabilities Education Act (IDEA) required the mainstreaming of physically and mentally disabled students, a revolutionary law that greatly enhanced the lives of disabled students but that nevertheless burdened school districts with enormous costs for retrofitting, special education instructors, and specialized equipment (a 2002 report from the National Association of State Boards of Education showed a per-student cost of $12,474 for a disabled student compared with $6,556 for a general education student). The law promised that the federal government would pay for no less than 40 percent of the new costs associated with mainstreaming disabled students, but Democratic Congresses had never provided more than 8 percent of such funding. Conservative Republicans argued that if Washington compelled school districts to comply with this law, it had to do its part to help local districts meet the needs of disabled students without taking resources away from the rest of the classroom population.

The Republicans did have an overarching goal when it came to education, but it had little to do with achieving real education reforms. They wanted to cut into the massive education bureaucracy to reduce federal spending and achieve their demand for a seven-year balanced budget. Republicans appeared all too eager to attack the bureaucratic edifice and the billions of dollars that propped it up each year, not so much as an exercise in reform (though that's how it was belatedly advertised) but as part of a wholesale assault on the budget to bring it into balance. This, at least, is where Republicans began on the question of federal education funding; in no other part of their agenda did they suffer a more humiliating defeat or have to spend more time retrenching and rethinking their approach.

Memorably, Republicans started by trying to shut down the Department of Education. Although two former secretaries of education, William Bennett and Lamar Alexander (now the junior senator from Tennessee), endorsed the idea, it was a symbolic gesture that could only be attributed to the fever-swamp enthusiasm of the times *(Hey, anything's possible, we're in charge!)*. Most Republicans didn't believe they could kill the department and most didn't believe they could destroy all vestiges of federal involvement in education. The move to shutter the Department of Education was *supposed* to stand as a symbol of Republican frustration with D.C.'s poor performance when it came to teaching children how to read and write, add and subtract. But revolutions can never be about totems or symbols.

Republicans had arrived in Washington carrying a bill of policy particulars, offering the nation a set of yes-or-no questions. But on education they committed the mistake bad attorneys often make, asking a witness a question they don't already know the answer to. Republicans didn't have the faintest idea what the country thought about the Department of Education or what it symbolized. All they knew was what *they* thought about the Department of Education, what it symbolized to *them*. When Republicans were assailing the department, they had no idea how their attacks would be heard, because they'd never asked the question, never pondered in the broadest possible terms how the country might interpret their condemnations. Remember, to the degree that Republicans had an education agenda, it was limited to two constituencies dying to get out of the education establishment: voucher supporters and home school families—hardly a cross section of the American electorate. Republican rhetoric worked well with this niche audience. It failed miserably elsewhere, because when

Republicans took aim at the Department of Education, the rest of the nation conjured images not of reformist crusaders protecting valuable tax dollars from gross inefficiency but instead of green-eyeshade ghouls strangling school budgets because they simply hated education, schools, teachers, and children. Can you say *politically injurious?*

The Republicans did introduce their fanciful proposal to close the Department of Education. They did so in the context of their assault on Goals 2000, the education act that President Clinton had signed the previous year. Goals 2000 created eight voluntary national education goals for elementary and secondary schools. The law did not make school districts' continued receipt of federal funds contingent on achieving the federal standards. In other words, it was a system with all carrot and no stick. And in 1994 Republicans had no desire to create a stick; they just wanted to get rid of the carrot. Rather than having the federal government set hard, measurable standards, they wanted to cede control over education entirely to states and school districts. Their goal: to redirect federal tax dollars from the Department of Education to the so-called front lines of education achievement.

On May 18, 1995, Republicans passed a budget resolution calling for the abolition of the Department of Education. On May 24, the special House task force on education, led by freshman Representative Joe Scarborough of Florida (now a talk-show host on MSNBC), laid down the specifics of the Republican plan: close down the Department of Education within a year; kill the Goals 2000 federal supervisory board and some higher education and elementary and secondary education programs; block-grant $9 billion of elementary and secondary education out of roughly $15 billion in spending; block-grant $2 billion out of $14 billion for higher education; and shift Pell grants and direct student loans to the Department of Health and Human Services. All of this was called the Back to Basics Education Reform Act. "The great federal experiment in education is over," Scarborough said. "It failed. It is the time to move on." Department reaction was suitably grave. "These kind of proposals would really end up hurting education, especially for the most needy students in our society," said Undersecretary of Education Marshall S. Smith. "The last thing we need now is to completely take away the national purpose, and the national voice, for improving schools."

The idea of abolishing the Department of Education made almost zero legislative headway. The next day, the Senate passed its budget resolution, which said nothing about abolishing the department. The debate dragged on for months, and by late summer, House Republicans began to accept the idea that the Senate would prevail.

During the budget showdown that year, President Clinton destroyed the Republicans' all-out effort to take down the federal education bureaucracy. Education was one of the vital pieces of spending he swore to protect in any balanced budget, and after he won that political battle, Republicans were left to negotiate their first full-fledged education budget in 1996 under the new political rules that dictated avoiding another shutdown at all costs (meaning no confrontations with Clinton over education spending). The 1996 bill was a complete repudiation of everything they had sought in 1995. The Department of Education's budget actually *rose* by 22 percent, to $26.3 billion. Spending went up across the board—on Goals 2000, on remedial education, on Pell grants, and even for the safe schools and drug-free schools program. Republicans had no chance of achieving victory by legalizing school vouchers. They faced intense political opposition and significant constitutional barriers.

As a backup, Republicans pressed for education savings accounts, which were essentially individual retirement accounts for education, in which families could set aside up to $2,000 per year tax-free to pay for future education expenses. Republicans wanted to allow families to use the savings accounts to pay for private school tuition, vocational training, tutoring, specialized school supplies, or college tuition. Critics saw it as a backdoor means of using the tax code to provide tax shelters to savings that would eventually end up paying for private religious school tuition. President Clinton vetoed the bill but reluctantly approved a smaller and more heavily regulated version in 1997 that limited tax-free set-asides to $500 per year. President Bush would increase the amount to $2,000 and streamline IRS compliance regulations in his first tax cut of 2001.

Republicans had come to Washington hell-bent on destroying the federal education bureaucracy and sending as much federal money as possible back to the states with strings-free block grants. But after the 1995 budget fiasco, Republicans reformed their ranks and tried to siphon funds from the Department of Education. Nibbling at the edges of federal education funding did not work either, since President Clinton would wave the bloody shirt of education cuts each budget cycle and Republicans would retreat. Sure enough, federal spending on education increased every year of Clinton's presidency that the Republicans ruled Congress.

But even after Clinton, congressional Republicans boosted federal education spending and greatly enlarged the busybody role of the federal government under the persistent demands of President Bush. As a candidate, Bush had campaigned heavily on education, the first Republican to do so since Democrats carved out a federal role in 1965. The candidate's most memorable line was to quote Phyllis Hunter of Houston, Texas, a reading specialist who called reading "the next civil right." Bush vowed to keep the Education Department and dramatically boost spending, but only if Congress agreed to impose specific, verifiable performance standards on reading, mathematics, and (ultimately) science and to tie future federal allocations to meeting those standards. Congressional Republicans saw Bush fight Vice President Gore to a draw on the education issue and, generally speaking, fell into line. They initially resisted the huge new investment in federal spending, but in the end the No Child Left Behind Act, which President Bush signed on January 8, 2002, provided a larger increase in federal spending on education than anything Clinton had ever sought.

The No Child Left Behind Act required all states to create and execute statewide reading and math tests by the 2005–2006 school year and to create a similar science proficiency test by the 2007–2008 school year. Schools that failed to meet standards of achievement on reading and math scores for every student for two consecutive years would receive increased federal technical assistance; schools that failed to meet standards for three consecutive years could lose students, as parents would be allowed to leave the school without sanction; after four consecutive years of failure to meet standards, the school districts would be allowed to take "corrective actions"; and after five consecutive years of failure, the state or school district could close the school.

When the president signed the bill, he was presiding over a revolution in which congressional Republicans had no real part. They didn't think of it, didn't set it in motion, wouldn't have even considered it upon first arriving in power. But it was a way off the frustrating policy treadmill Clinton forced them to walk after they made such a mess of education policy and education politics. Bush set out the new agenda. And he was joined by some highly unlikely liberal Democratic allies, among them Senator Edward Kennedy of Massachusetts and Representative George Miller of California, two of the most aggressive and effective critics of Republicans' education efforts pre-Bush. Bush saw the law as a path to forcing a public reckoning with the embedded inefficiencies of the public school system that would provoke even deeper reforms, such as vouchers and the expansion of charter schools. He was willing to increase federal spending if schools were forced to measure their ability to educate *every student*. In the speech he gave after signing the No Child Left Behind Act, Bush praised the three principles behind the new law: (1) accountability; (2) trusting parents "to make right decisions for their children," since the law would give parents options for getting out of failing schools; and (3) trusting "the local folks on how to achieve standards" and getting power out of Washington's hands.

The No Child Left Behind Act cemented a new Republican revolution in education, one unimaginable to the revolutionaries of '94. As Haley Barbour describes it, "Unlike abortion and gun control, education is a case of the issue capturing Republicans."

The story of the education revolution is a three-part story: the utter failure of grand proclamations about destroying the federal education bureaucracy; capitulation to Clinton stand-patism (Clinton brought few policy initiatives to education); and finally, a reluctant embrace of an intrusive federal mandate tied to the largest increases in federal education spending in history. There is no part of domestic policy on which congressional Republicans have ended up farther away from where they started. None.

But some revolutionaries have come to embrace the Bush education plan as ardently as any plank of the Contract.

Former representative Bob Walker of Pennsylvania, one of the architects of the Contract, told me, "The idea that every child should be given the same opportunity to be educated is an amazingly transformational concept that should be embraced by every conservative, because instead of offering victimization as the answer to long periods of discrimination, we're offering opportunity. It's setting up the framework where all of a sudden you have the educational community coming back and saying, 'We can't do it, we can't teach every child.' And now the answer can be, 'Why not, what's gone wrong in education, what do you need to do?' Doesn't this call for a transformation of what's happening in schools?"

Congressional Republicans hope so. If it does and if Republicans maintain their control over Congress, they may someday achieve some of the fundamental reforms in education that were part of their misbegotten agenda when they first took control.

# 11

# TWO GUYS NAMED TRENT

When conservatives and liberals begin to state the prosecution case against the Republican Revolution, many start at the same place.

Medicare.

To liberals and Democrats who opposed the Contract with America and the "revolution" it set in motion, the tale of Medicare and the new, aggressive Republican majority bears some resemblance to the story of any one of a number of one-dimensional Tom Cruise characters: The brash, know-it-all kid arrives in town, pushes everyone and everything around to get his way, succeeds in achieving his initial goals but discovers a new and even more alluring one, and pursues it with the same combination of no-holds-barred intensity, only to be rebuffed repeatedly until, finally, he comes to his senses, swallows his pride, and submits to the realities of humility, selflessness, and generosity and gets the girl.

Substitute "Medicare" for "girl" in our allegory and, Democrats would say, you pretty much have the story of Republicans and Medicare. With one exception: Republicans never really got the girl they wanted the way they wanted her.

In fact, the Medicare bill that Republicans fought for and passed in the fall of 2003 was almost *nothing* like the Medicare policy that had been drawn up in conservative think tanks and that the Republican revolutionaries had come to Washington championing. To many conservative Republicans who rose to power in 1994, Medicare was a fitting symbol of all that was wrong with Washington: a bloated federal bureaucracy that spent wildly, defrauded Americans on a massive scale, and prevented the sort of private-sector competition that breeds efficiency and brings better service to the American people. While many liberals called for Medicare to provide prescription drug coverage, conservatives balked at this, believing the costs of such an entitlement would be stratospheric. But instead of reducing the Medicare bureaucracy, streamlining the system to reduce costs and minimize fraud, opening it up to direct competition, and holding the line against prescription drug coverage, Republicans in 2003 did the exact opposite: *They enacted the single largest expansion of a government entitlement program since the Great Society.*

What further proof is there, critics say, that the Republican Revolution is dead and gone than the GOP's enlarging the legislative legacy of Lyndon Johnson? To many conservatives, the Medicare drug bill of 2003 was the triumph of politics for the sake of power. The Republicans' conduct, they fret, was all about winning elections (since President George W. Bush was desperate to pass some sort of Medicare drug bill, as he had promised in the 2000 campaign). It had nothing to do with helping the country or furthering conservatism, they argue. Many of those who were there at the Contract's creation, and who dreamed most ardently of how America would be changed for the better under the enlightened, fiscally sound, and ceaselessly inventive Republican majority, now look at the Medicare bill and throw their hands up in disgust.

The condemnation comes from both ends of the political spectrum. Democrats argue that in order to take home this "prize," Republicans had to resort to the most odious forms of intimidation, brute politics, and deception. Such heavy-handed tactics are particularly galling to critics because the Republicans had predicated their "revolution" on changing the way Washington worked—not just altering policy and budgets but actually bringing openness to the government to make politicians more accountable to the people. The preamble to the Contract with America begins, "Iron-handed one-party rule of the House of Representatives over the last four decades has led to arbitrary and often secretive procedures that disenfranchise millions of Americans from their representation in Congress. This autocratic rule is a direct attack on the free democratic principles upon which our nation was founded." And yet, critics charge, here were the Republicans employing "arbitrary and often secretive procedures"—or perhaps worse—to preserve their grip on power. The charges are numerous. Let's evaluate them one at a time:

*The Bush administration lied about the cost of the bill.* In March 2004, an actuary for the Department of Health and Human Services (HHS),

Richard A. Foster, claimed that his boss, HHS Medicare administrator Thomas A. Scully, had ordered him to withhold from congressional Democrats several pieces of information concerning the Medicare bill. Was Foster's cost estimate for the Medicare bill—which was more than $139 billion *larger* than the one the Republican-controlled Congressional Budget Office (CBO) provided to Congress—among the items to be withheld? Foster told me that Scully had not mentioned the cost estimate explicitly but that it was well understood that orders not to share data with Democrats extended to the cost estimates as well. And Democrats in Congress never did receive the HHS cost estimate. HHS secretary Tommy Thompson said GOP leaders knew of his department's higher cost estimates, and that was good enough for him. But in fact many rank-and-file House Republicans did not know, and if they had known, the bill might not have passed. The HHS inspector general concluded Scully threatened to fire Foster if he told Congress of the larger cost estimate. But the IG concluded Scully broke no laws. Whether it was outright lying, bureaucratic manipulation, or simply the shrewd compartmentalizing of data doesn't really matter. In no way can the handling of the Medicare drug bill costs numbers live up to the openness and accountability the new Republican majority promised upon its election in 1994.

*The House leadership held the vote open to allow time to pressure lawmakers into voting for a bill the GOP could not have passed under normal procedures.* This is absolutely true. House Republican leaders held open the floor vote for nearly three hours—something that had never been done since the House began electronically recording votes in 1974 (and possibly in the entire history of Congress). Technically, the GOP leadership did not violate House rules, which require only a *minimum* of fifteen minutes to record votes of this type. Recognizing this, the press secretary for House Speaker Dennis Hastert, John Feehery, justified the tactic by saying, "Seniors have been waiting thirty years for prescription drug coverage—waiting another three hours won't hurt anyone." But such an ends-justify-the-means approach negates the essential give-and-take that produces durable compromises. Although the majority party establishes House rules, those rules reflect custom and comity more than they do the majority's wishes. A legislative body must agree on the rules, boundaries, and customs for it to function well and for the minority party's participation in the process to be real. Republicans knew this, or should have known this, since it was under what they considered the oppressive yoke of Democratic rule that they united to overthrow the Democrats in 1994. The Republicans never should have resorted to such tactics, if for no other reason than that they had sworn in the Contract—a *pact* with voters—that they never would.

*Republicans tried to bribe members.* One Republican, Representative Nick Smith of Michigan, said other Republicans offered him an indirect bribe to change his vote. They allegedly offered substantial financial contributions to Smith's son Brad, who in 2004 would be running to succeed his father in the same House district. But the bribe came with a threat attached to it, according to Smith: If he did *not* fall into line, the Republicans would see to it that GOP donors boycotted his son's campaign. Smith later softened the accusation, but not before repeating it in a radio interview and in print. The allegation gave rise to the first full-blown Ethics Committee investigation since Republicans took control of Congress in 1995. On September 30, 2004, the committee admonished House Majority Leader Tom DeLay for his involvement, stating that he had tried to establish "a *quid pro quo* to achieve a legislative goal."

Let's see: Lying, brazen rule-bending, bribery—it doesn't sound like the open government Republicans promised to bring to Washington. The reformers and idealists had become the arm twisters and hacks they had so roundly denounced before their rise to power. The GOP's strong-arm tactics in pushing the 2003 Medicare bill were as bad as, and quite possibly worse than, any committed by the Democratic majorities whom the Republicans had justly reviled for subjugating and humiliating them.

Two Republicans say as much. Representative Trent Franks of Arizona told me that the push for the Medicare bill represented what he hoped was a "rare, horrifying moment" in Republican control of Congress. Another Trent, Senator Trent Lott of Mississippi, told me "there is no question" that the bill represented the triumph of power over policy. "And that is the part that just makes my stomach just churn."

In the entire history of the U.S. Congress, never before have two men with the first name Trent served at the same time. The two Trents—one in the House, the other in the Senate—couldn't be more closely linked with the intellectual and political wellsprings of the Republican Revolution. And these revolutionaries look on the Medicare episode with despair, recognizing how far it took the Republicans from the Contract with America, on matters of both policy and procedure.

And yet these two men are most responsible for saving the Medicare bill from defeat. At the last minute, they cast the deciding votes for the bill.

Quite possibly, at no time in American history have two politicians' voting records and political philosophies offered less of a sign as to how they would vote on such a critical issue. To call the Medicare votes of the two Trents at odds with their core philosophies doesn't begin to explain the chasm. Both believed the vote would define their legislative careers. They voted against themselves. Their stories better than any others explain how the revolution came to the crossroads known as the Medicare prescription drug bill.

### The Two Trents

Trent Franks was elected to the House in 2002, but make no mistake, he was a revolutionary. Franks ran for Congress in 1994 in Arizona's Fourth Congressional District Republican primary, losing to John Shadegg, who became one of Congress's most unyielding social and fiscal conservatives. Franks ran to the *right* of Shadegg in the 1994 primary. If Franks had won that race, he would have gladly signed the Contract with America.

Before running for Congress, Franks had aligned himself with the most conservative causes he could find. He led the unsuccessful effort to pass a statewide initiative to limit abortion access rights in 1992. He was the executive director of the Arizona Family Research Institute from 1989 to 1993. The institute was the Arizona political arm of Focus on the Family, the national social conservative network headed by James Dobson. Franks served one term in the Arizona House, from 1984 to 1986, and while there caught the attention of fellow legislators by wearing a tie tack in the shape of the feet of a fetus.

Franks told me that when he ran for Congress, both in 1994 and in 2002, he saw it as his mission to stop creeping socialism. When he first ran, Bill Clinton was in the White House and Democrats controlled both houses of Congress, and he "saw the entire Republic beginning to crumble," he says. "In 1994, our nation, I saw it as we were beginning to socialize our world to the extent that I was afraid that freedom and free enterprise would no longer survive. And when I ran in 2002 I ran to stop that from ever coming back."

Franks did not come to Washington to expand Medicare. He came to reform it—just as Shadegg and the revolutionaries of 1994 did. He didn't believe a prescription drug benefit was even necessary. In 2000, when the Bush-Cheney campaign team asked Franks to endorse its plan for drug coverage limited to cases of catastrophic illness, Franks refused. He said even that was too costly and the elderly should plan in advance to save for catastrophic drug costs that could wipe out family fortunes in a matter of months. Franks's conservative pedigree on Medicare and prescription drugs is unassailable. Yet as we will see, it was Franks who rescued the Medicare prescription drug bill in the House and kept it alive for Senate consideration. Without Franks's vote, the bill President Bush and the GOP leadership negotiated would have died.

The other Trent, Senator Lott, was first elected to the House of Representatives in 1972. He worked his way up through the minority power structure to become whip in 1980, when he allied himself with Jack Kemp and Newt Gingrich. In the mid-1980s, Lott more energetically devoted himself to the activist/conservative wing of the Republican conference and joined many of the battles against the Democrats that Gingrich waged.

But in 1987, Lott reached the end of his confrontational rope. The incident was the one Republicans came to call "Bloody Thursday"—when House Speaker Jim Wright rammed through the Democrats' budget bill by ordering the end of that day's legislative business and then ordering a new legislative day to be convened only twenty minutes later. It was a power play to get around House rules that would have made it nearly impossible to bring the defeated budget up for another vote that same day. After Wright had twisted enough arms and changed enough votes to pass the budget, an enraged Lott stormed to the well of the House and slammed his fist down on the dais with such force that part of the wood splintered and broken pieces fell to the carpeted floor.

"I knew right then and there I could not continue in that chamber. The animosity was too intense. I had to get out of there to save my sanity and my temper."

When Lott arrived in the Senate in 1989, he brought with him the House sensibilities of activism and conservatism. He positioned himself as one of the few young conservative Turks willing to challenge the party's moderate Senate leadership. In 1992 he ran for and won the number-four post in the leadership ranking, Republican conference secretary, and in 1994, after the GOP sweep, he challenged Senate Republican leader Bob Dole's protégé, Alan Simpson of Wyoming, for the number-two post of minority whip.

Simpson was no squishy moderate, but next to Lott's near-perfect lifetime record of conservative votes, he *looked* moderate. With the help of newly arrived conservative Republicans, Lott beat Simpson by one vote, becoming the first lawmaker ever to serve as minority whip in both the House and the Senate.

Lott wanted to push the GOP agenda harder and draw sharper ideological distinctions with Clinton, but his election to minority whip was the only tangible manifestation of conservative activism in the Senate in the immediate aftermath of the 1994 election. Despite his new clout, Lott was still overshadowed by Dole, whose instincts were for accommodation and compromise. That Lott was able to maintain near-perfect conservative voting records while ascending to leadership positions that (especially in the Senate) required a heightened degree of political flexibility is a testament to his willingness and ability to stick to the conservative line.

In short, a more unlikely vote to enshrine a Medicare prescription drug bill of the kind President Bush signed in 2003 you could not find.

Yet both of these Trents were the difference makers. They were revolutionaries who were there at what many regard as the unraveling of the revolution. Not only were they witnesses, they made it happen.

How? Why? What does it mean?

To answer these questions, one must understand the tortuous path of GOP-sponsored Medicare legislation after the 1994 election.

## Optics

Medicare was nowhere to be found in the Contract with America. Health care policy was nowhere to be found either, except indirectly through tax breaks for providing home care to an elderly relative. But this doesn't mean Republicans had not put together new Medicare policy before the 1994 election. Their 1993 budget alternative contained $57.5 billion in Medicare savings over five years, achieved through various cost-containment measures. These measures reflected how most Republicans, at this point, pursued Medicare reform as a budget-balancing exercise. Yes, some Republicans sought structural reform, but most just wanted to save money.

In their first budget after winning the majority, Republicans sought the biggest slowdown in future Medicare spending ever proposed, aiming to reduce the projected growth in Medicare spending by $270 billion over seven years. Although Republicans argued that Medicare spending would still rise by nearly $1.7 trillion over the seven-year period, Democrats called this proposal a "cut" in Medicare spending. The Democrats' claims inflicted some damage politically on the Republicans, but the bigger problem for the GOP was what Hastert spokesman John Feehery calls "optics"—that is, how their proposal appeared to voters.

As Republicans proposed reducing Medicare spending by $270 billion over the next seven years, they were also calling for $245 billion in tax cuts over the same time span. I attended town hall meetings across the country in which Democratic members of Congress would simplify the debate for constituents and local reporters by drawing the $270 billion Medicare figure on a chalkboard or an easel and saying something like, "This is what the new Republican majority wants to *cut* from your Medicare." Then the Democrats would write the $245 billion tax-cut figure just below the $270 billion Medicare figure and say something like, "And this is what the new Republican majority wants to *give* to its rich friends in tax cuts." And then with a snarling contempt they would say, "Well, I'm just a simple congressman, but it looks to me like they made the cuts to *your* Medicare almost the same size as the tax cuts for their rich friends. I don't remember hearing anything in that so-called Contract with America about robbing from Medicare to pay for tax cuts for the wealthy."

As Feehery dryly notes today, very bad optics.

"We tried to reform Medicare and cut taxes by almost identical amounts. It was a monumentally stupid thing to do. You had to pay for the tax cuts, but optically it was a stupid thing to do."

To defend their proposed Medicare reforms, Republicans conducted intensive focus groups. GOP pollsters discovered a soothing way to describe the cost-saving measures to nervous constituents: The Republicans were seeking to reduce future costs of Medicare only because the program was headed toward bankruptcy (in 1995 the Medicare trustees projected that Medicare Part A, which covers hospital visits, would become insolvent in six years). The pollsters instructed Republicans to inform voters they were only trying to "preserve, protect, and improve" Medicare— magic words that were reordered to form the acronym PIP. The Republican leadership gave GOP lawmakers instructional manuals and videotapes on Medicare, ordering them to conduct town hall meetings in their home districts to sell the gospel of PIP.

But as the budget battle heated up in 1995, the Clinton White House discovered a catchphrase of its own: "M-squared, E-squared," which stood for Medicare, Medicaid, education, and the environment—the four priorities Clinton swore to protect in any balanced budget. This was part of Clinton's shrewd political maneuvering during the 1995 budget showdown: He used Medicare's popularity as a weapon against Republicans in the final negotiations over a balanced budget. At the time, public relations specialist Bill Novelli was working in concert with House Democrats to wage a savage campaign against the GOP-sponsored Medicare reforms. Although Republicans would survive the assault in the 1996 midterm elections, the Novelli campaign and the White House's attacks made them leery of Medicare reform.

When Clinton and congressional Republicans agreed on a balanced budget in 1997, the deal included nominal Medicare savings—$115 billion in projected savings over seven years, compared with the $270 billion the Republicans had originally sought. And even these savings never materialized, because doctors and hospitals aggressively lobbied Congress in later years to reinstate planned cuts in Medicare reimbursements. The budget deal also contained provisions designed to entice seniors into Medicare + Choice programs, private insurance coverage that offered prescription drug coverage. Republicans hoped Medicare + Choice would be the beginning of a new era in free-market dynamism within Medicare. But the White House and congressional Democrats succeeded in writing rules so complex and limiting participation to such a small number of patients that the program never got off the ground. The old bureaucracy plodded on.

These experiences left congressional Republicans demoralized, frustrated, and listless. They wanted to change Medicare but they didn't know how. Though they had fought Clinton to a standstill, they were no longer interested in pushing for dramatic savings. Moreover, by 1998, the projected year of Medicare insolvency had moved back from 2001 to 2008, as the booming economy provided a new infusion of revenue. Even when, in 1998, a bipartisan commission that Clinton had appointed recommended increasing private competition against Medicare, Clinton rejected the idea.

The issue percolated through the 2000 campaign, but to neither party's apparent advantage. Al Gore advocated a fee-based system with the government paying for up to 50 percent of drug costs. Bush wanted to provide a narrow drug benefit, but he also sought Medicare cost-saving reforms of the kind House Republicans had fought for in their early, less politically sensitive days of activism.

In early 2001, after Bush took office, Senate Republicans proposed bills to allow private insurers to compete for Medicare beneficiaries if they offered prescription drug coverage. Democrats denounced the idea as a cynical means of undermining Medicare by attracting wealthier recipients able to pay for private insurance. They also argued that the failure of Medicare + Choice (which they had intentionally undermined) proved that seniors were not interested in private alternatives to Medicare.

In April, Senate Republicans approved the first-ever allocation of resources for a future Medicare prescription drug bill, $300 billion over ten years. It was merely a placeholder, since the Republicans did not write the legislation to provide the benefit. But the GOP had taken an important step toward integrating drug coverage into the Medicare bureaucracy. By including it in the budget resolution, Republicans were tacitly admitting their failure to develop private-sector alternatives to Medicare drug benefits.

In the summer of 2002, the more conservative House passed a budget with a $350 billion, ten-year placeholder for a Medicare drug benefit. Republicans were now on the record in both chambers as favoring the use of Medicare to provide at least limited drug coverage. These budget allocations only raised expectations that Medicare would provide drug coverage and made passage of some form of drug bill inevitable. The only remaining question was when.

### The Next Stage of the Revolution?

In his January 28, 2003, State of the Union address, President Bush called for a $400 billion Medicare drug benefit. The White House demanded passage that year, knowing Congress could never muster the will to debate and approve any changes to Medicare in an election year. The plan was more generous than what Bush had proposed as a candidate, which would have covered only drug costs associated with catastrophic illnesses.

Bush had traveled the country to marshal support for the drug benefit, but it was a tough sell. The new plan offered nearly blanket coverage for the poorest seniors (those with incomes at 150 percent of the annual federal poverty level) so long as they paid a $35 monthly premium and a copayment of no more than $5 per prescription. Those above this level would have 75 percent of their drug costs covered for drug costs ranging from $250 to $2,250 per year if they paid the $35 monthly premium, and they would receive full coverage for annual drug costs above $3,600. But seniors would lose coverage on drugs if their annual spending rose above $2,250 but below $3,600. This gap in coverage became known as the "doughnut hole," which would probably cause millions of seniors to lose drug coverage. Proponents of this plan said some coverage was better than none at all. But the plan wasn't nearly generous enough to satisfy Democrats, and despite dozens of trips and dozens of speeches, Bush could not create a groundswell for the Republican plan.

As difficult a time as the Bush White House had in pushing its Medicare drug benefit, it would have had a much harder time if Republicans had exposed the reality of the costs involved. Congress was allocating $400 billion over the next ten years for the new Medicare drug benefit, but that would not be nearly enough to cover consumer demand. CBO estimates said that seniors would spend $87 billion on prescription drugs in 2003 alone, and that by 2012, annual Medicare drug costs would rise to $278 billion. So while the White House and congressional Republicans talked about a world where Medicare drug costs could be kept under $400 billion over ten years, the harsh reality, at least under CBO projections, was that consumer demand would amount to $1.8 *trillion* over a decade. So the White House and GOP leaders built for themselves a *political reality* that ignored the disconnect between projected demand and benefits offered. (Demand was expected to grow so much that after the bill passed, the CBO said the same benefits coverage could cost $2 trillion in the *subsequent* ten years.)

For weeks in advance of the showdown vote in the House of Representatives, the Bush White House courted Republicans publicly and privately. But it could not generate sufficient pressure. If the White House was to win the bill, it had to rely on a Texas Republican the president didn't like and didn't trust: House Majority Leader Tom DeLay.

Although DeLay had not been a member of any of the committees that drafted the House Medicare drug bill, Speaker Hastert placed him on the pivotal House-Senate conference committee that was drafting the compromise bill. DeLay's job was to ensure that the final product could win the support of free-market conservatives worried about exploding Medicare costs and that the bill could actually win on the House floor.

The original House bill had passed by the slightest of margins, 216–215, on June 27, 2003. It contained numerous internal Medicare reforms, among them a concept to allow large private health plans to compete directly for Medicare patients, in part by offering drug coverage. The idea of bringing private health plans into competition with Medicare was known as "premium support" and was central to conservatives' efforts to contain future costs. A majority of Clinton's presidential Medicare reform commission had endorsed the concept back in 1998, but Clinton had rejected it. And now Senate Democrats, led by Senator Edward Kennedy of Massachusetts, worked strenuously to see it removed from the compromise bill. The fight over premium support dragged on for weeks and threatened to torpedo the entire bill. Representative Bill Thomas, chairman of the House Ways and Means Committee, and DeLay realized that many Republican moderates opposed premium support and would vote against the bill if it was included, which raised the very real prospect of seeing the bill die in the Senate. So they agreed to a watered-down pilot program that would allow private health plans to compete directly with Medicare in six metropolitan areas for six years but that would not begin until 2010. It was a fig leaf, and an insulting one to most conservatives. But it was the best deal DeLay and Thomas could make.

As the final deal began to take shape, conservatives had lost on almost every key issue. But there was one thing they liked: Health Savings Accounts (HSAs). Under the bill, all taxpayers could set aside, starting January 1, 2004, up to $4,500 per year tax-free in what amounted to a health insurance IRA. The money would stay in the account until it was needed to pay health care expenses, and it would allow individuals to avoid paying deductibles on small medical expenses like routine doctors' visits. Unused amounts would gain interest annually, allowing taxpayers to create their own financial shield against unexpected health care costs. In addition to giving individuals incentives to save for health care costs, HSAs would, proponents said, allow employers to concentrate most of their health care insurance expenses on large-scale illnesses instead of routine expenses, meaning they could more easily manage costs and provide broader coverage to a larger number of employees.

Congress had first put this idea into law in 1997, when the accounts were called Medical Savings Accounts (MSAs). But Kennedy and other Democrats had discouraged widespread participation in MSAs, and now, when Kennedy could not defeat Thomas's and other Republicans' demands for universal HSAs, he pulled his support of the bill, even after he had won virtually every policy skirmish. Kennedy's denunciation actually rallied conservatives around the bill, as it told them that HSAs were a potentially potent reform.

The section of the legislation dealing with HSAs was just a tiny portion of the bill, but within this provision Republicans found the next stage of the revolution, according to top GOP activist and lobbyist Grover Norquist. Norquist argues that before celebrating the death of the Republican Revolution on the jagged cliffs of the Medicare drug bill, Democrats should consider the significance of the GOP's victory on HSAs. He also questions those conservatives who see the end of the revolution in the 2003 Medicare bill. (In any case, he believes that those who are angriest about Medicare have no one to blame but themselves. In the 1990s, he says, conservatives "didn't do the work" on Medicare that they did on other issues like welfare, taxes, and defense, and therefore Republicans did not have their own alternative on Medicare around which they could rally and hold the line against the Democrats' specific proposals.)

Norquist agrees that liberals won on virtually every key Medicare battle except the one on HSAs, but he says that twenty to thirty years from now, the Republicans' one victory will transform Medicare, while all the victories won by liberals in 2003 won't matter. To many, Norquist's claim might sound ludicrous. But consider why Senator Kennedy, who knows as much about Medicare as anyone, turned violently against the bill and did everything he could to defeat it because of a single issue, *the inclusion of HSAs.* Why? Perhaps because Kennedy feared that Norquist just might be right.

Norquist explains, "There are three major government programs— education, health care, and Social Security. These are the three programs you cannot cut. These three have to be reformed, not cut. We started back in the late 1970s to push 401(k)s, IRAs, and mutual funds as useful alternatives to Social Security. Now we're in the process of debating the privatization of Social Security."

The "we" Norquist refers to is the conservative movement, comprising primarily free-market thinkers who have an appetite for ideas that can change political equations. Norquist, like Newt Gingrich, thinks and plans in cicada-like cycles. "I was always more comfortable with Gingrich than any other politician, because I could say, 'Fifteen years from now I want to be here,' and he was the only politician to say, 'Of course, I see that. I understand.' "

Norquist's reference to 401(k)s, IRAs, and mutual funds is telling. All had humble beginnings, but in a short period of time they have radically transformed the economy and Americans' notions of the best way to protect their financial security. Each of these devices was a way of using either the tax code or market incentives to accomplish one of two goals: increasing personal savings, thereby increasing personal autonomy and responsibility, or allowing individuals to invest small amounts of money without exposing them to the wild gyrations of an individual stock. And all three have achieved precisely what their proponents sought when they fought for their creation back in the late 1970s: greater individual comfort with the investment world; a larger, more expansive sense of financial security and financial well-being through self-managed investments; and an overall reduction in the suspicion of, and resentment toward, what used to be known quite pejoratively as the "investment class." Tens of millions of Americans now own their own retirement accounts or participate in some form of mutual fund. These investment vehicles are no longer just for the rich; they reach down to the middle and lower-middle classes. Personal finance is now a near-universal American topic. These profound changes occurred in the space of just a couple of decades, as Congress approved IRAs in 1974 and 401(k)s in 1978, and the first retail mutual funds appeared in 1976.

And as Norquist accurately observes, the nation is now seriously debating the value of partially privatizing Social Security, which was a topic George W. Bush campaigned hard on in 2000 and again in 2004. Privatizing Social Security for younger Americans appears a long way off, to be sure. But it's much closer than anyone would have imagined in the late 1970s. And it's certainly much closer than it would have been if Norquist and company for all those intervening years had simply complained about the Social Security system rather than creating an alternative structure that makes privatization a viable option. "If Social Security was in crisis back in the old days, we'd have just bailed it out [with higher payroll taxes]," Norquist argues. "Today if Social Security hit some sort of crisis, we'd get some sort of privatization."

And now, they plan to do the same thing for Medicare (or *to* Medicare, depending on your viewpoint). This is why Norquist bats aside the conservative angst over the Medicare bill. Yes, it's too expensive. Yes, it has almost no structural reform. Yes, Republicans caved on almost every principled fight they had waged throughout the 1990s. It's all true and lamentable, and would border on tragic if it weren't for one thing: HSAs are now in the law.

"As long as HSA is in this expansion, it's part of the revolution and a natural extension of it," Norquist says. "And if we can get HSAs expanded to 20, 30 percent of the population in the next five years or so, the more people who get into HSAs, the more people we can say, 'This is the alterna-tive.' We're going to give people HSAs now so we take them out of the pool of people who care about Medicare when they're sixty-five, but we do it when they're twenty, thirty, forty years old. That's what we did with 401(k)s, IRAs, and mutual funds. What we did do was insist that HSAs be in there. We've done our homework. We've been working on them for more than a decade. Our job as a movement is to ramp up the number of people in HSAs dramatically. . . . We will revisit Medicare, because it's going bank-rupt. We've got to get that done. In the life cycle of convincing people it's broken and needs to be fixed and giving them an alternative they are com-fortable moving to, that is how [we will change the dynamic]. We will not cut Medicare, we will move everyone into HSAs. We're talking about turn-ing Medicare and Social Security into forced savings plans, which turns them into massive tax cuts and massive spending reductions. That's 30 to 40 percent of the federal budget we could be replacing."

And there is the next stage of the revolution in a nutshell.

Almost no one sees it that way now, however. And the two lawmakers who played the biggest role in making sure the Medicare drug bill became law didn't see it that way when they played their pivotal role in the most sig-nificant shift in health care policy for the elderly since 1965.

But the story of why our two lawmakers voted for the 2003 Medicare drug bill must wait, of necessity, for the story of the vote itself.

### The Vote

In November 2003, I was covering the Medicare bill for Fox News, and I knew this House vote would be extremely tight. I knew Republicans had mobilized armies of lobbyists from every conceivable industry to push for passage. The pharmaceutical industry had assigned one lobbyist per Republican member of Congress, while major insurance companies had dispatched nearly as many lobbyists. The Chamber of Commerce was work-ing the hallways, as was the American Medical Association. Other powerful GOP interest groups with no apparent stake in Medicare or prescription drugs also worked the corridors, including defense contractors and the National Right to Life Committee. Defense contractors, like all major employers, were concerned about maintaining billions in corporate subsi-dies, and the National Right to Life Committee wanted to preserve as many free-market provisions as possible, because it sees any movement toward government-sanctioned rationing of care as a step toward limiting the options of the terminally ill and those who require life support.

But the most important lobby in favor of the bill was AARP, formerly known as the American Association of Retired Persons. AARP endorsed the bill and spent $8 million on a television campaign to build public support for it.

"That was the key to legitimizing the vote," says Tony Rudy, a former chief of staff to Tom DeLay who lobbied for the bill on behalf of the pharmaceutical industry. "It was a shot to the knees of Democrats. It was the Good Housekeeping seal."

It was an odd move for AARP. For years the organization had sided with Democrats over the prescription drug issue, but now it endorsed a bill Democrats denounced as the first step toward dismantling Medicare. Essentially, AARP made a political calculation about the future. It could not imagine when Democrats would next control Congress, so it wanted to use the GOP bill to put Medicare in the business of providing drug coverage. The drug bill could and probably would be enlarged later. Democrats ridiculed AARP and called it a stooge of the radical right-wing majority, but the organization held firm. No single voice was more important in building support for the bill within GOP ranks.

And yet even with AARP on board, the public reaction was tepid. Seniors remained skeptical. Even AARP's TV spots said the bill was far from perfect but the best seniors could hope for now—not exactly a ringing endorsement. Though AARP's campaign worked wonders on Capitol Hill, it appeared to sway very few voters. This was a case study in a powerful interest group separating itself from its members but retaining its clout on Capitol Hill by reputation. Many lawmakers endorsed the bill after AARP did, fearing seniors' backlash if they didn't. But if these lawmakers had waited for AARP to actually produce real voter pressure, they would have discovered that AARP couldn't do it. What turned votes was fear of a backlash that AARP had no hope of producing.

The afternoon of the House vote, Friday, November 21, I began an e-mail conversation with Tim Berry, House Majority Leader Tom DeLay's chief of staff. Berry was stationed in DeLay's conference room just off the House floor, working the floor and counting votes. I never tried to call him. Even cell phones were too much of an imposition. He spoke to me entirely through his BlackBerry.

At 4:30 P.M. I opened the conversation by asking about the status of the bill and when the vote would be. Berry wrote back, "Medicare is tough sledding but we always seem to hit the wall about this point. Depends on how all of our conservatives break and whether or not the Democrats ultimately break. We are hearing all over the place that there are about 20 Democrats that are nervous they will lose their seats over this and are furious with [House Minority Leader Nancy Pelosi]. If they vote against the bill we will do everything we can to make sure they do lose their seats. Vote sometime late tonight, probably 1 or 2 in the morning."

Pelosi was a huge problem for Republicans. She knew many conservative Democrats wanted to vote for the Republican bill because they were virtually certain it would pass and the president would sign it. They didn't want to vote against the first drug benefit added to Medicare. Many had worked the issue for years and pledged to constituents that they wouldn't demand perfection the first time around. With AARP's blessing, the bill met all legitimate criteria for at least twenty and as many as thirty Democrats. But Pelosi made opposition to the bill a test of party loyalty. She told a closed-door meeting of House Democrats that it would be "disastrous" if Democrats helped the GOP pass the bill.

"They threatened Democrats who might vote for the bill that they would lose committee posts and office space," says John Feehery, Hastert's spokesman.

At 5:19 P.M. I wrote back to Berry, trying to draw him out on what AARP and the White House were up to. Six minutes later he responded, "They [AARP] are not cutting nuts. The President has made some calls and will make more but it is tough all around right now. We have picked up a few conservatives in the last half hour and put a couple of hard no's in play. No question this thing could go down, but it is always bleakest right before folks start to break your way. Always. I've been through about a dozen of these. Not many this hard, but a handful."

President Bush had already been on the phone lobbying Republicans opposed to the bill. This was an early sign of just how dire the situation had become. Typically, presidents don't make personal calls to lobby for votes until the last minute. That Bush was on the phone ten hours before the House leadership would even put the bill up for a vote signaled that the White House and the GOP leadership were way behind. Nearly thirty conservative Republicans were still stubbornly opposed, which meant that

GOP leaders had to find at least fifteen crossover Democrats. But those votes were nowhere to be seen. Minority Leader Pelosi had given conservative Democrats permission to vote for the bill if that's what politics required, but she ordered that *under no circumstances* were they to provide the votes necessary to produce a majority before Republicans had produced it themselves.

Berry's line about AARP's inability or unwillingness to "cut nuts" revealed the organization's limited ability to move votes in the clutch. In the past, AARP could mobilize dozens upon dozens of votes. In some cases, its endorsement or rejection meant victory or defeat. Not this time. AARP's "Good Housekeeping" seal, as Tony Rudy described it, was of limited value. It kept Republicans in the game and gave the bill life it might not otherwise have had. But it was not decisive. By this time, GOP leaders now recognized that AARP couldn't deliver the majority they would need, either among Republicans or Democrats. This was a staggering setback, one that took GOP leaders by surprise and forced them to rely on much more brutish means.

Still, I recognized that Berry was right when he said "it is always bleakest right before folks start to break your way," since votes often move when lawmakers see that leadership has brought the issue to a head and there's no more room to hide. I've watched literally dozens of "absolute no's" turn to "yes" votes under the pressure of a real vote. Most lawmakers in both parties, regardless of ideology, don't have the stomach to contribute to the defeat of a leadership-backed bill. This is especially true in the House, where the majority party can dictate the schedule and move legislation. If the majority party's leaders can't be sure its members will stand with it on close votes for high-priority bills, those leaders become paralyzed and the minority party can more routinely exert influence over floor proceedings. The Republicans had seen this breakdown in Democratic discipline and unity in 1993 and rightly concluded that it foreshadowed the Democrats' political disintegration. Therefore, since the dawn of the Republican Revolution, a central organizing principle of the GOP majority had been that Republicans would not inflict wounds on their leaders. I also figured that most lawmakers would realize that the opportunity to pass a Medicare drug benefit might not come around again, possibly, for as many as four years.

I wrote to Berry again at 5:36 P.M., sketching out my plans to keep track of the vote and wondering whether he agreed that Republicans would be able to pull votes over to their side if they got within ten votes of the minimum needed for passage.

At 5:40 P.M. Berry responded, "I think we will get at least there [within 10 votes of passage] but everything we hear is that there is a big group, about 20, that are desperate to vote for the bill but won't go up until we go over 218."

GOP leaders and the White House were caught in a Catch-22. They had a theoretical majority, since a number of Democrats *wanted* to vote for the bill. But because of Pelosi's order, the Democrats who wanted to vote yes wouldn't do so until their vote wasn't necessary—that is, until Republicans *already* had a real majority. Meanwhile, the twenty to thirty conservative Republicans who wanted to vote no had no intention of switching, because they wanted the bill to die and the process to start all over again. So GOP leaders and the White House had to try to wrench conservative Republicans from the ranks of "no" in order to move the bill close enough to passage that conservative Democrats would catch this-is-going-to-pass-and-I-don't-want-to-be-against-it fever.

I wrote back to Berry immediately, again trying to draw out how far the Republican leadership had gone in threatening Democrats that they might lose out if they refused to switch their vote. Were the Republicans going to put out the word that those conservative Democrats had better not wait until the GOP got to the magic 218 votes, since the gavel would drop at that moment?

At 5:51 P.M. Berry wrote back, "We already have."

This message left me stunned. From this point forward I couldn't see how the leadership or the White House could turn the vote around. AARP had shot its bolt. Bush had made calls but was still at least twenty and maybe even thirty votes away. Democrats weren't breaking and weren't buying GOP threats to pass the bill without them. This told me that the House Republican leadership and the White House were miles away from assembling a majority *and the Democrats knew it.* Unity was now easy for Democrats to impose because the threat of a GOP victory appeared so puny.

The Republican leadership and the White House decided to gamble: They would throw the bill on the floor and see what would happen.

I left Fox and headed home. I wasn't working Saturday, but I had an intense curiosity about the vote and I considered the entire issue the best prism to judge the revolution of '94. I wanted to be as close to the final outcome as I could, and keeping in touch with Berry was the best way to do this. I e-mailed Berry from my BlackBerry just as the House was preparing to vote on the rule that would set the stage for final debate and a vote on final passage. It was 10:09 P.M., and I checked in to see if the Republican leadership had made any progress in the intervening four and a half hours.

Berry wrote back at 10:28 P.M., "If we get the Democrats we are told we will get, we are there. Unfortunately, we can't depend on that. We are working a handful of remaining votes."

I knew then that the leadership and the White House had made almost no progress. Less than a half hour before this e-mail exchange, Nancy Pelosi had flatly declared, "They don't have the votes." And they didn't. But they pressed on, unsure of the outcome and hoping against hope they could somehow prevail.

Floor debate droned on until 3 A.M., when vote on final passage began. By roughly 3:30 A.M., Democrats had 218 votes, enough to defeat the bill. A short time later, Democrats had 219 votes and Republicans had 215 votes, with only one lawmaker whose vote was unrecorded. Yes, the GOP leadership had pulled some of its wayward members back onto the reservation, but the Republicans were still stuck.

At 4:13 A.M., bleary-eyed and disbelieving, I unsheathed my Black-Berry, turned on a light by the TV, and wrote Berry for another update.

At 4:29 A.M. he wrote back, "We aren't having much luck. Could go down."

This was ninety minutes into the vote. It was already becoming clear that Republicans had tried everything and none of it was working. The situation was desperate. They had few alternatives.

Berry's message underlined the gravity of the situation. I'd never known DeLay's team to concede defeat. As Berry had pointed out in earlier e-mails, he'd been through many tough votes when they achieved victory after defeat had appeared certain. He had never actually seen defeat. No one on DeLay's staff had. But now, on the president's number-one legislative priority, defeat appeared all too real. The fate of the president's domestic agenda and the GOP majority's ability to govern hung in the balance. And no one knew quite what to do.

I wrote Berry back at 4:33 A.M., asking if POTUS—the President of the United States—was calling House members to try to win them to his side. Given how bad things were looking for the Republicans at that moment, I also asked about the next step: Would the bill resurface if it was voted down now?

Berry wrote back at 4:40 A.M., "No POTUS right now. No real negotiations, just arm twisting. No way to tell if it will resurface."

The vote count did not move. The bill was dead. But because Republicans would not call an end to the vote, it remained technically alive. For more than an hour Democrats had registered the absolute majority necessary to kill the bill, and although House rules specified only a *minimum* time to record votes, the long custom was for floor votes to last no more than an hour. By every conventional application of the House rules, the bill had long since been rejected. But Republicans were breaking all customs and conventions. They would not accept defeat. And because they had the majority and thus were able to enforce rules in their favor, the vote stayed open. In all, Hastert would hold the vote open for 171 minutes—nearly three hours.

I wrote Berry back at 4:50 A.M., hoping to learn the next strategic steps the leadership would take and asking if the president was actively involved at this point. Berry wrote back at 5:05 A.M., "He is up and making calls."

The president was now back in the game, calling lawmakers on their cell phones. But even this wasn't working. Bush called Michigan's Nick Smith at 5:30 A.M., but the congressman rebuffed the president as he had Hastert and DeLay. Nothing was working.

Then something changed. And it changed while I was asleep on the couch.

With only the glowing TV lighting my living room, I'd drifted off around 5:30 A.M. At 5:53 A.M., I awoke to the sound of a pounding gavel. I grabbed my glasses just in time to see the final count: 220 yes, 215 no. In less than thirty minutes, the Republicans had gained five votes and the Democrats had lost four.

The vote had lasted some three hours. At 5:59 A.M. I wrote Berry, "There's a helluva story in that three hours."

Berry wrote back at 6:29 A.M., "Maybe you should end your book with it."

## The Difference Maker

How did the House leadership do it? What did the president say? What happened in those pivotal twenty-three minutes when the bill had seemed sure to die?

Trent Franks knows. Because he turned the tide. He was the difference maker. Without him, the bill wouldn't have passed.

I spoke to Franks to find out what had happened behind the scenes.

Before the vote started, Hastert, DeLay, and former Speaker Newt Gingrich lobbied Franks, the Arizona congressman recalls. He told them all no. He said he wouldn't budge, no matter what.

About two hours into the floor vote, Hastert approached Franks again. "He said, 'Trent, can't you help me?' "

Franks said he told Hastert, "Mr. Speaker, the more time you are spending with me, the more time you are spending away from someone who may be able to help. So please don't do this."

Pressure was building on the floor and members were getting testy. One Republican came up to lobby Franks and Franks told him he couldn't vote for a bill that would increase the pace toward socialism. According to Franks, the member shot back, "You calling me a communist?" Franks said no, but the conversation ended on unsettled terms.

After Hastert left, Franks says, DeLay approached.

"Then comes the majority leader. I really love him. I think he's a champion."

DeLay repeated all the arguments, but Franks wasn't buying. The Arizona congressman considers himself an ideological conservative, one willing to lose his seat in Congress on principle. He doesn't consider himself a waverer. He possesses no self-doubts, he says. The principle in this case was that the GOP bill was creeping socialism, something Franks specifically promised in his 2002 campaign to oppose. But DeLay kept the heat on.

"It wasn't the political pressure," Franks says. "I've always been what I consider to be pressure bulletproof. I was being pressured but I wasn't feeling it. Did they try to use every argument they could? Yes. But there was no, absolutely no, absolutely no inappropriate pressure. And I said no many times. Was it intense? Yes. They were trying to get everyone."

In truth, Franks and the other conservatives never believed they would hold out long enough to actually kill the bill. They didn't have a leader and they hadn't organized coherently to defend against leadership pressure. They always assumed the leadership or the White House would peel enough of them off with all variety of legislative goodies. But it didn't happen. The conservatives stuck it out.

"We really didn't think we'd be able to stop it," Franks recalls. "But when it came down to the last hour, the leadership concluded it was going to lose. They absolutely thought it was going down. I heard the majority leader say, 'We're done, let's call it.' " Franks says this was in the final hour of the vote, which is consistent with Berry's e-mails to me. But as Franks tells the story, DeLay did not give in at that point.

"He wasn't playing games. Then they said, 'Wait.' They approached some Democrats. Some offers were made. Were they unethical? No. But were they inappropriate? Yes."

Franks will not discuss the offers made to conservative Democrats. Whatever they were, they failed to move votes.

About this time, Franks assembled a group of about six conservatives to discuss options in the aftermath of the bill's death. But suddenly Franks and conservatives grew anxious that the bill would rise again in a much less attractive form.

"Something then did happen," Franks says. "[The Republican leadership] made the decision the bill was going to go down. We became aware— incontrovertibly aware—that an understanding had been reached that this bill was going to go down and the leadership was going to bring the Senate version to the floor and let the House vote on it. And we learned the Democrats were able to guarantee 200 votes, more than enough from their side for passage. We became aware of this plan. We were absolutely, fundamentally aware."

Conservative Republicans loathed the original Senate Medicare bill. It contained no provisions for market competition and no HSAs, and it provided far more generous drug benefits. While Republicans feared that the House-Senate conference report would cost much more than the CBO's $400 billion estimate, they were convinced the Senate version could cost as much as $1 trillion. Interestingly, President Bush had endorsed both the House and Senate bills. He had sent word that he hoped to sign the most conservative bill Congress could produce, but he kept his options open because he insisted on passing *some* Medicare drug bill that year.

Franks says that the GOP leaders decided to go along with a White House request to drop the House-Senate conference report and call up the Senate alternative. In fact, he says, they had negotiated a deal with Democratic leaders.

"They had already made provisions to let the Senate version pass," Franks says. "Here's what was scary. Three Democrats in the House leadership, they had agreed and would supply as much as 200 votes. There was no doubt about being able to stop it."

It was now well past 5:30 A.M., and Franks and other conservatives in his group suddenly grew squeamish. This unholy alliance of GOP leaders, the White House, and the Democratic leadership looked all too real, and the prospect of seeing the Senate bill become the vehicle for Medicare drug benefits left them all terrified.

"I said out loud, 'Oh my God, we can't stop this.' "

Franks says he bolted out of the House chamber's north door and was followed by several conservative Republicans: John Shadegg and Jeff Flake of Arizona, Jim Ryun of Kansas, C. L. "Butch" Otter of Idaho, and Mike Pence of Indiana. They huddled off the floor.

"I said, 'You know what's happening? They could call the vote anytime.' Flake said, 'You're right.' These guys that were in the room were not the guys who were wavering. We opposed the bill. But this was panic time. It was panic time for the country. We were panicking. They could have dropped the gavel anytime. And someone said, 'Do they [the GOP leaders] know that we know?' We said, 'No, they don't know that we know.' And I said we had to get something good for what we're going to do."

According to Franks, he and the other five conservatives went to Tom DeLay's conference room just off the House floor, where they met with DeLay, Dennis Hastert, Bill Thomas, and HHS secretary Tommy Thompson.

"We said there might be a way we'd support the bill if we could get certain assurances from the president. Some of them had to do with some good things on free-market principles later on. The Speaker said, 'No, the president wouldn't go for it.' But the majority leader said, 'Maybe. All we can do is call.' So DeLay called the president and handed the phone to me. I talked with him for fifteen minutes. I was dedicated to getting the best thing for the country. Some of the things had everything to do with Medicare and some of the things had nothing to do with Medicare. But we tried to do something good for the country. We tried to get as many free-market dynamics into Medicare [as we could]. We knew if we failed to get this bill passed, something really bad would happen to the country. This was something we could build on. I had to make an incredibly difficult choice that wasn't selfish, that wasn't political. All I had to do was go to my office and go to sleep. And I would do it again, even though I'm sorry we had to choose between the imperfect and disastrous."

Even so, Franks has confronted no end of critics back home.

"I have taken a pretty good licking on this," Franks says. "One of my longest and most faithful supporters came up to me and said, 'If you, one of the truest believers, caves, then what hope is there?' "

The hope for Franks and conservatives like him is that, as Grover Norquist argues, the small toehold of free-market reforms in the bill, primarily the HSAs, will allow more Americans to use their own savings (HSAs) and make their own choices (premium support) when it comes to health care. To free-market conservatives, a health care system of pooled resources and pooled risk simply cannot pay for all Americans' health care needs, particularly since more and more Americans demand instantaneous relief from pain and discomfort, no matter how minor. If individuals or families begin using the advantage of tax-free savings to set aside their own rainy-day funds for immunizations, well-baby visits, or prescription drugs for a seasonal cold, they can choose health care plans with higher deductibles and pay lower premiums. The more individuals and families make these kinds of choices, the less employers will have to spend on kitchen-sink health care plans, conservatives argue. According to proponents of HSAs, that will reduce the premiums businesses pay and allow more of them to provide health insurance to employees who don't have it now. And while Democrats derided HSAs as health care for the rich, the history of regular IRAs and IRAs designed to help pay for college indicates that individuals and families from all income brackets can benefit from tax-free savings.

"You know, as I looked at the final bill, I almost looked at in disgust," says Tony Rudy, the lobbyist and former DeLay chief of staff. "When we started in 1995, we wanted hard-core free-market reforms. But the country's not there. You can't govern too far ahead of the American people. It's incrementalism that's important now. Even though it was a massive enlargement of the Medicare entitlement, I think at least 25 percent of the Medicare market will be covered by the private market in twenty years."

But that's not why the other Trent saved the Medicare bill. The other Trent saved the Medicare bill because that's what loyal Republicans do.

## Party Loyalty

Trent Lott of Mississippi performed one of the greatest acts of party loyalty in recent memory less than a year after his own colleagues and a Republican White House stripped him of his position as Senate majority leader. Lott had caused an uproar with a comment he made at a party celebrating the hundredth birthday of Senator Strom Thurmond of South Carolina, a comment that some interpreted as racist but that Lott swore was spoken in jest. The party, held in December 2002 in the Senate Russell Caucus Room, was a jovial occasion filled with witticisms about Thurmond's longevity in life and ribald commentary about his legendary procreative capabilities (he sired his fifth and last child at the age of seventy-four). Lott was clearly enjoying the frivolity and hijinks, but he got a bit wound up. He said Mississippi was still proud of voting for Thurmond for president in 1948, when the South Carolinian ran as the leader of the segregationist Dixiecrat Party. Lott said the nation would have been better off in 2002 if other states had followed Mississippi's lead and elected Thurmond president. "And we wouldn't have had all these problems we've had over the years," Lott said, leaving the notion behind that the "problems" segregationists would have spared the nation from included integration, civil rights, and voting rights.

The White House did not abandon Lott immediately after the ensuing uproar began. It gave Lott several days to remedy the situation, in fact. But Lott handled the matter clumsily and only made matters worse. Finally, the White House sent word that Lott could be replaced—but only if the replacement was Senator Bill Frist of Tennessee. This instruction reflected the president's commitment to winning the fight over the Medicare drug benefit. Frist was the only physician in the Senate, a world-famous lung and heart transplant surgeon who spoke with an unrivaled credibility on all matters of health care policy and politics. What's more, Bush knew that Lott was not well versed on the Medicare issue, and he doubted whether he could rely on Lott to support an imperfect compromise. So with the White House's support, Frist—who had been elected in the 1994 revolution and had held no Senate leadership roles before—leapfrogged over all his colleagues to supplant Lott and take control of the GOP agenda. Not surprisingly, when he became Senate majority leader he said his top priority in 2003 was the passage of a Medicare drug benefit.

Many Washington observers thought Lott would resign in disgrace. He did not. He relinquished his leadership post and settled into life as one of a hundred senators. Lott was determined to make a difference his way and rebuild a reputation he had done so much to sully.

Lott has given few interviews about his role in the Medicare bill. He refused to talk to reporters after playing the pivotal role in saving the bill from certain defeat in the Senate. He has shied away from interviews in part because he considers the vote to save the bill "one of the worst of my life."

Here's how it happened:

As majority leader since 1996, Lott was all too familiar with the political pressure to provide prescription drug coverage under Medicare. The Senate Republican conference is less conservative than the House conference, and the internal pressure to produce credible Medicare drug alternatives to those put forth by Democrats had been nearly constant since the late 1990s.

"I came to the conclusion several years back that we were going to have to deal with the need for prescription drug assistance for low-income elderly only," Lott told me, "and to help pay for that, we were going to have to couple that with some reforms. And we made a couple of runs at it."

But the GOP "runs at it" failed to attract much Democratic support and did not even unify all Senate Republicans. Lott and other Senate Republican leaders had been fending off a Democratic Medicare drug bill but knew they couldn't hold the Democrats back forever. In the run-up to the 2000 election, House and Senate Republicans feared that a Gore victory could snap the GOP resistance but thought a Bush victory would provide a respite.

Lott was willing to accept a prescription drug benefit but *only* if it was limited to the poorest Medicare beneficiaries and cases of catastrophic illness, since the costs of a universal benefit would be prohibitive and would assuredly accelerate Medicare's headlong rush to insolvency. After his election, President Bush said he wanted such a narrow drug benefit, but he also wanted important cost-saving reforms: higher premiums on wealthier Medicare beneficiaries, stringent antifraud measures (Medicare wasted tens of billions annually in overcharges), and less-generous reimbursement rates.

"When I met with the president in the fall of 2002 with [Oklahoma Republican and Senate Majority Whip] Don Nickles and [Iowa Republican and Finance Committee chairman] Chuck Grassley in the Oval Office, the president said, 'We need to do prescription drugs and it's *got* to be coupled with Medicare reform,' " Lott recalls. "So I thought that was the marching order."

But the politics of universal drug coverage proved too strong. When seniors heard Medicare, they thought universal coverage. One equaled the other. Severing the two, it appeared, was politically impossible. By the time the decisions were being made with how to proceed with a Senate version of the Bush Medicare drug bill, Lott was no longer the majority leader, no longer the broker. But he still had his one vote. In the end, it would count more than any other.

"Well, 2003 the bill comes up here [to the Senate] and the president's proposal is just summarily shot down, first on making it universal and second on blowing off most of his reforms," Lott remembers. "The key Republican leaders were saying, 'No, no, it's too hard, it's politically unacceptable.' The mistake the president and the White House made was saying, 'Well, okay, do the best you can and we'll sign any damn thing you get through and send us.' And that was a *huge* mistake. He started with a good program, it had good principles, and the Congress brushed it aside and he said, 'Okay.' . . . There's no justification for high-income people or even people in the middle-upper income to be getting subsidized prescription drugs. There's no justification for it and you can't afford it. So that was the beginning of the end, early on."

As the bill made its way through both chambers, Lott grew more and more discouraged. He saw the ideas behind Medicare reform—ideas Republicans had kept alive throughout the Clinton presidency—pulverized by a coarse politics of expediency. *Republican expediency!* Lott voted against the Senate's Medicare bill because he considered it far too expensive. He had no intention, initially, of voting for the compromise bill worked out by House and Senate negotiators, because he considered it only slightly less expensive and slightly more reform-oriented than the Senate version. Regardless of the CBO's $400 billion cost estimate, the figure Congress was by law compelled to use, Lott felt quite sure the bill would cost at least half as much more in its first ten years.

"By the time we get to the floor, I felt very confident the cost of the bill is not going to be $400 billion but $600 billion to $800 billion," Lott recalls. "I thought there were many sleights of hand, the payoffs to the industry."

The bill came to the Senate floor on November 22. Democrats knew that any Republican defections might torpedo the bill, so they did what any aggressive minority would do: They used every parliamentary tactic possible to drive a wedge into GOP ranks and kill the bill. They argued that the bill would cost much more than the $400 billion Congress had allotted to cover Medicare drug costs over ten years, which would violate the 1974 budget act. Democrats produced numerous outside analysts who projected the bill's costs from $600 billion to $1 trillion. (The Democrats used this argument simply as a procedural tactic to kill a bill they opposed; even according to the ultraconservative CBO estimates, the Democrats' own Medicare drug bill would have cost *$1 trillion* over ten years.) In response to the Democrats' maneuver, Republicans had to vote in sufficient numbers to say, *No, the bill doesn't violate Congress's budget.* On votes of this kind, it doesn't matter who is technically correct; it only matters who has enough votes. Republicans needed votes to prevail, and they realized they might need Trent Lott's vote.

This put the White House, Senate GOP leaders, and Lott in a very strange position indeed. The White House and some of the same Republicans who had cast Lott aside and replaced him with Frist would now have to come to him on bended knee to save the president's bill—and, by extension, to save the president's bid for reelection. Talk about awkward.

"I made clear I was going to vote [against the Republicans], but I held my fire as much as I could because I did not want to appear that this was me confronting Frist," Lott recalls. "This was his baby. Big baby with a bow in its hair. So I didn't want it to appear that this was sour grapes because of what happened."

The vote was drawing near. GOP vote counters were now almost certain they would need Lott. Without Lott, the bill could lose on the Democrats' procedural vote, which would force the bill to be redrafted and the process to start all over. Losing on this vote would mean total defeat for President Bush and the GOP leadership in both chambers. Supporters of the bill believed that the mass media would say the president was too weak to lead, too weak to make good on a campaign promise (never mind that the bill was far more generous than what Bush had campaigned on behalf of).

"I knew by the time the vote occurred that was going to be the key vote and my vote could be the vote," Lott says. "And it came right down to me. And when I went to the floor, I told two of my best buddies, [Kentucky's] Mitch McConnell and [Pennsylvania's] Rick Santorum, 'All right, I'm going to give you one last chance to convince me to vote on this.' They both made their case; I was unpersuaded. I went back into the back of the chamber, like on the second row, and was surrounded by people I do respect and people I do listen to. [Arizona's] Jon Kyl, [Texas's] Kay Bailey Hutchison, Chuck Grassley. You know, lots of people. I was unpersuaded by all of it and was intending to walk down and vote [saying the bill would violate Congress's budget]. Part of their argument was, 'We need this, we have to show we can produce a result, we told the people we were going to do this, we've just go to do it.' And I said, 'But we're doing the wrong thing. You're asking me to vote for a good-sounding title, but the substance is all wrong.' "

In the Senate, the majority party does *whatever it can* not to lose on procedural votes of the kind Republicans were now facing—votes not related to the substance of a bill. If the majority party can't enforce internal discipline to stop the minority party from using procedural votes to derail its agenda, then its majority power simply ceases to exist, and legislative anarchy reigns. This is why Senate Republicans were making such impassioned appeals to Lott.

"They reminded me of all the times I had asked them to cast a tough vote," Lott recalls. "The best argument was, 'Look, you have repeatedly said over the years, *Don't vote for technical motions by Democrats that are used to kill a bill,* and we're asking you the same thing.' "

Lott still thought the bill was "a big mistake," but he knew how many times in his years as majority leader he had implored his fellow Republicans to defend against a Democratic procedural assault simply to protect the Republicans' majority power. Whether he was beseeching a conservative to stick with the party on moderate policy or a moderate Republican to resist a procedural assault on conservative policy, Lott himself had often asked Republicans on the fence to cast a vote *against their convictions but with their party.*

That wasn't the clincher, however. The clincher was the senior senator from Massachusetts, the personification of liberal excess.

"I'll tell you the defining thing was I looked over on the Democrat side and there was Ted Kennedy looking right at me with a smile as big as a mile," Lott recalls. "And I thought, 'If I do this and take this bill down, there's going to be a huge press conference with Ted Kennedy and Hillary Clinton and Tom Daschle jumping up and down celebrating the defeat administered to President George Bush,' and I just could not stand that thought. And so I said, 'All right.' I walked down the well, cast my vote, and stormed out of the room. And [I] was in a severe state of depression. And it was one of the worst votes I've cast in years. And I'll regret it the longest day I live."

### The Revolution: Dead or Alive?

Trent Lott's vote defeated the Democrats and saved the president's Medicare bill. It's a bill Lott believes George W. Bush and Republicans will live to regret for years. He knows that Newt Gingrich, with whom he used to be close, lobbied for the bill and changed votes on the House side. It all leaves Lott stone-cold.

"I think maybe that vote was the clearest signal I've seen yet that the revolution is over," Lott says. "In fact, I've only spoken to Newt Gingrich once since that and I basically said, 'What were you doing?' The Moses who led us into the Promised Land helped end the revolution. It is a major form of socialism and government control. Subsidized medicine for upper-income people, budget busting—I mean, good gravy, what is it we stand for?"

Gingrich no longer has a vote. But one of his fellow revolutionary leaders, Tom DeLay, still does. He not only has a vote, he has a voice. DeLay was there at the dawn of the revolution, and he was there when Lott and many other Republicans believed it died. To them, DeLay says, *Don't despair, the revolution lives on.* But if the revolution lives on, some of the revolutionaries no longer display the almost pathological antipolitical instincts they did in those heady early days. DeLay's comments reflect his awareness of the importance of political pragmatism.

"If you're going to change entitlements, if you're going to change politically sensitive issues, you do it the way we did it with welfare reform and you do it the way we did it on Medicare," DeLay told me. "What we did was significant and profound because what we did was completely redesign health care for senior citizens by using market principles and our philosophy."

Like Grover Norquist, DeLay believes that the small free-market reforms in the Medicare bill will lower costs in the future. He also hopes that the law will improve diagnostic care and preventive medicine. Perhaps most important, he believes that parts of the law will change how seniors look at health care—such as the reforms that should encourage seniors looking for drug coverage to turn away from Medicare and to health maintenance organizations (HMOs) or preferred provider networks (PPOs), which work more aggressively to control costs. Most of these savings and improvements will not come immediately, but as Norquist points out, sometimes the most important changes come over time.

DeLay reveals his political pragmatism when he lashes back at critics such as Lott.

"How would they do it?" DeLay asks bitterly. "Repeal Medicare—that's good. You'll get twenty votes for that."

Nobody, least of all Trent Lott or Trent Franks, ever proposed repealing Medicare. What they would have preferred was a bill that would have reformed Medicare in the ways they had hoped for and the ways their party used to demand. That bill never materialized, because of political concessions by GOP leaders early on in the legislative process.

What will they get for their reluctant votes for a bill they didn't believe in?

Only time will tell.

# EPILOGUE

Arguing that the Contract with America changed the country and will continue to shape its future requires challenging two separate ideological orthodoxies, Left and Right.

The Left never took the Contract seriously and has downplayed the Republican majority's influence. To them, the real source of change was President Bill Clinton, whose superior political skills allowed him to claim more political victories and who consequently survived impeachment and left the White House nearly as beloved, in their eyes, as Ronald Reagan was. As this book has shown, Clinton bested congressional Republicans on key policies—beating them back on education and environmental regulations, to name just two. Clinton remains a demigod within the Democratic Party, while many of his "revolutionary" foes have seeped quietly into lobbying or think-tank wonkery, and some have left (or been driven out of) politics entirely. By these conventional standards, arguing that the Contract made a lasting difference seems foolhardy.

What's even more interesting in assessing the Contract's impact is that so many of its original cheerleaders find themselves disgusted, discouraged, and demoralized. They see the past decade as a nightmarish tale of Republican renegades losing their nerve, of hell-for-leather leaders settling into moderation and accommodation, of young Turks transformed into grandees concerned with acquiring perks and examining polling data rather than with discerning right from wrong and pursuing what in the Contract era was referred to as commonsenseconservatism (back then it sounded like one word) no matter the political cost. (Just a year apart, two erstwhile revolutionaries—both maverick freshmen from the Republican class of '94—wrote books calling out their former congressional colleagues for having betrayed the Republican Revolution: September 2003 marked the release of former

Oklahoma congressman Tom Coburn's *Breach of Trust: How Washington Turns Outsiders into Insiders,* while September 2004 brought a scathing indictment from former Florida representative Joe Scarborough, the cable talk-show host, titled *Rome Wasn't Burnt in a Day: The Real Deal on How Politicians, Bureaucrats, and Other Washington Barbarians Are Bankrupting America.*)

The Left never took the Contract seriously. And now much of the Right doubts its importance.

Which is all the more reason to study this fascinating document and distill its real-world impact—why it mattered, where it mattered, and how political pressure forced necessary compromises. As this book has shown, the Republican Revolution was real and widespread. It defined core economic and social policy for both parties (Democrats now call only for tax increases on the wealthiest 2 percent, live with the GOP-defined welfare reform, endorse tax credits rather than universal government control to expand health insurance, seek large defense budgets, and would make Medicare drug benefits more generous). The mainstream Left operates within a political bandwidth defined by the 1994 election and the Contract with America.

Meanwhile, the Right has achieved policy successes so wide and deep that it's almost impossible for many conservatives to fathom the change. Welfare reform broke cycles of dependency. Family-targeted tax cuts helped alleviate the burdens of payroll taxes on two-earner families, allowing the middle class to expand. Early spending cuts and the near-death struggle over balancing the budget steeled both parties in the politics of deficit reduction (the Clinton White House didn't call economic growth that fed deficit reduction and debt reduction "the virtuous cycle" until a GOP congressional majority made such choices more than virtuous—they made them politically mandatory). Unlike the Democratic architects of the Great Society, Republican Party leaders (and the country at large) have little buyer's remorse with what the Contract wrought.

When there's no buyer's remorse, the appetite quickens for a subsequent agenda equally daring, equally satisfying. And this defines the Right's dyspepsia over what a decade of power has wrought. What comes next? Many on the Right don't quite know, but they fear that what will fill the vacuum is what always fills the vacuum on Capitol Hill: the vulgarisms of unchecked power. Politicians going native, increased federal spending, expanded government entitlement programs—these failings and setbacks, not the achievements, define the revolution in many conservatives' minds.

And yet focusing on the setbacks, on the trappings of power, ignores the jaw-dropping changes the Contract with America has produced. Controversial as it was, the Contract represented a singular act of clarity, a moment of derring-do without modern precedent. It also invited serious appraisal by the press and the public and exposed conservative ideas to the purifying heat only free debate in a free society can apply. What emerged is a center-right consensus that at present has no serious political opposition. Almost every one of the dozens of Republicans interviewed for this book believes that the GOP continues to live off the accountability and "promises made, promises kept" ethos of the Contract, and *all of them* agree that Republicans would not have held on to power for a decade *without* the Contract. A good number of Democrats agree, which accounts for John Kerry's stab at a Contract of his own (with the middle class) during the 2004 presidential campaign.

A decade after the Republican Revolution, this much is certain: We are a different country because of the Contract with America, and our direction will continue to be shaped more durably and more profitably by the Contract than by any other manifesto of the twentieth century.

Where does it lead? How will the Contract change America in the next ten years? Specifically, not at all. But in tone and spirit it has already defined the next decade of Republican domestic policy. When President George W. Bush and top GOP figures spoke of an "ownership" society in the 2004 campaign, they were describing a world defined by the core precepts of the Contract: individual choices; government incentives to save and invest for life's exigencies; and freedom from government-produced forms, rules, or allocations when it comes to retirement security through Social Security, medicine through Medicare or Medicaid, education through public schools or college loans, or starting a small business or building an alternative to traditional one-company pensions. This isn't the Contract in word or deed, but it is in spirit. One is descended from the other, just as the Contract is a descendant of Reaganism. And since the Republicans have solidified and expanded their power—after their stunning success in the 2004 elections, they now hold even more seats in the House and the Senate than they did after the historic 1994 elections—they have positioned themselves to put their imprint on American society.

One Republican operative deeply versed in the history of Western civilization once described it this way: Reagan represented the Greeks, who created and defined the broadest swaths of enlightened civilization; the Contract and those who carried it out represented the Romans, who borrowed from the Greeks but added a muscularity and practicality that spread civilization across much of the known world; and President Bush's ownership society represented the Byzantines, who moved away from some aspects of Roman rule but remained faithful to the Greek definition of civilization. The analogy is by no means perfect, and reducing centuries-old civilizations to the crudities of American executive and legislative politics is, one must confess, more than a bit garish. But if you think of Reagan as the center of the GOP universe, the wellspring of its intellectual and political identity, then, yes, the Greek analogy applies. Similarly, the Republican congressional majority was nothing if not Roman in its ferocity and take-no-prisoners approach to politics, and it has remade the political landscape, bringing the GOP into parts of the country where, at least legislatively, it had never or rarely trod before, so the Roman analogy roughly fits. As for the Byzantines, they moved the geographic center of the Roman empire eastward and thereby cut the cords with Rome and its militaristic and expansionist ways; they also offered a softer version of that culture, borrowing more from Greek culture and Greek politics. In this the Bush reign—the first time a Republican president enjoyed a concentrated Republican congressional majority since the time of Herbert Hoover—can be seen as at least partially Byzantine: It has paid homage to Reagan with tax cuts and a strong defense, but it has also sloughed off some of the harsher forms of the early GOP congressional revolutionaries (the Romans), adapted to real-world political realities by spending more on domestic programs (education chief among them), and redefined the approach to conservatism by adapting limited free-market concepts to pre-existing entitlement programs such as Medicare.

Greek. Roman. Byzantine. It may seem an almost ludicrous stretch, but Republicans who have been living through this period and pondering its future don't think so. And perhaps the best place to end this dissection of the Contract with America is with a question: Can any other period in American political history ascribe to itself such an epochal intellectual and cultural heritage? I for one can't think of any.

# APPENDIX

# PATH TO REVOLUTION

The Contract with America, which congressional Republicans signed on the front steps of the U.S. Capitol on September 27, 1994, has reshaped American life in ways even those who drafted it did not expect. Liberal and conservative critics have declared the Contract with America dead so many times over the past decade that it is easy to overlook the profound changes that the Republican Revolution and the Contract have brought. The inescapable historical reality is this: the Contract changed the power equation in Washington and the national agenda on a host of issues—taxes, defense, welfare, budgets, crime, health care, education, entitlements, and gun control, among others. Quite simply, America is a vastly different place after the Contract than it was before it.

One impediment to understanding the significance and durability of the Republican Revolution is an inability to grasp what the Contract was and how it came into being. Often dismissed as just another election-year publicity ploy, the Contract, in fact, constituted a detailed legislative agenda, and it resulted from an extremely rigorous process that lasted months. As the documents shown in the following pages will demonstrate, Republicans devoted countless hours to developing a set of ideas not simply to win an election but also to create an ideological and political benchmark that would last for years to come. These never-before-published internal memoranda from high-ranking Republican officials reveal the intense planning, debate, issue development, research, team building, coalition outreach, and fund-raising that went into the document that has so profoundly changed our nation.

October 21, 1993


Memo
To: Newt
Fr: Dick
Re: Planning

     First of all, congratulations.  While I know you won't take
anything for granted, for all practical purposes you will be our
next leader.  We have many talented people in our Conference, but
I strongly believe that you are the best person for the job of
leading us to the majority.  You not only understand the enormity
of the task, but you understand strategy, tactics, teamwork, and
countless other ingredients that go into building a winning
effort.  And, just as important, you have the energy and inner
drive to get us from here to there.  The next few years may be
our best chance to capture a majority, and I want you to know
that I will be giving it everything I've got to help make it
happen.

     We are almost surely going to have a strong and effective
leadership team.  Whatever the final line-up, if I am re-elected
to leadership I will do everything I can to make it a solid team
effort.

     I appreciate your comments and your outline of a plan for
the next several months.  As I knew you would be, you have
already begun the process of planning for us to be effective for
the remainder of this Congress and after you become Leader.  I've
looked at your outline and I would like to offer a few comments
about the outline and other things as well.

     **RAC.** I need to study your RAC in more detail.  I haven't
seen the tapes or had a chance to read the book yet but I intend
to in the next several days.  I will then be in a better position
to comment on that.

     **Planning.**  You and I both share a strong disposition to plan
ahead.  I totally agree that we need to use the upcoming recess
period to prepare for next year.  The sessions you list (November
2, January 11-12, and January 28-29) sound fine to me.  We should
seriously think about how to structure these sessions to make
them productive.  We should strive for not only solid legislative
and campaign plans, but we should instill in our Members the need
to really go all out next year to gain as many seats as we can.

*Planting the seeds:* In this October 1993 memo to Newt Gingrich, Dick Armey shares his ideas of how House Republicans should draft a plan to win the majority for the first time in four decades. Gingrich has just announced that he will run for House Republican leader, and there is little doubt he will win. This memo marks the beginning of an important political partnership, because until this point Armey has not aligned himself with Gingrich's guerrilla style of politics. Notice that Armey does not portray a Republican majority as something likely to be achieved in the 1994 elections. Equally notable are Armey's concluding remarks, a prescient analysis of the weaknesses that will haunt Gingrich as a leader. *(pp. 278–282)*

Regarding staff training, we have already begun drafting a
plan for a more intensive staff training program.  We have
revised the "Hitting the Ground Running" book and before we put
it to all the offices I would like for you to look at it and
suggest any additional chapters or other changes.  We would like
the finished product to be the basic "textbook" for the staff
training course.

As we plan for the end of this year and next year, I believe
we should focus on:

**NRCC.**  As you mentioned, Bill will be struggling
financially all year.  We cannot, however, let our support for
candidates slip this next year.  You and I along with a few
others will have to take up the slack.  We must be heavily
involved in not only the fundraising end of things, but helping
to set the message and tone for the campaign year.  With all the
other elections and referendums and initiatives, we have a great
chance to pick up seats (although I believe realistic gains are
15-20 rather than the wild numbers we hear others suggest).

**End of year Issue Development.**  I believe we have made a
good start in developing positive GOP proposals on major issues.
Contrary to what many in the media have said, Republicans are not
"brain dead" when it comes to an agenda.  My article in the
Washington Times on "The Emerging GOP Agenda" highlights our
renewed vigor on the issues.  But we need to keep moving.  I
would like for us to have strong, dramatic GOP proposals on
congressional reform, regulatory relief, economic growth,
immigration, as well as our vision for the post-cold war era.
How we get this done may depend on the next item...

**Re-energizing the Roundtable.**  The Leader's Roundtable
has at times been productive, but more often than not it has
degenerated into being simply another Tuesday morning leadership
meeting.  As originally designed it was supposed to manage
projects, maximize our use of resources, and keep us ahead of the
curve.  As we discussed in the meeting we need to find a way to
either get the Roundtable rejuvinated or find another mechanism.
If you recall, during the final weeks of the budget debate the
Roundtable was canceled four times out of five.  We can't afford
for this group not to be effective in the heat of a campaign
year.  As you suggested, perhaps a meeting of the old
Coordinating Group should be called to discuss how we can get
back on track.

**Coalitions.**  One of our biggest shortcomings this year
has been the failure to get our coalitions effort on track.  We
are way behind on coalition efforts on health care, NAFTA, and
many other issues.  Tom DeLay really wants to get our coalitions
effort moving, but I believe he feels his hands are tied since he
is not the head of the coalition group.  Perhaps we can find a
way to get DeLay more involved similar to my new role as
communications chairman for health care.

**End of year communications.** We need to start planning now on how we control the year-end assessments of the first Clinton year and House Republicans' first year. My staff has already started this process but we need to focus on it as a leadership project.

**Energizing Ranking Members.** Our ranking Members and their staffs should be much better prepared than they are to develop proposals, coordinate their opposition plans, effectively oppose the Administration, and conduct relevant research and investigations to promote our cause. The Ranking Members might be in a listening mood next year as they know many restless Members might consider a challenge to certain Members. At the very least we should develop job descriptions and prepare a game plan for at least the most important committees for next year.

And for the longer term, I believe we should begin thinking about:

**Overall plan for reaching a majority.** I would like for you and the rest of the leadership to propose a comprehensive plan (well thought out and prepared in advance) for House Republicans to reach the majority. At this point, I'm afraid that a large number of our Members just don't understand the intensity and sheer effort that will be required for us to be successful. We need to lay out a plan and sell them on it. I believe most of our Conference is hungry for direction and is hungry for a full scale effort to try to gain control of the House. It may take a long time to persuade our Conference that the sacrifice it will take is necessary, but I believe we can do it. Your efforts and mine over the years helping candidates and engaging in all the important policy fights gives us unique standing among the troops to explain the hard work it will take to be successful and to encourage others to play a bigger role. This leads into the next topic...

**Contingency plan for when we take over the House.** When the Republicans won the Senate in 1980 they were woefully unprepared. We must not make that same mistake when we take over the House. Kerry is already working on a draft plan covering most everthing including audits needed, Conference and House Rules changes, media plan (for post-election, pre-swearing in), committee ratios, physical space questions, appointment power and expirations, etc. I would like for him to include someone from your staff in researching and completing the plan. A comprehensive plan will take an enormous amount of work. The time frame we are working under is to be finished by next August. When it actually happens, the Democrats will be fighting tooth and nail to hang on, and after the election they will be attempting to cover up everything in sight. We need to be ready to cover every base. Good planning now will keep us from making serious mistakes during the heat (and excitement) of the moment.

**Structure for bold, dramatic issue development.** If we are to become the driving force behind a bold and innovative issue agenda, that should be the key to whom you place on any Leader task force. In the past, too many times the task forces have served mainly as early warning devices for the leadership -- to make sure all factions in the Conference had a voice. And frankly the most vocal moderates were placed on virtually every Leaders task force and usually in much higher proportions than their representation in the Conference. The result can easily lead to "lowest common denominator" proposals. It's important that all factions have a voice, but that process is different from developing flagship issue proposals. We need strong thinkers who are in line with the Conference who will work with key outside experts and leading think tanks (along with other coalition groups) to develop the best possible issue proposals for our Party to push. The task forces should utilize (but not be a slave to) solid polling data from the RNC and other sources.

**How best to work with the moderates.** My theory for handling the more moderate Members of our Conference is to find issues where their position is in line with the Conference as a whole and give them a high-profile position on that issue. There is a lot more that unites us than divides us. We should focus their attention on the part that unites us. And surely we can find issues that need solid work (but are maybe not our flagship issues) but are not necessarily philosophical issues, i.e., certain communications issues, pensions, oversight, etc., where we could encourage good work that benefits them but also the Conference as a whole. And the moderates that work within the system without trashing the leadership should be rewarded, not the other way around.

Also, if I may, a few words of caution.

You have the unbelievable ability to see the big picture and the vision for where we should be going. My strength is seeing a shorter term objective and moving heaven and earth to get there. The two approaches are complemetary. If I have any criticisms of your style at all (and any criticisms are greatly outnumbered by your positive abilities) it would be that you sometime allow the forest to obscure the trees. I would encourage you to make sure that doesn't happen with RAC. We need to get your concept and philosophy into manageable projects that we can get our arms around. I will be glad to pledge my time and the time of my staff to help develop your objectives into manageable projects.

Also, I'm a firm believer in "Ockham's razor." The straightforward and oftentimes more simple approach is usually better. A simpler strategy is easier for the troops to understand and to follow. In watching you over the years the only times I've seen you make mistakes (in my opinion) is when you've been too smart by half. I.e., you sometimes complicate a strategy or want to change it too late in the process. In fairness, your mistakes are like mine -- errors of commission and usually not omission. This is not a big problem, but I feel compelled to point it out.

Finally,

I'm extremely excited about our chances over the next few years. You, as the revolutionary leader of our group, can lead us to a majority. I want to be there with you every step of the way.

12/20/93

Memo
To: Newt
Fr: Dick
Re: Professional development projects for next year

I've been working on a couple of new professional development
project ideas and wanted to run them by you.  For the projects to
be successful, it would be helpful to have your tacit approval at
least and, preferably, your enthusiastic support.  I would
certainly be open to any of your comments, criticisms, or
suggestions for improvement.

The overall idea for these projects is not only to produce solid
work that will help our leadership and all our Members be more
productive, but also to begin creating the mindset and energy
necessary for GOP Members to visualize actually being in the
majority.  Actively preparing for the majority is the first step
in gaining the majority.  As I told a reporter the other day, we
are not hoping for a majority or wishing for a majority, we are
planning for a majority.

As part of an overall professional development plan, the new
projects are:

1.  **A Conference Journal entitled "Building a Majority"** to help
build the skills and morale of Members and staff, focusing
primarily on the skills that will get us to a majority or help us
be effective once we gain the majority.

The journal will highlight and analyze successful projects (such
as the Inhofe petition project), include interviews with
successful leaders from business, sports, other levels of
politics, etc., review useful books on leadership, organization,
strategy, etc., include lists of "rules" or "lessons learned"
from successful managers and leaders, and include letters to the
editor or other articles submitted by House GOP Members on
professional development.

Several of these ideas were inspired by watching your RAC tapes,
particularly the tapes on personal strength and entrepreneurial
free enterprise.  I would hope that I could count on you to
submit some of your RAC material for the journal.

*The plan:* In December 1993, Armey follows up with Gingrich to offer more concrete ideas on how to put a political and legislative plan into action. Specifically, he recommends that Republicans develop a "Project Majority Contingency Plan." Gingrich will seize on Armey's ideas and use the upcoming January 1994 House Republican retreat in Salisbury, Maryland, to begin selling the idea of a unifying agenda. Gingrich, Armey, and other "young Turks" challenge Republicans to stop deferring to the Democratic majority and start thinking in terms of how the GOP can actually win and keep control of the House. The Contract with America begins to take shape even before it has a name. *(pp. 283–284)*

The journal will have an advisory board of several House Republican Members from all factions within the Conference. Each advisor will be encouraged to actively work on not only the journal, but a wide range of professional development projects over the next year. **(Outline of Journal is attached)**

2. **A "Project Majority Contingency Plan."** We need a well thought out, comprehensive plan of what needs to be done when we win the majority. We absolutely cannot be caught flatfooted like the Senate was in 1980 (or worse, like the last time the GOP won the House in 1954 and then promptly lost it in 1956).

I've been working on an outline for a plan and had intended to develop it quietly and privately over the next several months. After thinking more about it, however, I would like to enlist ranking Members and other key GOP Members in the process. By doing it this way we will probably get a better plan, plus more of our Members will have an investment in the process. Much like Kasich rounded up assistance on the budget, I want to round up assistance on this project.

This plan does not focus on what issues to push or setting a legislative timetable. Rather, this plan will cover specifically how we handle the transition, including information on key appointments, organization of key offices (such as JTC, CBO, Architect, Clerk, Postmaster, Sergeant-at-Arms, GAO, etc.). It will also include necessary Conference rules changes, how to handle committee ratios, budgets, etc.

The plan also focuses on the critical time between the election in early November and our taking control in January. The Democrats will be in a panic and will shredding more documents than Oliver North ever thought about. We will need a legal strategy, an auditing strategy, a media strategy, and a continual campaign strategy (assuming our margin will be very thin).

The plan will have to have the support of you, the rest of leadership, and the Conference as a whole. By developing it with a larger group, our chances of full support go up dramatically.

If done properly, this project will create energy, a sense of excitement, and a belief that we can actually win. By focusing on how we'll operate as a majority, I believe we have a higher likelihood of getting the majority.


These two projects are in addition to the professional development seminars we are planning, the manual you saw earlier (any more comments on the manual are welcome), and other Conference publications designed to help Members run their offices more smoothly.

Please let me know what you think of these ideas and if you would be willing to assist on these efforts. Thanks.

4.   Follow up to the above.  As Armey/Kasich will cover the
economic ends (as well as some of the family needs), I suggest a
companion bill (Family Freedom Bill?) that would be the
morality/family values/culture equivalent to Armey/Kasich.  I've
not thought this through completely, but it should include such
things as legal changes to strengthen the two parent family,
support adoption not abortion, replace many of the welfare
provisions with work ethic provisions, strong paternity language,
an end to quotas, etc.  Basically, it would be a bill to bias the
laws toward personal responsibility, not irresponsibility.  I
think this could be done in a creative way that would not get
into too many "federalist" problems.

     The reason I thought of this is primarily due to the
influence of Bill Bennett.  His recent article in Policy Review
(the same edition your recent article was in), and his book at
number 1 on the best seller list, along with various comments I'm
picking up from other sources, tells me that there is a new
thread of morality popping up in all areas of society.  I've seen
several newspaper articles about high school girls joining in a
pledge to abstain from sex until they're married.  Churches with
popular youth departments are filling up on Sundays.  Something's
happening out there that we can't quite explain.  The ethical
problems of the Clinton administration will just exacerbate this
issue.  Maybe a longer chat with Bennett could help us get a
better handle on it.

5.   The next "Freedom" article is shaping up to be extraordinary.
I'm not sure how much time you've had to work on it, but the
draft I saw really moves the freedom theme along.  I told Brian
one of the most ingenous parts of the article is how he
successfully argues that the moral high ground belongs to the
capitalists in battles against the state, environmentalists,
civil rights organizations, unions, etc.  There are also several
fascinating explanations of key events in history.  I suggested a
few additions, but the piece overall is really impressive.

6.   Please read the Pete du Pont article on "Conservative
Manifesto."  I think you will find it very helpful.

7.   Post-Salisbury working group.  Newt has asked Pete Hoekstra,
John Boehner, and Jim Nussle (along with me, Dan Meyer, Boehner's
AA, and Nussle's AA) to work in a small group to work out the
plans to follow up the ideas generated at Salisbury.  This group
is going to develop an overall plan for Member and staff
training, a "product development" plan (decide what new issues or
bills need to be developed), a marketing plan, a communications
plan, and a computerization plan.  The contingency plan you are
heading up is technically part of this group but has been
separated to run on a different track.  One of the key products
this group will develop is the "10 things House Republicans Will
Do If We Take Over In January."  Newt asked you to take that
project on in the Roundtable today (culminating in a mass event
on the steps of the Capitol in late September).

*A ten-point agenda:* On March 17, 1994, Dick Armey's chief of staff, Kerry Knott, writes to
his boss about a working group that will lay the foundation for a detailed, point-by-point
legislative agenda. At this point, what will become the Contract with America has the
awkward handle "10 Things House Republicans Will Do If We Take Over in January."
Putting together such an agenda will require massive organization of lawmakers, staff,
and outside experts, and Knott will be the point person for these and other tasks. Every
one of Knott's suggestions in this memo will eventually become part of the Contract,
and almost all will become law.

: *GOP CONFERENCE*                                              MAY 94

D-R-A-F-T

### September 27th Project

### GOP House Majority Agenda

**Event:** Republican Members and candidates stage an event on the Capitol steps to announce the agenda for the House if Republicans are in the majority next Congress. The agenda has two parts -- an opening day agenda, and a first 100 days agenda.

**Purpose of the event:** To show the American people that the House GOP is different from the Democrats who have controlled the House for over 40 years. The event will raise our credibility level by guaranteeing to the American people that House Republicans take this seriously and pledge to run the House in a dramatically different fashion. If successful, this event (along with other activities) will enhance the environment to help elect more House Republicans. By pledging support for our agenda, we will give GOP candidates an agenda to support, and give our allies a more concrete agenda to campaign on. In developing our agenda, we must take into account the likely effectiveness of each item on 1) degree of real change it will bring, and 2) will it help us actually gain seats in November in order to become the majority party.

**Possible event message:** "If you don't like the way Congress is run, change the people who run it." Headlines echoing this message, along with the 10-point GOP agenda, should be the norm if this event is successful.

**Coordinator:** Dick Armey (Kerry Knott, staff) RNC War Room
Working with: Newt, NRCC, RNC, House Republican Leadership

**Plans needed for event:** Develop best list of opening day and first 100 day legislative priorities; develop coalition support plan, and effective communications plan.

### Developing Agenda Items

Step One:  Survey all Members and Candidates

1. Develop Criteria for agenda items (to be approved)
2. Develop survey listing most likely issues/proposals. Staff
     to meet with Party officials, consultants, allies, etc., to
     draft initial list.
     --Deadline June 15
3. Planning Group approve draft list for survey.
     --Deadline June 22
4. Mail survey with cover letter from Armey/Gingrich/Paxon to
     all  House GOP Members
     --Deadline July 1

*Aggressive and specific:* In May 1994, Kerry Knott presents the first comprehensive memo on the House Republican leadership's plans for seizing the majority in November. In the months since Armey wrote his initial memo to Gingrich, Republicans have grown more optimistic about their chance for a majority. The excerpts from Knott's memo shown above—including detailed timetables—reveal how the Republicans intended to use the plan not only to get elected but also as an agenda once in control of the House. *(pp. 286–292)*

Developing agenda items (continued)

5.  Mail survey with cover letter from Armey/Gingrich/Paxon to
    all GOP congressional candidates
    --Deadline July 1

    **Note: In order to keep our candidates involved regular
    conference call with Gingrich, Armey and Paxon and others should
    be held over the next several weeks.**

5.  Follow up calls and letters as necessary.

6.  Tabulate all responses
    --Final tally by August 1 (for input only)

Step Two: Meet with outside allies and party representatives

1.  Conference staff meet with key outside allies to gather input
    for agenda items.
2.  Armey/Gingrich (and others) meet with outside allies
    (including Party officials) to discuss the agenda.
    --Ongoing throughout year

Step Three:  Member working groups formed to develop specifics

1.  For likely agenda items, begin forming Member groups to flesh
    out legislative language
    --beginning July 15
    --one lead Member per group
    --Leadership staff assigned to each group
2.  Conference develop specific instructions for Member working
    groups to follow
    --criteria for each item
    --list of key outside allies to consult with
    --list of key Members to work with
        --how to handle problem areas (turf, etc.)
    --broader coalition strategy given for communication
    --micro media and micro coalition instructions given
    --timetables for completion
3.  Member group presentation to Leadership and Roundtable Group
    --By beginning of August recess

Step Four: Approval of agenda

1.  Planning Group to approve "First cut" agenda items ASAP
    --working groups immediately established for those items
2.  Planning group to agree on "Second cut" agenda items
    --by mid July
3.  Planning group to make final approval of items
    --by beginning of August recess
        --final working groups established
3.  Leadership presentation to full Conference
    --ASAP after August recess

Press and Communications plan (continued)

4.   Pre-event press
        --Gingrich/Armey/other Leaders meet with key reporters to
        "sell" them on the seriousness of the effort
                --David Broder
                --George Will
                --Network news reporters
                --Fred Barnes
                --Sunday Talk Show guests
                --Conservative press (magazines, Limbaugh, etc., to
                promote event)

        --Delegation press briefings
        --Candidate press briefings

5.   Day of event and post event press

        Day of event

        --Radio talk shows (remote broadcasts from site)
        --Limbaugh special shows
        --C-Span coverage
        --CNN special coverage
        --GOP-TV
        --NET
        --Network morning shows (Today, GMA, etc.)

        Post event press activity

        --Key House Republicans to aggressively push for time on:
                --Crossfire
                --Equal Time
                --Sunday
        --Aggressively work syndicated columnists to cover post
        event activities
        --Work local press in key areas
        --conservative press follow ups
                --National Review
                --American Spectator

6.   Additional coordinated events to keep message going for
        several days
        --bus trip with key GOP leaders through one or two states
        --follow up events with each state delegation (back in home
        state)

        **Note: Keeping the message going is extremely important.
Whether bus trips, satellite hook-ups, fly-ins, etc., some
aggressive effort must be undertaken.  As many Members of our
Conference as possible should participate.**

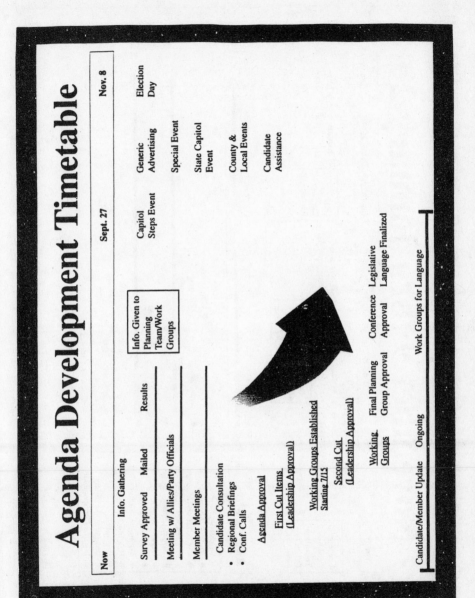

# Agenda Development Timetable

| Now | | | Sept. 27 | Nov. 8 |
|---|---|---|---|---|

Info. Gathering

Survey Approved    Mailed    Results

Meeting w/ Allies/Party Officials

Member Meetings

Candidate Consultation
· Regional Briefings
· Conf. Calls

Agenda Approval
First Cut Items
(Leadership Approval)

Working Groups Established
Starting 7/15

Second Cut
(Leadership Approval)

Working Groups    Final Planning    Conference    Legislative
                  Group Approval    Approval      Language Finalized

Candidate/Member Update    Ongoing    Work Groups for Language

Info. Given to Planning Team/Work Groups

Capitol Steps Event    Generic Advertising    Election Day

Special Event

State Capitol Event

County & Local Events

Candidate Assistance

# November 9 thru January 2

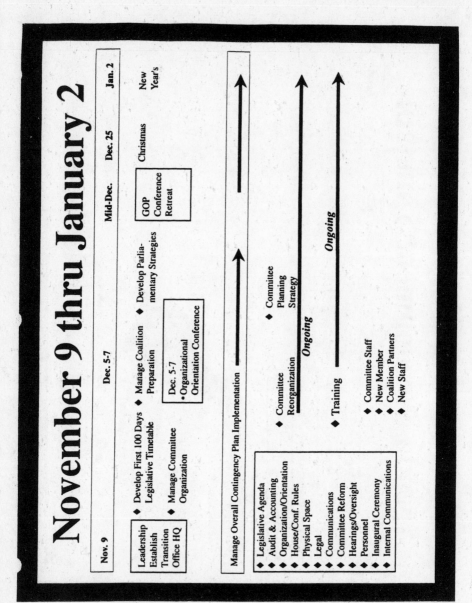

| Nov. 9 | Dec. 5-7 | Mid-Dec. | Dec. 25 | Jan. 2 |
|---|---|---|---|---|
| Leadership<br>Establish<br>Transition<br>Office HQ | ◆ Develop First 100 Days<br>   Legislative Timetable<br><br>◆ Manage Committee<br>   Organization | ◆ Manage Coalition<br>   Preparation<br><br>◆ Develop Parlia-<br>   mentary Strategies<br><br>GOP<br>Conference<br>Retreat | Christmas | New<br>Year's |

**Dec. 5-7**
• Organizational
  Orientation Conference

Manage Overall Contingency Plan Implementation

◆ Committee
   Reorganization

◆ Committee
   Planning
   Strategy

*Ongoing*

◆ Training

*Ongoing*

◆ Legislative Agenda
◆ Audit & Accounting
◆ Organization/Orientation
◆ House/Conf. Rules
◆ Physical Space
◆ Legal
◆ Communications
◆ Committee Reform
◆ Hearings/Oversight
◆ Personnel
◆ Inaugural Ceremony
◆ Internal Communications

◆ Committee Staff
◆ New Member
◆ Coalition Partners
◆ New Staff

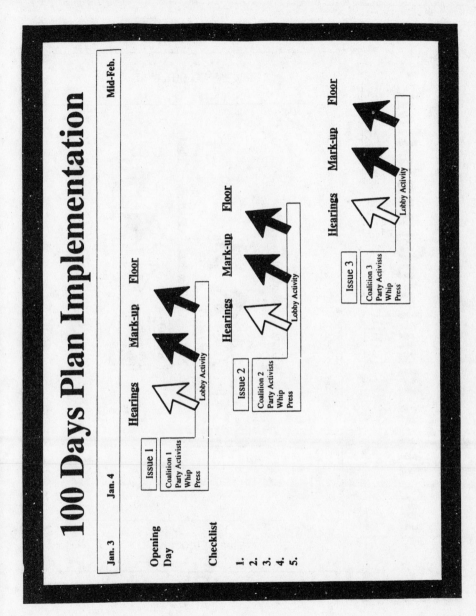

# 100 Days Plan Implementation
## (continued)

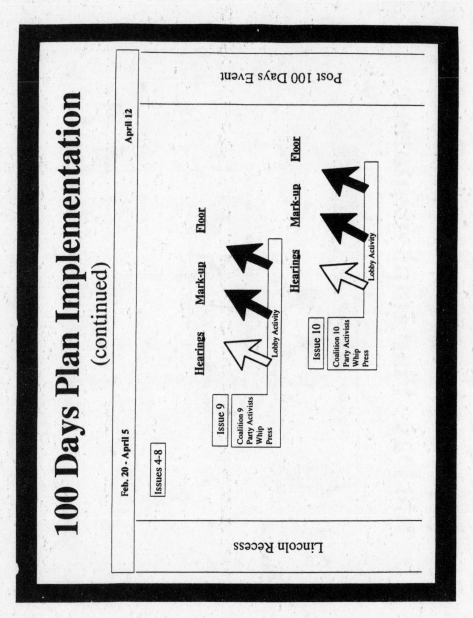

June 2, 1994

Contingency Group →
I. Most Important Goals: (that are achievable by control of House)
  ① Change image of GOP --

  ② Create House as center of GOP activism -- springboard
        to taking Senate ∴ WH
  ③ Break up iron triangle --


Trouble area: conflict btwn. institutional changes vs. 100 day leg. agenda

  - vote on Comm reorg. in Jan., but doesn't take effct until Sept.


I. Organization
  - adopt new rules before Nov. elections ?
      problems: gives opponents time to organize
          - distract from election efforts
          - divides conf.
          - may be scanned & thought, but not taken seriously.
  - Steering & Policy Comm. could be appointed

  - Move up top 3 leader elections to T-giving - w/ mandate
    to set up temp. Steering comm.

  - Org. comm. mtg. would be week of Nov. 14

II. Rules Reform -
  ① Super-majority for tax increase / problem of precedent or super-maj.


*The "center of GOP activism":* In these handwritten notes from June 2, 1994, Peter Davidson, legislative aide to Dick Armey, shows how the Republicans see taking control of the House as a "springboard" to taking the Senate and ultimately the White House. In other words, they are planning well beyond November 1994. Davidson also notes six items on "auditing and accounting," which are similar to the "reforms" of Congress that will become part of the Contract. *(pp. 293–294)*

Comm. Reform Project — Dreier & Dems working on it:
    Bipartisan Comm to Study Reorg. of Exec. & Leg. Branches
    — to take effect 6 yrs. late
    — merge ____ into

2 options – radical & achievable w/ less disruption.

Audit & Acct'g —
① Temp. IG on each committee
② Require each Comm. have an oversight subcom.

③ After election — send letter to Dem. chairs that
    all Dem. Comm. employees will be let go — so take
    care of them before Jan. 3 — re: severance pay, etc.
④ Policy: cut, then flip allocation
⑤ Get Dan to appt. a Personnel director —
⑥ Get them to put Q's in recommendation form —

Legal Group —
① to be able to use Cap. Police / S-A-A — make announcements
    on who will be in charge in Jan. to get them to
    suck up —
② Go through equip. expense accounts to look for
    shredders ⟶ club report should have it.

## VI. Summary

<u>Legislative Package Project Group</u>

House Republicans will develop a "contract with the American People" to guarantee passage of an opening day agenda, and promise to bring to a vote 10 key bills in the first 90 days if Republicans are the majority party.

This section will cover the opening day agenda and the first 90 day agenda, as well as other legislation that needs to be passed in the first session of the new Congress.

This section will discuss the criteria to be used in developing the agenda, a plan for working with a variety of House GOP Members, and a plan for working with key outside allies.

This section will cover the plans for developing the agenda this year, as well as plans for actually implementing the agenda next year, including the development of hearing schedules, committee mark-up schedules and floor schedules for the first 90 days.

*Leaving nothing to chance:* In the summer of 1994, the House Republican leadership produces a closely guarded document that lays out every single detail of how Republicans will take working control of Congress almost immediately after Election Night, should they achieve a majority. This is no small matter, since the GOP has been out of power for forty years and Democrats have controlled everything from committee assignments to personnel to payroll records. In the section shown above, the leadership explains how the Republicans will develop a "contract with the American people"—a detailed agenda for the Republican majority to "bring to a vote 10 key bills in the first 90 days."

## XII. SUMMARY

### Hearings/Oversight

The purpose of this section is to explore how a Republican majority in the House should use committee oversight authority.

We know the wrong way to do the job: the way Senate Republicans functioned in 1981 and later years. Their priority was making the legislative trains run on time. They ignored the Carter/Democrat past, did not expose wrongdoing within the institution, did not discredit their eminently discreditable opponents. They blew it.

To do the job right, House Republicans have to start with the right job description. They should consider oversight hearings as both a tool for building constituencies and a weapon to expose and punish bad people and their bad policies.

Yes, bad people, not just people with whom we disagree. House Republicans must be willing to let the world know that great evil has been done in the Congress over the last 40 years of Democrat rule. To exaggerate a bit, this will be our Nuremberg. Month after shocking month, the Democrat past must be put on trial.

Astute management of the oversight process will:

    o  Concentrate on defining issues for the public rather than tinkering with existing government programs.

    o  Give individual Republican Members a media bully pulpit which, properly used, can be far more powerful than that of a no longer creditable president.

    o  Both rally and reward key constituencies.

    o  Discredit, not just the agenda of the Left, but its organizations and key personnel as well.

That agenda -- apart from any legislation House Republicans may pass in the process -- is critical for maintaining GOP control of the House.

It is also the best way to reincorporate what might be called Perot-Americans into the Republican coalition - and to finally leave behind us the baggage of 1992.

The opposite approach, the classic "good government" approach of Senate Republicans in the 1980s, is the fast route back to minority status.

*Overreach:* In another section from the document explaining what the Republicans will do when they control the House, the GOP leadership describes how a Republican majority can use one of Congress's most fearsome powers—oversight hearings—to "expose and punish bad people and their bad policies." The document says the Democratic majority has done "great evil" and deserves a "Nuremberg" of its own. This ruthless language reveals how, even while the GOP revolutionaries remain committed to their ideas, they hunger desperately for power. But once in power, the Republicans won't use oversight to punish congressional Democrats or to make government more accountable; they will instead try to score political points against the Clinton White House.

---

**Working Group on Strengthening Defense**

Lead Member:  Livingston

*Attending :*

Working Group Members:     Hunter ✓
                           Spence ✓
                           Stump ✓
                           Kasich
                           McDade ✓
                           Hansen
                           Cunningham
                           Gilman
                           Hyde ✓
                           Combest    *(staff)*
                           Rogers ✓

Republican Conference Staff Contact:  Peter Davidson

Outside Groups Participating:

Coalition for Peace through Strength
Richard Perle
Heritage Foundation
Frank Gaffney
Center for Strategic and International Studies      *Rodman*
AEI                                                 *wolfowitz*
                                                    *Bob Zoellick*

Criteria for final product:

   1. Be sound public policy
   2. Excite our base and key allies
   3. Be dramatic enough to show real change
   4. Be easy to explain
   5. Not split our Party
   6. Be doable
   7. Fit within our overall message

General timetable:

   1. Initial Member meeting (week of July 11)
   2. Members and outside groups (week of July 18)
   3. First conceptual draft of component parts (July 22)
   4. Second draft of component parts (July 29)

---

*Outreach:* Though Democrats do not realize it, in the summer of 1994 the Republicans are constructing the Contract with America as a rigorous policy document. The GOP has set up task forces to craft a *complete bill* to stand behind every plank of the Contract. The document shown above underscores the fact that Republican members are conducting extensive research on all the issues. The "working group on strengthening defense" has reached out to numerous outside experts, including (according to a handwritten notation) Paul Wolfowitz, a former official in the Departments of State and Defense—who will also become undersecretary of defense in George W. Bush's administration.

## III. EVERYONE HAS A PART TO PLAY

*"The Team that doesn't break in the fourth quarter wins."*
- Vince Lombardi -

### The Winning Team

- Chairman Bill Paxon has improved the economic ship at the NRCC and has provided an impressive foundation of Member involvement upon which we must now build;

- Requires a scale so large that it requires an unprecedented commitment from members;

- RNC and Chairman Haley Barbour have committed unprecedented candidate assistance to take advantage of this extraordinary opportunity;

- **The minimum goal for candidate assistance is $8.5 million.**

### The Ideal Member Role

*Individual Member Commitment*

**OPTION A:**
- Commit $148,000 to challenger and open seats
  (This covers the challenger and open seats)

**OPTION B:**
- Participate in the "Buddy System;"

- Help to reshape the political environment with business leaders, political action committees, trade associations, and successful people;

- Raise $50,000 for the NRCC;

- Contribute $5,000 to challenger / open seat candidates;

- Meet incumbent support obligation for 93-94;

**OPTION C:**
- Do both Option A & B

**OPTION D:**
- Design a fundraising program based on your personal strengths and interests that will yield $65,000.

7

*Play or pay:* In this memo sent to every Republican House member on July 18, 1994, Newt Gingrich lays down the gauntlet on fund-raising. Declaring the goal to be to raise the astonishing sum of $8.5 million for Republican candidates in 1994, Gingrich writes that *every* member must contribute and lists four different options for doing so. It is the first time in party history that incumbents are ordered to raise money for other Republican candidates. Most senior Republicans hate the idea, but to Gingrich and other revolutionaries, that resistance to helping other candidates explains why the GOP has remained in the minority for decades.

WASHINGTON, D.C.                                                                        HOUSTON

# THE TARRANCE GROUP

**Research for Decisions in Politics and Public Affairs**

Edward A. Goeas, III
*President, CEO*

Brian C. Tringali
*Senior Vice President*

David J. Sackett
*Senior Vice President*

Michael D. Baselice
*Vice President*

William H. Cullo
*Research Analyst*

Lorraine Gudermuth
*Research Analyst*

Patricia J. House
*Research Analyst*

**M E M O R A N D U M**

TO:        Republican Conference

FROM:      Ed Goeas

DATE:      August 30, 1994

RE:        A Contract With The American Voters

---

"I'd love the idea of voting for a platform as opposed to a person..."

"Yes, I would be more than willing to say, forget the party, I'm willing to vote for these ten things to get done in the next few years. That would be a real nice thing to do..."

"You have to fix the institution (Congress) before you fix the policies."

The previous quotations are taken from a series of focus groups conducted on behalf of the Republican National Committee among participants with a history of splitting their ticket. The focus groups were conducted on July 20 & 21 as part of a project for the ad hoc Learning & Planning Team in their effort to develop messages around both legislative activity and the upcoming elections. The specific subject under discussion was the potential for a Republican contract with the American voter, which is now the thrust of the September 27th event on the Capital steps.

Focus group findings are qualitative in nature. Our findings cannot be extrapolated to the ticket-splitting voters across the country, nor to the electorate as a whole. But these findings do offer some insights into why the voters might be drawn toward the scheduled September 27th event and supportive of the ideas behind a Contract with the American electorate.

The following are some of the key insights that limited discussions of a Republican contract with the American voters revealed:

211 North Union, Suite 200, Alexandria, VA 22314   (703) 684-6688   Fax (703) 836-8256

*Testing the concept:* While the Contract with America is shaping up to be much more than a publicity stunt, the Republican leaders do pay close attention to whether the idea of a "contract" resonates with voters. This August 30, 1994, memo from Ed Goeas, of the research firm the Tarrance Group, to Republican leaders confirms that focus groups find the notion of a "contract with the American voter" to be extremely attractive. According to Goeas, voters respond powerfully to the idea that politicians will be "held accountable for their actions." *(pp. 299–301)*

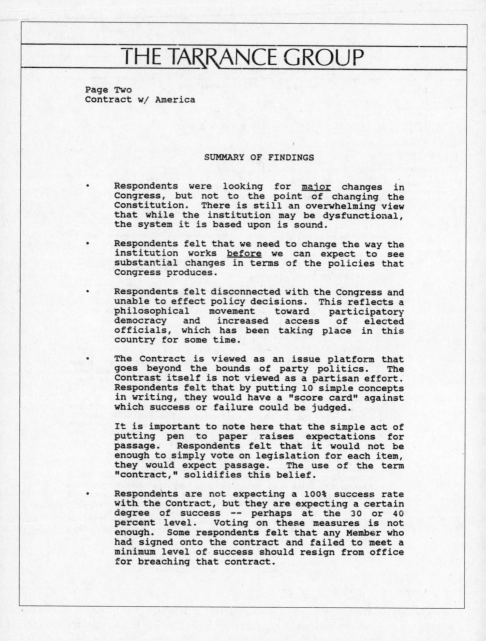

# THE TARRANCE GROUP

Page Two
Contract w/ America

### SUMMARY OF FINDINGS

- Respondents were looking for <u>major</u> changes in Congress, but not to the point of changing the Constitution. There is still an overwhelming view that while the institution may be dysfunctional, the system it is based upon is sound.

- Respondents felt that we need to change the way the institution works <u>before</u> we can expect to see substantial changes in terms of the policies that Congress produces.

- Respondents felt disconnected with the Congress and unable to effect policy decisions. This reflects a philosophical movement toward participatory democracy and increased access of elected officials, which has been taking place in this country for some time.

- The Contract is viewed as an issue platform that goes beyond the bounds of party politics. The Contrast itself is not viewed as a partisan effort. Respondents felt that by putting 10 simple concepts in writing, they would have a "score card" against which success or failure could be judged.

  It is important to note here that the simple act of putting pen to paper raises expectations for passage. Respondents felt that it would not be enough to simply vote on legislation for each item, they would expect passage. The use of the term "contract," solidifies this belief.

- Respondents are not expecting a 100% success rate with the Contract, but they are expecting a certain degree of success -- perhaps at the 30 or 40 percent level. Voting on these measures is not enough. Some respondents felt that any Member who had signed onto the contract and failed to meet a minimum level of success should resign from office for breaching that contract.

# THE TARRANCE GROUP

Page Three
Contract w/ America

- The most important concept revealed in the focus groups was <u>accountability</u>. Respondents felt that government and Congress are no longer held accountable for their actions. The hope of the Contract is that it will offer some method of accountability -- if only in the short term.

- The top legislative priority for respondents is term limits. It is the first issue they would like to see brought to the floor for debate in a new Congress.

- One of the issues mentioned in the Contract is an independent audit of the Congress. Third party oversight is something fully endorsed by respondents -- partially because it offers another avenue for accountability.

- As we have seen in polling data, neither political party has a particularly good image. But respondents felt that the Republican Party has been remiss in not providing proper explanations for the policies they oppose. They felt that more effort should be made to discuss consequences of policy decisions -- particularly with regard to cost.

- While positive movement on key issues was considered important to the respondents, change for the sake of change was not embraced. To many of these respondents <u>gridlock</u> is just a political term for the system of checks and balances that our political system is designed around. With that in mind, many respondents felt that gridlock might be a positive thing and a proper role for a minority, depending upon which policy or program was under discussion.

THE
# LUNTZ RESEARCH COMPANIES
Luntz Research & Strategic Services ■ The Public Opinion Company ■ Luntz Corporate ■ Luntz Worldwide

**MEMORANDUM**

TO:            Republican Leaders
FROM:          Frank Luntz
RE:            Public Reaction to "The Contract"
DATE:          September 2, 1994

---

### SUMMARY

In politics, as in commercial advertising, it is rare for all elements of a market test to complement each other. In this case, that is exactly what happened.

Americans are skeptical of everything partisan and political, but "The Contract with America" is an exception. After completing both an extensive telephone survey and focus group session with swing voters, I can say with confidence that <u>the "Contract" is our best hope of winning back Perot voters, disgruntled Republicans and conservative Democrats.</u> It is real, credible, and deals with the issues most important to the electorate. Furthermore, the concept, wording and execution could not have been designed more effectively.

The process used to help test the document you now see was comprehensive and thorough:

--     To help determine the Contract's **content**, we designed and tabulated the Congressional Canvass that was filled out by more than 100 Members and over 100 challengers.

--     To help determine the Contract's **wording**, we interviewed 1,000 registered voters by telephone. They were read competing statements about each of the ten Contract items and asked which statement they preferred.

--     To help determine the Contract's **format**, we convened a focus group in Denver of Perot and independent voters.

<u>While the notion that politicians would actually sign their name to a promise is valuable, what truly sets the Contract apart from past political documents is the *"If we don't accomplish what we've pledged, throw us out -- we mean it"* clause. This graphically demonstrates our seriousness, and it will surely appeal to swing voters on Election Day.</u>

---

1000 Wilson Boulevard ■ Suite 950 ■ Arlington, Virginia 22209 ■ Phone (703) 358-0080 ■ Fax (703) 358-0089

*The public's reaction:* In this confidential memo to the Republican leadership, delivered eight weeks before Election Day, pollster Frank Luntz reveals that focus groups respond not only to the concept of a contract with voters but also to the specific issues included in the Contract with America. Luntz reports that even people who voted for H. Ross Perot in the 1992 presidential election—"literally the most negative, hostile voters I have ever assembled for a focus group"—have been convinced by the Contract. *(pp. 302–305)*

## THE CONCEPT

To say that the electorate is angry would be like saying that the ocean is wet. Voters in general and our swing voters in particular, have simply ceased to believe that anything good can come out of Washington. Politicians are the second least trusted profession (used car salesmen are still stuck at the bottom), and a candidate's promise has about as much credibility as Roger Altman at the Whitewater hearings.

The Contract is different. As the opening statement emphatically proclaims, "A campaign promise is one thing. A signed contract is quite another." No one expects such a document, and the element of surprise works to our advantage. **The idea that candidates -- incumbents and challengers alike -- would sign at the dotted line is highly appealing to the voters we wish to reach.**

## THE WORDING

Once the ten salient issues were determined by the Conference, we set out to find the most effective communication strategy to outline the Republican position. Using both quantitative research and focus group transcripts from the past year, we created two competing phrases for each issue. We then asked a thousand registered voters to pick the phrase they preferred. By conducting the telephone survey rather than focus groups, we were able to **quantify** the impact of each phrase among independents, Perot voters, likely voters, weak Democrats, weak Republicans, and other important electoral subgroups.

**Most of the phrases you see in the final Contract earned significant majorities**, a strong indication that we really are using the best language possible. However, an equal number of people want term limits "to replace career politicians" as do those who think "politicians shouldn't be a lifetime job." So instead of choosing one or the other, we decided to combine them.

The reaction to the content and text by the focus group participants was nothing short of startling. Having spent 60 minutes venting their frustration with politicians, parties and partisan politics, they did an about-face and responded extremely favorably to the substance of the Contract. I am convinced that if the electorate reads the Contract, they will respond in a similar fashion. What's more, focus group responses indicate that a significant number of voters will in fact read the document if they get the chance.

## THE EXECUTION

A focus group of Perot voters and self-described "strong independents" was convened in Denver to determine the most effective "leverage points" available to Republicans in the Fall campaign, as well as to determine the correct layout for "The Contract." All participants were between the ages of 30 and 54 -- the swing vote population -- and all claimed to be active voters. None had anything nice to say about Bill Clinton, Congress, or either of the political parties. In fact, they were literally the most negative, hostile voters I have ever assembled for a focus group (and I have conducted 97 focus groups over the last three years). If the Contract can convince them, it can convince anyone. **It did.**

Each focus group participant was given the choice of five different first page Contract "formats" and then asked to rank them from best to worst. We were specifically looking for respondent "agreement," "interest" and "likelyhood of turning the page." All five styles were designed by expert advertising personnel, and all five were excellent, but **every focus group participant (but one) chose the document you now see before you.** The odds against that happening are quite high.

A number of additional findings are worth noting:

--     The 1-800 telephone number is important to Perot voters because it adds credibility to the message. You should be prepared for a significant number of calls, particularly from these voters.

--     The Contract items have been ranked in order of importance to swing voters. However, term limits (the second most popular issue) was put at the end to "bookend" the document for those who will read the first and last item and skip the body of the text.

One important caveat, however. **Not a single focus group participant liked the word Republican -- not even the registered Republicans!** In fact, if the focus group had its way, the word Republican would have been removed from the text in its entirety. Again, **any appeal to partisan politics draws an equally strong negative reaction from the very voters we need to win over.** This is a difficult obstacle to overcome, and it should convince you that the party name should not (and does not) appear frequently. Readers should realize that this is a Republican document, but the party name should not be so prominent that it destroys the message. The document you now have strikes a perfect balance.

## A FINAL POINT

The Contract works not because of the individual components but because it is a complete package. In other words, the sum is greater than the parts. Remove a single component and you destroy the entire effort.

To those voters who have had an opportunity to take part in the market testing, **the Contract represents the willingness of certain politicians to come together over a set of important issues and put their names and careers on the line. This is an exercise in unity and integrity not seen in recent political memory.** That's why the "Contract with America" works.

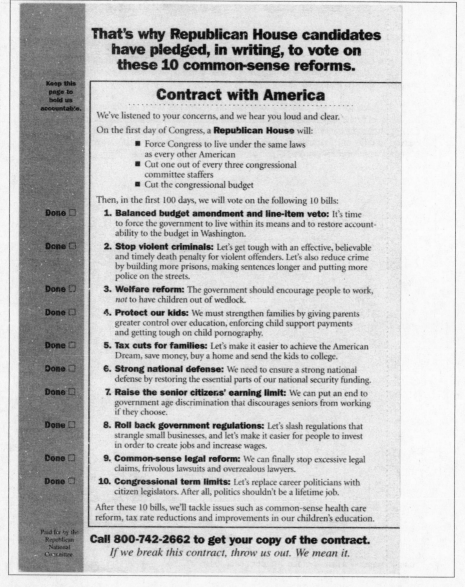

**That's why Republican House candidates have pledged, in writing, to vote on these 10 common-sense reforms.**

## Contract with America

We've listened to your concerns, and we hear you loud and clear.

On the first day of Congress, a **Republican House** will:

- Force Congress to live under the same laws as every other American
- Cut one out of every three congressional committee staffers
- Cut the congressional budget

Then, in the first 100 days, we will vote on the following 10 bills:

Done ☐  **1. Balanced budget amendment and line-item veto:** It's time to force the government to live within its means and to restore accountability to the budget in Washington.

Done ☐  **2. Stop violent criminals:** Let's get tough with an effective, believable and timely death penalty for violent offenders. Let's also reduce crime by building more prisons, making sentences longer and putting more police on the streets.

Done ☐  **3. Welfare reform:** The government should encourage people to work, *not* to have children out of wedlock.

Done ☐  **4. Protect our kids:** We must strengthen families by giving parents greater control over education, enforcing child support payments and getting tough on child pornography.

Done ☐  **5. Tax cuts for families:** Let's make it easier to achieve the American Dream, save money, buy a home and send the kids to college.

Done ☐  **6. Strong national defense:** We need to ensure a strong national defense by restoring the essential parts of our national security funding.

Done ☐  **7. Raise the senior citizens' earning limit:** We can put an end to government age discrimination that discourages seniors from working if they choose.

Done ☐  **8. Roll back government regulations:** Let's slash regulations that strangle small businesses, and let's make it easier for people to invest in order to create jobs and increase wages.

Done ☐  **9. Common-sense legal reform:** We can finally stop excessive legal claims, frivolous lawsuits and overzealous lawyers.

Done ☐  **10. Congressional term limits:** Let's replace career politicians with citizen legislators. After all, politics shouldn't be a lifetime job.

After these 10 bills, we'll tackle issues such as common-sense health care reform, tax rate reductions and improvements in our children's education.

**Call 800-742-2662 to get your copy of the contract.**
*If we break this contract, throw us out. We mean it.*

*The execution:* The Republicans pay attention to every detail in crafting the Contract with America. The final version of the Contract that runs as a full-page advertisement in *TV Guide*, shown on this page, differs in significant ways from earlier mock-ups, two of which are shown here (on pages 307 and 308). Pollster Frank Luntz's September 2 memo provides the rationale for the final order of the ten items: "The Contract items have been ranked in order of importance to swing voters. However, term limits (the second most popular issue) was put at the end to 'bookend' the document for those who will read the first and last item and skip the body of the text." *(pp. 306–308)*

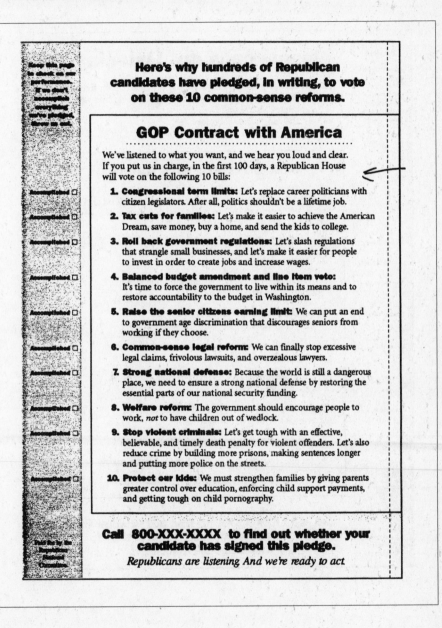

**Here's why hundreds of Republican candidates have pledged, in writing, to vote on these 10 common-sense reforms.**

## GOP Contract with America

We've listened to what you want, and we hear you loud and clear. If you put us in charge, in the first 100 days, a Republican House will vote on the following 10 bills:

1. **Congressional term limits:** Let's replace career politicians with citizen legislators. After all, politics shouldn't be a lifetime job.

2. **Tax cuts for families:** Let's make it easier to achieve the American Dream, save money, buy a home, and send the kids to college.

3. **Roll back government regulations:** Let's slash regulations that strangle small businesses, and let's make it easier for people to invest in order to create jobs and increase wages.

4. **Balanced budget amendment and line item veto:** It's time to force the government to live within its means and to restore accountability to the budget in Washington.

5. **Raise the senior citizens earning limit:** We can put an end to government age discrimination that discourages seniors from working if they choose.

6. **Common-sense legal reform:** We can finally stop excessive legal claims, frivolous lawsuits, and overzealous lawyers.

7. **Strong national defense:** Because the world is still a dangerous place, we need to ensure a strong national defense by restoring the essential parts of our national security funding.

8. **Welfare reform:** The government should encourage people to work, *not* to have children out of wedlock.

9. **Stop violent criminals:** Let's get tough with an effective, believable, and timely death penalty for violent offenders. Let's also reduce crime by building more prisons, making sentences longer and putting more police on the streets.

10. **Protect our kids:** We must strengthen families by giving parents greater control over education, enforcing child support payments, and getting tough on child pornography.

**Call 800-XXX-XXXX to find out whether your candidate has signed this pledge.**

*Republicans are listening And we're ready to act*

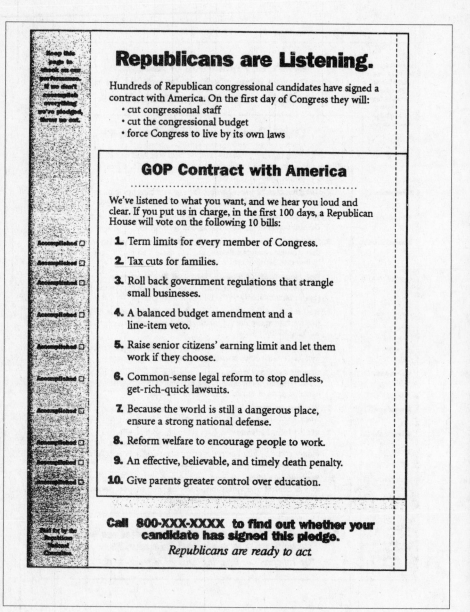

# Republicans are Listening.

Hundreds of Republican congressional candidates have signed a contract with America. On the first day of Congress they will:
- cut congressional staff
- cut the congressional budget
- force Congress to live by its own laws

## GOP Contract with America

We've listened to what you want, and we hear you loud and clear. If you put us in charge, in the first 100 days, a Republican House will vote on the following 10 bills:

**1.** Term limits for every member of Congress.

**2.** Tax cuts for families.

**3.** Roll back government regulations that strangle small businesses.

**4.** A balanced budget amendment and a line-item veto.

**5.** Raise senior citizens' earning limit and let them work if they choose.

**6.** Common-sense legal reform to stop endless, get-rich-quick lawsuits.

**7.** Because the world is still a dangerous place, ensure a strong national defense.

**8.** Reform welfare to encourage people to work.

**9.** An effective, believable, and timely death penalty.

**10.** Give parents greater control over education.

**Call 800-XXX-XXXX to find out whether your candidate has signed this pledge.**
*Republicans are ready to act*

November 7, 1994

Memo
To: Dick
Fr: Kerry
Re: Tomorrow night and beyond

Odds are very good that tomorrow night will herald the biggest political shift since the 1930's.  In the 30's, the underpinnings of big government liberalism were firmly established and, while short term roll backs were attempted, it has essentially continued unabated since.  This election has clearly been fought over the size and scope of the federal government, and if we win both the House and the Senate, the American people will have overwhelmingly chosen our side at virtually every level of government.

Odds are that conservative Republicans will be elected governors in over half of the states, including the 10 or 12 largest states in the nation.  It could happen that the largest state still hosting a Democrat governor could be North Carolina.  Amazing.

Numerous state legislatures will fall to the Republicans, and this will happen in all regions of the country.  The South will become perhaps our strongest region, and after this election we will see a new wave of state and local offices falling to Republicans over the next few years, finally breaking the "lock" that existed for so long in the South -- the tendency for Southerners to vote Republican for President but Democrat for everything else.

A hundred years from now, historians may look back and see this election as the real beginning of the Republican counterrevolution.

This is our big chance.  This country can't afford for us to blow it.

The responsibility that is about to rest on your shoulders will be immense.  Between you, Newt Gingrich, Bob Dole, Phil Gramm, Haley Barbour, and a few others, you will shape this counterrevolution.  Your efforts, and occasionally your efforts alone, may determine whether or not this counterrevolution succeeds or whether it is simply a short-lived blip on the political landscape.  Forty years ago, Republicans were turned out of the House majority after a two year stint.  I'm sure the Republican leaders at that time thought they would be back in power in a few short years.  I'd be surprised if more than a handful of them will be alive to watch Republicans finally take it back.

*Victory at hand:* This memo from Kerry Knott to his boss, Dick Armey, written on the eve of the 1994 elections, demonstrates that the Republicans now believe that they are on the verge of accomplishing something historic. Knott conveys his excitement but also reminds Armey that the Republican leadership bears a heavy responsibility to ensure that the revolution does not falter. *(pp. 309–312)*

Since these opportunities come so rarely, we absolutely must succeed. You and your colleagues must rise to the occasion.

Should this dream come true Tuesday night, everything will start happening very quickly. The media scrutiny will start with Newt (building on the attacks already begun), but then they will turn to other new leaders, primarily you. This will be the opportunity to define yourself to the public at large.

Over the next several months and perhaps years, the image you and Newt project will become the image of the Republican Party. You can start building that image tomorrow night. Here are some of my suggestions for the next several weeks:

1. All your comments Tuesday night and Wednesday must be on a high level, i.e., turning government back to the people, bring renewal, respect, and responsibility to government, etc. It is extremely important that no one in the leadership look boastful or petty in their comments. And keep in mind that while our policies goals are quite different from Clinton, he is still the President. The important thing is to define to the American people what the election results mean -- and this election was about the issue of big government. It does us no good at all to say the election was about Clinton's character, the lies in the campaign, or anything like that. I suggest that you, Newt, and the other leaders have a conference call Tuesday to go over the messages you want to deliver.

2. You must nail down the Majority Leader position immediately. You can't get complacent at all about this. You've come too far to take anything for granted now. You need to make the calls to your colleagues and the new Members and gain the necessary commitments. I wrote a memo last week on this in more detail (copy attached). The main thing is to treat this in the proper perspective -- you are not entitled to this position, you must humbly ask you colleagues to allow you to help lead them during this historic period. They must get a sense that you understand that this is very important and that you are up to this new and much more difficult task. Part of that job will be instilling in your colleagues that same sense of this historic opportunity.

You should call Bill McCollum and Jerry Solomon quickly. You should ask for their support. If you find out they are not running against you, you can use this in your other calls to colleagues. If they are thinking about running, you can talk them out of it, pointing out that you already have significant support lined up, etc.

3. Attacks on the Contract will come win or lose. If we fail to capture forty seats, the pundits and most of the losing candidates will blame the Contract. You must answer this charge not in a defensive way (don't belittle the losing candidates for not pulling their share, etc.), but in an analytical way that lays out why the Contract was valuable. If we win the House, you need to really talk up the virtues of the Contract. (Talking points will be prepared on Tuesday for this).

4. Handling the transition. How you handle yourself during the transition will be very important. You must act with a strong sense of purpose and confidence, but never with arrogance. The press will be looking for instances where they can write stories about Republicans not being to assume control, etc. Exude a quiet confidence, stating that we have an organized plan we are following (without giving out details) and that we will keep the press advised as we go along. Always keep the tone on a high level, emphasizing that we are committed to reforming Congress and to pass reforms that are important to the American people.

5. Handling your colleagues. Many of your colleagues will not handle the transition well. Many will see the GOP majority as their chance to pass their pet pork barrel projects or build their little empire on a committee or subcommittee. You must become a leader and a teacher for your colleagues, constantly moving them to the higher purpose. Building the Party for long term control will require that we all work together and share a sense of purpose. When Members call you asking for personal favors or protection (against the Boehner Rule, for example), you must let them know that the leadership will discuss these things, but you will do what's best for the Conference as a whole.

Also, it's very important that you and Newt avoid making off-the-cuff commitments to any Member who calls. The transition needs to be orderly, not run on the fly. I don't think you will have a problem with this, but Newt might. Your reinforcement of this to Newt will help.

6. Handling your new stature. Every word you say will now carry much more weight. Off hand comments about health care, GATT, taxes, etc., will be big news, particularly if it differs from the ongoing strategy. You must be incredibly disciplined. think things through before speaking, and don't get caught off guard. Learn to say "no comment" without feeling guilty. The press understands that you can't talk, but they will badger you. Frankly, letting them think you know what's going on without telling them builds you up in their eyes.

Comments to your colleagues and to others (non-press) must be disciplined as well. I noticed just in the four days I traveled with you numerous comments that could have been blown into national negative stories had they been repeated to a reporter. Remember, if you say something in a private meeting and then someone tells the press, you will have to admit, deny, or somehow respond. As Majority Leader, that's a much bigger deal. You have to be constantly careful, and simply learn not to make dangerous comments.

7.  Handling your new relationship with Newt.  Newt will get so much press in these next several months it will be amazing.  A great deal of it will be negative, but a lot of it will be about how he "singlehandedly" brought Republicans to power.  You may start to feel somewhat resentful of the attention he will get.  That's only natural.  But you can't let if affect your working relationship with Newt.  Instead of it bothering you, I would suggest you look at it as somewhat of a blessing.  Newt will be the lightening rod, while you learn your new job.  The press will especially be looking for any comment from you to show a split between you and Newt.  Whatever you say about Newt, it must be positive.

The above points (and cautions) are important.  After saying that, let me also say that I believe you are ready for this responsibility.  You have grown tremendously over these last two years.  You've gained the respect and appreciation from a large number of your colleagues, and I believe they will elect you Majority Leader if we gain forty seats.

I would recommend you take a few moments alone tomorrow to reflect on what this all means.  Collect your thoughts, think about the big picture and how you will now fit into it.  Think about your country.  Think about what you can do to leave a lasting legacy for your country and your Party.

With Ronald Reagan now fading rapidly towards the "sunset of my years" in his words, you have a chance over these next few years to be the intellectual leader for your philosophy.  I have no doubt that you can do it and be successful at it.

Finally, I want to thank you for the opportunity to be a part of all this.  In the 1984 campaign, you always said you were going to Washington to "save America."  Now you'll get a chance to do just that.

Best of luck Tuesday night.

**MEMORANDUM**

TO:        **Republican Members of Congress**
FR:        **Dick Armey and John Boehner**
DATE:      **12/26/94**
RE:        **Contract Coalitions and Outreach**

As we discussed at our Republican conference meeting on December 22, we should not underestimate how crucial coalitions and citizen outreach will be to our success in passing the Contract. If you take just a moment to recount some of the most effective GOP initiatives over the past two years, you will remember how crucial coalitions were to their success: the GOP budget plans in '93 and '94, Kasich-Penny, defeat of the EPA cabinet-status rule, defeat of the crime rule -- and most importantly, defeat of the ponderous Clinton health care plan.

The scale of coalition effort needed to pass the Contract dwarfs these previous efforts. It is also much more complicated, because the Contract is a comprehensive plan to reform nearly every aspect of government, not a single issue. In order to start organizing such a massive and complicated coalitions support movement, we've come up with the following plan.

## I. Lines of Authority

Although Armey as Majority Leader will be ultimately responsible for the effort, Boehner as the Conference Chairman will be overseeing the day-to-day operations of the coalition and will run the major meetings. The Chairman may, of course, delegate certain responsibilities to the Vice Chair and Secretary of the Conference. *But, overall, the Conference will be the central clearinghouse for both communications and coalitions for the Contract.* The day-to-day operations of the Contract coalition will be transferred from my office to the Conference as soon as we are settled in our new offices.

## I. Structure

The Contract is itself a rebuff to business as usual, and we are asking Contract supporters to throw out business as usual in building coalitions as well. Specifically, we are asking supporters to get behind the Contract as a whole; not just their traditional interest area. By creating a legislative juggernaut, we make it more likely that <u>all</u> items of the Contract get passed -- like the old adage that a rising tide lifts all ships.

Toward that end we will form a core coordinating group to map out strategy, and which will be composed of those fully committed to the Contract as a whole and have "grass roots armies" to mobilize. The next level is composed of three different issue-oriented groups that also fully support the Contract as a whole: 1) economic

*Living up to their pledge:* Just before the Republicans formally take control of the House, GOP leaders Dick Armey and John Boehner, who will handle the communications strategy for the Contract, urge their colleagues to focus on pushing to the House floor all ten items in the Contract with America. The Republicans have made a pact with the American voters: "If we break this contract, throw us out. We mean it." The leaders now want to ensure that Republican members do everything in their power to fulfill that promise. And the Republicans will bring all ten Contract bills to a vote within the first hundred days, though only two will pass in that time period. *(pp. 313–314)* growth/business; 2) grass roots and values groups; 3) think tank and academic groups.  The contact points for each of the three groups are as follows:

> 1) **economic growth/business**:  Dirk Van Dongen and Alan Kranowitz (National Wholesalers)
>
> 2) **grass roots and values groups**:  Grover Norquist (Americans for Tax Reform, et al.)
>
> 3) **think tank/academic groups**:  Mike Franc (Heritage Foundation)

Finally, we realize that no matter how we ask some groups to stretch their areas of interest, they either don't have the resources or the institutional interest to work on behalf of the entire Contract.  These "single-issue," or satellite, groups will gear up on a bill-by-bill basis, and work their issue as it moves throughout the process.  The attached diagram illustrates the structure.  These groups will serve as the real footsoldiers as we move from battle to battle in coordination with the core coordinating group.  Some of these groups are up and operating already (such as the balanced budget group and the legal reforms group), and we will provide more information to you on each new group as it becomes available.

Coalitions are by their nature governed by inspiration, emotion, idealism, and a good dose of chaos.  No structure could impose too rigid a discipline on groups of citizens trying to improve their government -- nor should it.  This structure is simply meant to channel energy in the most productive ways.

So, here's the bottom line:  *if you have an interest in participating in one of the coalitions outlined above, or if you know of groups that are interested in supporting the Contract, please put your thoughts or recommendations into a memo and submit it to John Boehner.*

I hope all of you will play *some* role in the communications or coalitions aspects of the Contract, and I encourage you to take the plunge early -- remember, the first big test, the balanced budget amendment, comes up around January 19th!

# ACKNOWLEDGMENTS

L ike Oscar speeches, acknowledgments sound tedious to everyone but the author and the intended audience. Unlike Oscar speeches, there is nothing forced or feigned about my gratitude to the following.

This book is about a crucial moment in history, and I wish to thank those who first made the history and later took time to speak candidly about what worked, what didn't, and why. In addition to reviewing hundreds of pages of internal Contract-related documents, I conducted more than fifty interviews for *The Enduring Revolution*. I interviewed the Republican lawmakers, legislative staff, strategists, and pollsters who developed the Contract. I interviewed the top Democrats in Congress and in the Clinton White House who fought the Contract tirelessly. Republicans and Democrats still disagree about what the Contract stood for when it was signed and what it has meant to the country in the decade since the Contract contributed to the broadest GOP victory of the late twentieth century. On one thing, however, Republicans and Democrats agree. The Contract and the legislative push behind it made for consequential times. There is an almost universal wistfulness for those days of titanic political struggle. Both sides remember the intense energy, the high sense of purpose, the audible crackle of ideological conflict. The people I interviewed helped me recapture the pulse and passion of that time and see more clearly how the struggles for power that followed reveal the Contract's continued relevance and potency now.

Before there is a book, there is an idea. Agents transform the idea into a commodity a publisher will buy. (This is not a vulgarism but a truism, one no honest author disdains or ignores.) My agent, Jan Miller, has thrice performed this literary alchemy and, in so doing, allowed me to realize my highest ambition.

Jan has always been my agent, but this book introduced me to a new editor, Crown Forum's Jed Donahue. Jed is without question the best editor I've ever had. He knows what works and never shies from a fight over what doesn't. And woe be the author whose editor doesn't care enough to fight over content, voice, and usage. Jed also knows which fights to pick, meaning ties typically (but not always) were broken by my sense of narrative voice.

A book of this kind relies heavily on research. As a full-time reporter covering the presidential campaign through much of 2003 and 2004, I would have found the research required to complete this book overwhelming had it not been for my research assistant, Michael Wussow. Michael's work was thorough, his counsel cogent, his analytic advice precise. Michael is a superb writer and a tireless worker. Were I starting any journalistic enterprise and Michael were available, I would hire him on the spot (and I would bid aggressively if he were already well situated).

I also wish to thank those at Fox News who encouraged this project and believed me when I promised it would not undermine my day-to-day work for the network: Roger Ailes, John Moody, Kevin Magee, Brit Hume, Kim Hume, and Bruce Becker.

Finally, as any author with a family knows, there is the "family" who helps bring the book to market and the family who gives you every ounce of human sustenance required to survive the rigors of writing the manuscript. To my wife, Julie, and my children, Mary Ellen, Luke, and Audrey, I offer humble, heartfelt thanks for all you give me: patience, love, support, enthusiasm, and, most of all, undying laughter.

Major Garrett
Washington, D.C.
November 2004

# INDEX